THE TEACHINGS *of* MASTER WUZHU

TRANSLATIONS FROM THE ASIAN CLASSICS

THE TEACHINGS *of* MASTER Wuzhu

Zen and Religion of No-Religion

WENDI L. ADAMEK

COLUMBIA UNIVERSITY PRESS *NEW YORK*

COLUMBIA UNIVERSITY PRESS
Publishers Since 1893
New York Chichester, West Sussex

Library of Congress Cataloging-in-Publication Data
The teachings of Master Wuzhu : Zen and religion
of no-religion / Wendi L. Adamek.
p. cm. — (Translations from the Asian classics)
Includes translation from Chinese.
Includes bibliographical references and index.
ISBN 978-0-231-15022-4 (cloth : alk. paper) —
ISBN 978-0-231-15023-1 (pbk.) —
ISBN 978-0-231-52792-7 (electronic)
1. Zen Buddhism—China—History. 2. Wuzhu, Master, 714–774.
3. Li dai fa bao ji. 4. Buddhist sects—China—History.
I. Adamek, Wendi Leigh. II. Title. III. Series.
BQ9262.9.C5L5313 2011
294.3′85—dc22 2010039929

♾
Columbia University Press books are printed on permanent
and durable acid-free paper.

This book is printed on paper with recycled content.
Printed in the United States of America

Design by Shaina Andrews

For MY DEAR DOLPHINS, *who piloted me through shark-infested waters*

you know who you are

With warm thanks to the STANFORD HUMANITIES CENTER *and* THE TEAM *at* COLUMBIA UNIVERSITY PRESS, *with special thanks to Leslie Kriesel and Michael Brackney for stellar editing and indexing*

CONTENTS

PART I | MASTER WUZHU AND THE DEVELOPMENT OF CHAN/ZEN BUDDHISM 1

CHAPTER 1. INTRODUCTION TO THE *LIDAI FABAO JI* AND MEDIEVAL CHINESE BUDDHISM 3

The *Lidai fabao ji* (Record of the Dharma-Jewel Through the Generations) 3

Overview 4

Soteriology and Politics: Salvation and Power 5

Medieval Chinese Devotionalism and Merit Practices 8

A Foundational Chan Narrative 12

CHAPTER 2. QUESTIONING WUZHU'S TRANSMISSION 15

Transmission 15

Bodhidharma's Robe 18

Constructing Patriarchal Lineages 20

A Special Transmission 22

Wuzhu's Life and the Transmission Controversy 24

CHAPTER 3. RADICAL ASPECTS OF WUZHU'S TEACHINGS 30

From Bodhisattva Precepts to Formless Precepts 30

Indian Mahāyāna Bodhisattva Precepts 31

Precepts Texts Written in China 32

Chan Reinterpretation of the Precepts 33

Wuzhu's Teachings on the Precepts 36

The "Three Phrases" Controversy 37
Critiques of Wuzhu's Style of Practice 39

CHAPTER 4. WUZHU'S FEMALE DISCIPLES 46

The Background of the Nun's Order 46
Women in the *Lidai fabao ji* 47

CHAPTER 5. WUZHU'S LEGACY 53

Later References to the Bao Tang School 54
Tibetan Traces 57
Sichuan Chan and the Hongzhou School 59
Conclusion 61

PART II | TRANSLATION OF THE *LIDAI FABAO JI* (RECORD OF THE DHARMA-JEWEL THROUGH THE GENERATIONS) 67

SECTION 1. SOURCES AND THE LEGEND OF EMPEROR MING OF THE HAN (*T.* 51:179A1–179C4) 69

SECTION 2. BUDDHISM IN CHINA (*T.* 51:179C4–180A2) 73

SECTION 3. TRANSMISSION FROM INDIA TO CHINA (THE *FU FAZANG ZHUAN*) (*T.* 51:180A2–180C2) 74

SECTION 4. THE FIRST PATRIARCH BODHIDHARMATRĀTA (*T.* 51:180C3–181A18) 77

SECTION 5. THE SECOND PATRIARCH HUIKE (*T.* 51:181A19–181B18) 79

SECTION 6. THE THIRD PATRIARCH SENGCAN (*T.* 51:181B19–181C8) 81

SECTION 7. THE FOURTH PATRIARCH DAOXIN (*T.* 51:181C9–182A10) 82

SECTION 8. THE FIFTH PATRIARCH HONGREN (*T.* 51:182A11–182B5) 84

SECTION 9. THE SIXTH PATRIARCH HUINENG, PART 1 (*T.* 51:182B6–182C16) 86

SECTION 10. DHARMA MASTER DAOAN AND SCRIPTURE QUOTATIONS (*T.* 51:182C17–183C1) 88

SECTION 11. HUINENG, PART 2 (*T.* 51:183C1–184A6) 92

SECTION 12. ZHISHEN AND EMPRESS WU (*T.* 51:184A6–184B17) 94

SECTION 13. CHAN MASTER ZHISHEN (*T.* 51:184B18–184C2) 96

SECTION 14. CHAN MASTER CHUJI (*T.* 51:184C3–184C16) 97

SECTION 15. CHAN MASTER WUXIANG (*T.* 51:184C17–185B14) 98

SECTION 16. THE VENERABLE SHENHUI (*T.* 51:185B14–185C26) 101

SECTION 17. DISCOURSES OF THE VENERABLE WUZHU (*T.* 51:185C26–186A14) 104

SECTION 18. WUZHU AND WUXIANG (*T.* 51:186A15–187C7) 105

SECTION 19. DU HONGJIAN'S ARRIVAL IN SHU (*T.* 51:187C7–188B21) 112

SECTION 20. DU HONGJIAN AND WUZHU MEET (*T.* 51:188B21–189B22) 116

SECTION 21. CUI GAN'S VISIT (*T.* 51:189B22–190B16) 121

SECTION 22. DIALOGUE WITH CHAN MASTER TIWU (*T.* 51:190B16–190C18) 126

SECTION 23. DIALOGUE WITH CHAN MASTER HUIYI (*T.* 51:190C18–22) 128

SECTION 24. DIALOGUE WITH MASTERS YIJING, ZHUMO, AND TANGWEN (*T.* 51:190C22–191A27) 128

SECTION 25. DIALOGUE WITH MASTER JINGZANG (*T.* 51:191A28–B17) 130

SECTION 26. DIALOGUE WITH MASTER ZHIYI (*T.* 51:191B18–C2) 131

SECTION 27. DIALOGUE WITH MASTER ZHONGXIN (*T.* 51:191C2–15) 132

SECTION 28. DIALOGUE WITH DHARMA MASTER FALUN (*T.* 51:191C15–192A7) 133

SECTION 29. DIALOGUE WITH THE BROTHERS YIXING AND HUIMING (*T.* 51:192A7–24) 134

SECTION 30. DIALOGUE WITH CHANGJINGJIN AND LIAOJIANXING (FEMALE DISCIPLES) (*T.* 51:192A24–B18) 135

SECTION 31. EXCERPTS AND QUOTATIONS, PART 1 (*T.* 51:192B18–193A15) 136

SECTION 32. EXCERPTS AND QUOTATIONS, PART 2 (*T.* 51:193A15–B2) 140

SECTION 33. TEA VERSE (*T.* 51:193B2–19) 141

SECTION 34. DIALOGUE WITH DAOISTS (*T.* 51:193B20–194A20) 142

SECTION 35. DIALOGUE WITH DHARMA MASTERS (*T.* 51:194A20–194B1) 146

SECTION 36. DIALOGUE WITH VINAYA MASTERS (*T.* 51:194B1–194C15) 146

SECTION 37. DIALOGUE WITH TREATISE MASTERS (*T.* 51:194C16–195A2) 149

SECTION 38. TRADING QUOTATIONS WITH MASTERS DAOYOU, MINGFA, AND GUANLU (*T.* 51:195A2–12) 150

SECTION 39. TAKING ON CHAN DISCIPLES WHILE DRINKING TEA (*T.* 51:195A12–29) 151
SECTION 40. DIALOGUE WITH MASTER XIONGJUN (*T.* 51:195A29–B3) 152
SECTION 41. DIALOGUE WITH MASTER FAYUAN, ACCOMPANIED BY HIS MOTHER (*T.* 51:195B3–22) 152
SECTION 42. DISCOURSE TO LAY DONORS (*T.* 51:195B23–C13) 153
SECTION 43. PORTRAIT-EULOGY AND FINAL SCENE (*T.* 51:195C15–196B6) 154

NOTES | 159
BIBLIOGRAPHY | 177
INDEX | 185

PART 1

MASTER WUZHU & THE DEVELOPMENT OF CHAN/ ZEN BUDDHISM

CHAPTER

1

INTRODUCTION TO THE *LIDAI FABAO JI* AND MEDIEVAL CHINESE BUDDHISM

THE *LIDAI FABAO JI* (RECORD OF THE DHARMA-JEWEL THROUGH THE GENERATIONS)

It is, perhaps, one of the earliest attempts to implement a "religion of no-religion." However, even sympathetic Zen historians are tempted to dismiss the *Lidai fabao ji* as a self-promoting fiction. It was discredited soon after it was written in the late eighth century and still provokes occasional disparaging comments. The sharpest early critic was Shenqing (d. 814), whose views are discussed in chapter 5. He voiced his objections in the *Beishan lu* (Record of North Mountain), his voluminous book on the current state of Buddhism in China.

The *Lidai fabao ji* was long considered lost. It was resurrected from among manuscripts accidentally discovered in 1900 in a hidden cache at the Mogao caves, near the Silk Road oasis of Dunhuang. By then there were few other traces of Chan Master Wuzhu (714–774) and his group, the Bao Tang (Protect the Tang Dynasty) school of Jiannan (Sichuan). The text was probably compiled within a few years after Wuzhu's death, which makes it one of the most immediate accounts of a Zen master in early Chan/Zen[1] history. Its obscurity also means that it is one of the least reworked. The *Lidai fabao ji* gives us remarkably lively glimpses of Wuzhu and his interlocutors, both adoring and hostile. It also gives us a window into a world of complex religious and cultural battles, many of which continue to resonate today.

OVERVIEW

In this first chapter I discuss fundamental aspects of medieval Chinese Buddhist practice in order to convey something of the context from which Chan/Zen emerged. In the second chapter I focus on Dharma transmission and its role in the contested account of Wuzhu's life. Throughout the book, I highlight the significance of the practices of merit, repentance, precepts, and transmission, aspects of traditional East Asian Buddhism that have not always assimilated smoothly into contemporary contexts.

In the third and fourth chapters I turn to the unusual aspects of Wuzhu's teachings and community: "formless practice"—Wuzhu's version of "no-religion"—and his validation of female practitioners. Through the *Lidai fabao ji* we get a view of the dynamics of a little-known group in the eighth century whose members were involved with some of the same issues that animate contemporary Buddhist practice groups: the consequences of abandoning set forms of practice and the roles of lay and female practitioners.

Wuzhu's exclusion from the emerging Chan orthodoxy is an important theme in chapter 5. There are multiple intriguing factors involved. Most provocative are the accusations by fellow clerics that the Bao Tang disciples misunderstood Chan practice and that they or Wuzhu himself lied about his having received transmission from the Korean Chan master Wuxiang. I also discuss Wuzhu's controversial role from a broader perspective: the "formless practice" of the Bao Tang community placed limits on its institutional development, and thus could not contribute to the collective and competitive project of building a socially legitimate Chan network.

Another issue pertinent to the question of Chan orthodoxy is the uneven writing style in the *Lidai fabao ji*. Some passages are almost shockingly colloquial, while others are pastiches drawn from a variety of formal Buddhist sources. Wuzhu's dialogues are rendered in a manner that suggests both scribbling down of lecture notes and dependence on a repetitive template. However, the *Baolin zhuan* (Transmission of the Baolin Temple), also of questionable literary merit, went on to become a cornerstone text in the development of an orthodox Chan genealogy, while Shenqing's highly erudite *Beishan lu* remained relatively obscure. The literary weaknesses of the *Lidai fabao ji* were probably less determinative than its unreliable transmission account and the radical nature of its practices.

I argue that Wuzhu was in many ways ahead of his times, particularly with regard to his abandonment of Buddhist devotionalism and ritual and his willingness to include female practitioners in his informal community. However, the Bao Tang community does not seem to have developed effective alternative means to transmit their ethos. In the long run, it was the creation of Chan rituals and institutions that ironically or mock-violently pointed to their own groundlessness that proved most successful.

SOTERIOLOGY AND POLITICS: SALVATION AND POWER

Before turning to specific features of medieval Chinese Buddhism, I would like to reconsider the often-raised question "What do Buddhists do?" In a Latin-derived English nutshell, they do soteriology. "Soteriology" means "pertaining to salvation," linking *soter,* savior, and *logos,* word. "Soteriology" designates a field in which it is impossible to separate practice from philosophy, doctrine, ideology, or theory.

Soteriologies may have physical, institutional, and doctrinal forms that make them into recognizable self-sustaining networks: religions. A soteriology may also be individual and private. The word does not necessarily indicate a spiritual, therapeutic, or psychological orientation, but it does connote transformation. It is thus an appropriate designation for the Buddhist approach, which is founded on the quest for liberation from suffering—in other words, salvation.

We will be exploring a particular soteriological approach articulated by an eighth-century Buddhist teacher and his community. The baseline Buddhist definition of liberation is the realization that suffering arises from attachment to the illusion of a permanent and essential self. All Buddhist communities might agree that they are oriented toward liberation from suffering arising from delusion, but there are many different kinds of "social contract" for working collectively on liberation. Social contracts inevitably involve questions about the distribution and circulation of authority and resources—in other words, power.

Does this mean that social contracts, politics, and questions of power and resource allocation are the bottom line, all that's "really" happening in a religious endeavor? When one tries to include politics and economics in the picture, one encounters a divide between academics and Buddhist practitioners regarding the true nature of Buddhist traditions. On the one hand, current academic and cultural practice is founded on a critique of religion, an important aspect of the Western Enlightenment project from the eighteenth century onward. Critiques of religion sometimes become remarkably reductionist: "Religion is all about maintaining power." On the other hand, Buddhism and especially Zen often appeals to modern sensibilities (or post-, non-, alternate-variations thereof) because Buddhism seems like it should be immune to such critiques. In both practice groups and classrooms, one hears people expressing the desire to separate "religion" from true or "pure" spiritual aspirations.

Zen becomes a focus of this desire. People are taken with the idea that it's not about God, not about sin and faith, priests and rituals. It's just meditating, "just sitting." Just sitting, *shikantaza,* was a phrase coined by the thirteenth-century Zen master Dōgen to express the immediate yet ultimate nature of Buddhist meditation practice. Wuzhu may have anticipated Dōgen with his insistence that what he was doing was *kongxian zuo,* "sitting in idleness," a phrase that also connotes sitting in emptiness.

In Zen contexts, realization of emptiness and "just sitting" are characterized as nondual. How pure! At the same time, inevitably, disputes arise over how to *teach* people to experience nonduality. How to express and transmit the inexpressible is a challenge in all soteriological contexts. Paraphrasing the famous *Heart Sūtra* phrase "form is emptiness, emptiness is form," we could also say, "soteriology is politics, politics is soteriology." One can't separate the Way from the means, and the means lay claim to the Way.

The *Heart Sūtra* phrase captures a dilemma at the heart of the development of distinct Chan forms of teaching and practice. Chan developed out of Mahāyāna (Greater Vehicle) Buddhism, a watershed that was later characterized as Buddhism's transformation into a universalist soteriology.[2] In Mahāyāna terms, one can't separate *bodhicitta,* an insight into interdependence/emptiness that triggers one's aspiration to attain buddhahood, from the conditions and forms that are the path to buddhahood. But who decides who has the authority to set the forms and teach buddhas-in-the-making?

A key Mahāyāna claim is that buddhas and buddhas-in-the-making (bodhisattvas) are no longer bound by appearances because of their insight into the nature of reality. Buddhas and bodhisattvas work with appearances in order to help other beings overcome the delusions that give rise to suffering. *Upāya* (expedient means) is self-aware engagement with the illusion that there are independent, selfsame entities. *Upāya* is strategic deployment of illusion in order to overcome attachment to illusion. Because forms and conditions change, there always have to be new means of conveying the Dharma (Buddhist teachings), which are forms of *upāya*. There are always disputes over what is true *upāya*—soteriologically skillful illusion—and mere attachment-based delusion.

How does this relate to the functioning of a community? Hierarchy becomes a key issue, often contentious. Hierarchies of privilege and responsibility are embodied in leadership roles. Who gets to tell whom to do what, and how? In any community, there are different levels of experience and commitment, so hierarchy is "natural." However, the desire for control and continuity arises endlessly, so hierarchy is naturalized.

Let us take a moment to distinguish between "natural" and "naturalized." The hierarchy is the same, but we view it from different perspectives. On one level, differences in commitment and responsibility are functional differences that emerge from causes and conditions; a Buddhist might say that they arise from karma, the momentum created by one's past actions in this life and previous ones. On another level, power differentials are integral to structures that maintain continuity, and they have to be rationalized. Differences in degrees of autonomy and authority have to be made to seem natural.

In this regard, there are key cultural contrasts between medieval China and the present. In imperial China, rituals that regularly marked distinctions in social rank were considered essential to the harmonious ordering and continuity of the state, for the benefit of "all under Heaven." In contrast, in the cultural context that most reading this book inhabit, hierarchical systems are required to function through practices that represent the essential equality of all members of the group. We tend to react (ritually) against overt, institutionalized hierarchy and authority.

Does this mean that representations of legitimate authority and representations of equality are always empty lies masking exploitation? Whether in Zen groups, families, or theaters of battle, rituals of hierarchal ordering and rituals of recognizing all the participants are interdependent and necessary functions. How does one distinguish *upāya*, skillful ritual/representation/illusion, from what Buddhists call the "three poisons"—greed, hatred, and ignorance? Several of the most prominent Zen groups in late twentieth-century America have generated significant and long-lasting abuse and trauma. Chan

Master Wuzhu was a former military officer whose disciples and patrons included military officers fighting the Tibetans along the Sichuan border.

Soteriology is politics. Politics is also soteriology, but that is another book. Investigating medieval Buddhism, the birth of Chan, and the teachings of Master Wuzhu is not a matter of distinguishing one from the other, but of understanding the varieties of "skill" invested in these creations.

MEDIEVAL CHINESE DEVOTIONALISM AND MERIT PRACTICES

Wuzhu's signature teaching was no-thought (*wunian*) as the practice of no-practice. In his own words: "At the time of true no-thought, no-thought itself is not." He warned against attachment to any form of practice, especially devotional rituals. This was a stance he shared with other early Chan teachers; eighth-century Chan developed in large part as a reinterpretation of and reaction against devotional practices. These included bodhisattva-precepts vows, repentance rituals, visualizations, and *samādhi* (meditation) techniques. A common thread running through devotional practice was the concept of generating and accessing merit.

The notion of merit (Chin. *gongde,* Skt. *puṇya*) has always been central to Buddhism. Early Buddhist sūtras (scriptures) taught that offerings to the Buddha and to the saṅgha (community of the ordained) gain merit for the devotee. Merit offsets the negative effects of past actions and helps create favorable future conditions in this life and the next. In traditional Buddhism, the most meritorious act was to become a monk. The highest reward for merit was to be reborn as a monk and then attain liberation from rebirth.

For laypeople, the most important merit-gaining activity was supporting the community of monks and nuns. This took many forms, including providing facilities and supplies, sponsoring vegetarian feasts and memorial services, and helping support family members who became monks and nuns. Building and maintaining devotional sites was an increasingly important form of generating merit. Donations for objects and structures were provided by both lay and ordained devotees.

Meritorious reproduction of images and texts was a key feature of Mahāyāna Buddhism. Mahāyāna images and scriptures began to trickle into China in the second century, and Chinese devotees soon began to develop their own forms of representation and practice. Due in part to the appeal of the notion of meritorious donation, by the middle of the fifth century Buddhism was powerful enough to be perceived as a threat. Emperor Taiwu (r. 424–452) of the Northern Wei carried out the first persecution of Buddhism in China, but this was followed by an enthusiastic renaissance.

From the devotional perspective, not only images of buddhas and bodhisattvas but also the sūtras themselves function as manifestations of the Dharma, with a salvational power accessible to all devotees. The soteriological function of objects was not considered contrary to the Buddhist doctrine of no-self and emptiness. How did this work?

Mahāyāna Buddhism achieved a remarkable synthesis of philosophical analysis and faith through formulations like the "Two Truths." According to this rubric, on the ultimate level of truth there are no individual beings; in fact, there is nothing that could be called either being or nonbeing. Things that appear to be separate phenomena are the virtual effects of interrelationship.

In Chinese Huayan Buddhism, this was explained through a positive visual analogy: it is as if the universe is a vast net with glittering jewels hung at every intersecting point. Every jewel is reflected in all other jewels, and all jewels are reflected in each. However, in reality there are no jewels and no net. Each apparent phenomenon arises moment by moment, by virtue of limitless interdependent reflective functioning.

The level of "seeming" is the level of so-called conventional truth, the appearance of beings, time, and space. Ordinary beings perceive the illusory manifestations produced by interrelation and, believing them to be real, suffer delusions. Buddhas and bodhisattvas perceive both the lack of reality of these phenomena and their provisional functioning.

In medieval Chinese Buddhism, the doctrine of ultimate and conventional truth was wedded to the early Chinese notion of sympathetic resonance (*ganying*) in order to explain how people, texts, images, verbal formulae, and contemplative visualizations have the power to deliver the devotee and his or her loved ones from suffering. On the conventional level of seeming duality between subjects and objects, buddhas and bodhisattvas manifest various forms in order to aid devotees. Devotion to buddhas and bodhisattvas and to the images that represent them naturally elicits a response. The salvific figure is moved to deploy the power of his or her vast stores of merit to relieve suffering, and this creates karmic connections that will ultimately lead the sufferer to realize his or her own liberation.

According to this view of reality, both the cosmic buddhas and the images that represent them are illusions, but they are illusions created through merit and thus have the power of skillful means. For example, the Buddha Amitābha, residing in the Pure Land he has created through his compassionate vows, is just as "virtual" as the stone carvings and murals representing him. However, because the merit sustaining the Pure Land is the product of Amitābha's vows as a bodhisattva, it has a more powerful effect. The aim of both philosophical-contemplative analyses of reality and devotion to the buddhas is to enable all beings to realize that these effects are produced through interdependence. They are empty of qualities, including the quality of "emptiness."

Thus, ultimate and conventional truth are not different layers of reality. The "Two Truths" are inseparable, but they appear to refer to each other. They are illusions working through truth, and also truth working through illusions. For Chinese Buddhists, this mutual reference meant that "transfer of merit" for the benefit of another was possible and desirable. Giving a gift to the Buddhist saṅgha and then dedicating the merit of that action for the benefit of others, the donor compounds individual merit into inexhaustible merit. This is accomplished through appealing to the mediation of a buddha or bodhisattva, who enables the devotee to sow seeds of individual merit in the universal merit field (emptiness). The buddha or bodhisattva also mobilizes the inexhaustible universal merit field in order to benefit the devotee and his or her family.

Practitioners, including monks and nuns, usually did not see any conflict between directing their merit-sweetened prayers toward worldly benefits like health and wealth and praying for transfiguration of themselves and their loved ones into purer realms or conditions. In orthodox doctrinal terms, merit is not considered sufficient cause for liberation, but it does direct karmic momentum toward liberation. The practice of generosity was considered especially powerful in that it both generates merit and aids in overcoming attachment to the notion of an essential self.

Various kinds of donation to gain merit were practiced by lay and ordained Buddhists in medieval China. Many of the donated objects included dedicatory inscriptions naming the donor and recording his or her prayers for family members living and deceased, prayers for the emperor and empress, personal health benefits, and favorable rebirths for all concerned.

Because of these mundane concerns, merit-gaining practices are often labeled "popular" in contrast to the contemplative and scholarly practices of monks and nuns. However, these practices were just as popular with monks and nuns, and they were far from simplistic. The self-serving quality of merit-gaining practice was also intended to be self-transformative. As a form of *upāya,* it was meant to function both gradually and pivotally: trying to get conditions to work in one's favor becomes/is working with conditions as they are.

Merit-oriented practices were unquestionably a major impetus for the spread and growth of Buddhism in China. However, by the time the *Lidai fabao ji* was compiled it had become clear that Buddhism's power and prestige created problems as well as opportunities. In a well-known scene, Bodhidharma, the putative first Chan Patriarch, is welcomed by an emperor and then brusquely dismisses the meritorious activities of his host. This episode was probably created by the monk Shenhui (684–758), but it enjoyed many retellings. This is the *Lidai fabao ji* version:

> Emperor Wu came out of the city to welcome [Bodhidharma] personally. He had him ascend to the audience hall and asked the Venerable, "What teachings to convert beings have you brought from the other country?" Great Master Dharma replied, "I have not brought a single word." The emperor asked, "What merit have We gained in having monasteries built and people saved, scriptures copied and statues cast?" The Great Master responded, "No merit whatsoever." He added, "This is contrived goodness, not true merit."[3]

It is important to note the historical context of this fictive exchange: the formative Chan criticism of merit-seeking is conveyed through a conversation between the mythical Chan Patriarch Bodhidharma and the first historically verifiable imperial patron of Buddhism, Emperor Wu of the Liang (r. 502–549). The story is effective because it reflects a tension that continues to manifest in Buddhist associations to this day: attracting wealthy patrons is a sign of success, but it is also a sign of compromise.

From the beginning of Buddhism's Chinese adventure, the relationship between Chinese elites and the Buddhist saṅgha was empowering and threatening for both sides. At times those in power cooperated with the saṅgha to the point of merging operations. At other times the wealth and power of Buddhism triggered regulatory measures and even persecutions. Controlling the growing Buddhist community presented difficulties even when Buddhism was just beginning to be established in China. As Buddhism underwent phenomenal expansion and bewildering diversification in the fifth through eighth centuries, there were periodic attempts at systematization and calls for reform from both inside and outside the saṅgha. Chan criticism of merit-making and devotionalism can be viewed as a successful response—or a successful strategy—in the context of demands for less expensive and explosive forms of Buddhism.

A FOUNDATIONAL CHAN NARRATIVE

Chan schools from the late eighth century onward were eager to trace descent from the so-called "Southern School" of the Sixth Patriarch Huineng (638–713). The ideology of an exclusive succession of Chan patriarchs and claims for the superiority of the Southern School of Huineng were initiated by Shenhui, the above-mentioned author of the Bodhidharma mythos. In 732, Shenhui launched a series of criticisms against disciples of the monk Shenxiu (d. 706), denouncing them as followers of an inferior "Northern School." Shenhui's criticisms and assertions were taken up by other clerics, and by the late eighth century there were a number of competing Chan lineages in circulation.

None of Shenhui's own writings attained the status of a classic text. Nevertheless, he changed the course of Buddhist history by linking the notions of "sudden" awakening and patriarchal lineage. Shenhui championed the notion of direct and spontaneous realization of the truth of one's own nature. According to him, Shenxiu's Northern School followers were "gradualists" who deluded people into thinking that awakening was a condition to be achieved through meditation and purification. Instead, all one had to do was realize that one's inherent reality was emptiness, the same as the buddhas. One's own mind nature was, therefore, buddha nature.

At the same time, Shenhui claimed that there was only one transmission that enabled a master to teach the true Dharma of sudden and direct awakening. This transmission was invested in one patriarch per generation, and

Huineng was the sixth patriarch to receive transmission on Chinese soil. In promoting a man he claimed as his teacher, Shenhui may well have been motivated by personal ambitions. However, as noted, Buddhists were perceived as having become unmanageably populous and diverse. Other clerics of the seventh and eighth centuries were also trying to devise means to define authoritative transmission of the Buddhist teachings.

A key text that promotes Huineng, his teachings, and its own version of the Chan patriarchal lineage is the *Liuzu tanjing* (Platform Sūtra of the Sixth Patriarch). Written at the same time as the *Lidai fabao ji* and expanded over the centuries, it became the representative early Chan text. The question of authoritative transmission forms the backdrop for a famous graffiti battle in the *Platform Sūtra,* in which Shenxiu and Huineng write competing verses on the walls of the temple where they both reside. In this account Shenxiu is depicted as earnest but not very bright, although the actual Shenxiu was a highly respected monk of profound insight and integrity. The story of how Huineng received transmission is not verifiable from other sources. However, this compelling fiction is undoubtedly a cornerstone of the Chan tradition, with lasting inspirational effect.

The *Platform Sūtra* opens with Huineng ascending the platform at a precepts-reception assembly and telling the story of his own life. He relates how he was a poor laborer in the far south, his family having fallen on hard times, when he happens to hear someone reciting the *Diamond Sūtra.* Though illiterate, he is instantly awakened. This profound taste of Buddhist truth draws him north, to the temple of the Fifth Chan Patriarch Hongren. After a short exchange at a public assembly, Hongren recognizes Huineng's worth, but he puts him to work threshing rice in the kitchens. Huineng spends nine months in the kitchens, and then Hongren announces to all the monks that he is ready to transmit the patriarchy to anyone able to successfully demonstrate his awareness in the form of a verse.

Shenxiu is the head monk, and the other monks assume he will receive transmission. However, lacking the confidence to present his verse directly, he writes it on the temple wall at night. When Huineng hears Shenxiu's verse recited, he asks someone to help him by writing up a verse he composes instantly in response, though he is unable to read or write.

These are the two verses in the *Platform Sūtra,* first Shenxiu's and then Huineng's:

The body is the bodhi tree,
The mind is like a clear mirror.
At all times we must strive to polish it,
And must not let the dust collect.[4]

Bodhi originally has no tree,
The mirror has no stand.
Buddha-nature is always clean and pure;
Where is there room for dust?[5]

The first verse, expressing a "gradualist" view, argues that one must strive to continually clear and purify the mind, while Huineng's "sudden" verse makes the point that there is nothing to clear, no "there" there. Huineng's verse supports the practice of not reifying any practice, including meditation, which is seen as a form of "polishing." Instead the *Platform Sūtra* supports the practice of "no-thought," which is also Master Wuzhu's key practice.

Buddhist references to "no-thought" predate the creation of this mythic conflict between paradigmatic representatives of gradualist and subitist (sudden awakening) positions. In the Chan context, however, no-thought came to refer to the nonconceptual realization of the nonseparation of practice and enlightenment. This begs the question: how do you teach and transmit a teaching, a practice, if you are supposed to not-think of it as anything in particular? This is the challenge Chan presented to itself: how to carry on a tradition of no-tradition. In light of Chan's long and multifaceted history, one can see that impossible challenges may be an asset. This paradox has kept a large number of practitioners busy over the course of some twelve centuries.

CHAPTER 2

QUESTIONING WUZHU'S TRANSMISSION

TRANSMISSION

The meaning of "transmission" in Buddhist contexts is by no means self-evident. There are at least three levels involved: transmission of a particular practice-approach to the Buddhist teachings of liberation from suffering, transmission of a doctrinal tradition claiming superior efficacy and authority, and transmission of an ideology that legitimates a particular approach, efficacy, and authority. All these levels involve contestation and may be represented by talismanic texts and images. If one approach to liberation, one form of Buddhist soteriology, is promoted, then others are explicitly or implicitly pushed aside. If something, a text or exegetical tradition or object, has a special aura attributed to it, then one must ask how and why it is invested with this privileged function. And finally, most subtly: when we identify transmission as an "ideology," what goes into that designation?

Chan notions of patriarchal transmission encompassed both the mystique of wordless rapport between master and disciple and an effective political tool to invest a relatively small number of males, Chan masters, with spiritual and institutional authority. When we frame Chan transmission as an ideology, we take the mystique as a function of the politics and focus on competitive relationships and rhetorical strategies. As noted, this kind of critical approach to religious history is a key feature of modernity. However, throughout this exploration of the meanings of transmission at work in the *Lidai fabao ji*, I also ask readers to remain reflexively aware of the rhetorical work involved in critique.

What cultural values and authorities do we transmit, intentionally or otherwise, when we choose frameworks for studies of soteriology, ritual magic, and competitive sectarian politics? Are we implicitly or explicitly assuming that one level is more "real" than the others? Can these levels be easily separated?

In the early centuries of Buddhism's spread in China, transmission of a large variety of forms—monastic rules, rituals, magic, and texts—conveyed authority and a sense of continuity. Transmission of the Vinaya, the rules for monks and nuns, gave practitioners a sense of assurance that Buddhism was proceeding properly, according to standards laid down by the Buddha. Rituals such as recitation of sūtras, devotional offerings, and vows were events in which ordained clergy and the laity participated together, creating a sense of Buddhist community. Mantric arts like *dhāraṇī* (incantations) contributed to the circulation of Buddhist symbolic capital. As noted above, image-making was an essential aspect of the transmission of Buddhism throughout Asia.

Scholarly traditions have tended to focus more narrowly on the translation and transmission of particular texts and doctrinal affiliations from one generation to the next. Traditions of textual transmission are reconstructed from several kinds of sources, most importantly prefaces to sūtra translations by the translator, his disciples, and later exegetes; collections of biographies of eminent monks; and Chinese commentaries on South Asian and Central Asian sūtras and treatises. Doctrinal and text-based affiliations were often associated with particular places—the courts of pious emperors or the mountain temples of renowned monks.

To return to a question raised earlier, if Buddhist traditions assert that under the right conditions a person has the capacity to realize the truth directly, then what is the soteriological purpose of all these forms and productions? This was a question that Chan masters posed as their own special challenge to tradition, but it was a challenge that had been in play from the beginning. Both clergy and laity were continually engaged with questions of legitimacy. What methods for transmitting the Dharma of liberation were to be considered trustworthy, effective, and worthy of support? Who would be considered legitimate guarantors of efficacy and how would they be maintained without corruption? By what means are the conditions for realization reproduced through time? How is continuity ensured from one generation of practitioners to the next and from one place of practice to the next?

Buddhists often evoke the "Three Jewels" of the Buddha, the Dharma, and the Saṅgha as a way of designating what carries Buddhism across space and time. Each of these "jewels" can be understood in both tangible and intangible terms. In most Buddhist traditions, it is said that the practitioner "takes refuge" in the Three Jewels and is enabled to share in the merit generated by collective Buddhist practice in order to ultimately achieve liberation through his or her own practice.

Master Wuzhu inherited a subitist stance toward the Three Jewels, which is reflected in his challenge to a group of traditional Dharma masters:

> He asked the Dharma masters, "What is the Buddha-Jewel, what is the Dharma-Jewel, what is the Saṅgha-Jewel?" The Dharma masters were silent and did not speak. The Venerable explained, "Knowing the Dharma is precisely the Buddha-Jewel, transcending characteristics is precisely the Dharma-Jewel, and non-doing is precisely the Saṅgha-Jewel."[1]

Chan Buddhism was radical in its rejection of the notion of taking refuge in the Three Jewels as outside supports, recommending that the practitioner go straight to her or his own mind. This paradigm shift is expressed more elaborately in the *Platform Sūtra,* the popular sibling of the *Lidai fabao ji* that was introduced at the end of the previous chapter. Let us look at each refuge and its reformulation as presented in the *Platform Sūtra.* Concretely, Śākyamuni is the physical representation of the Buddha-Jewel in our era. Images of cosmic buddhas and bodhisattvas also came to represent the Buddha-Jewel: they were actual (virtual) sources of aid for devotees, but they also represent *bodhi,* the potential for awakening, in each person. Thus, the refuge of the Buddha-Jewel is both other—salvific buddhas and bodhisattvas—and one's own realization. In the famous passage from the *Mahāparinibbāna-sutta,* Śākyamuni's last words are "Be a lamp unto yourself."[2] In the *Platform Sūtra,* Huineng says, "The sūtras say that oneself [as Buddha] takes refuge in the Buddha; they do not say to take refuge in other buddhas."[3]

The second jewel, the Dharma or teachings, can be considered concretely as Buddhist texts and lectures, but also ineffably as the "Law," the nature of truth to teach and realize itself. Early Buddhist scriptures are presented not as revelations or systematic compositions but as oral transmissions based on the memories of disciples who heard the Buddha speak. This is why early Buddhist sūtras begin with the phrase "Thus have I heard." However, each Buddhist country and era developed its own version of a Buddhist canon, and Buddhist texts written today may eventually become part of some future version of a Buddhist body of scriptures.

The *Platform Sūtra* teaches that everything in the scriptures is the nature of one's mind, but one may need the help of a teacher to activate it: "Therefore, although the buddhas of the three worlds and all the twelve divisions of the canon are within human nature, originally itself in complete possession [of the Dharma], if one cannot awaken to one's own nature, one must obtain a good teacher to show one the way to see the nature. But if you awaken to yourself, do not depend on outside teachers."[4]

The third jewel, the Saṅgha or Buddhist community, is in its narrowest sense the community of ordained monks and nuns and in its broadest sense all Buddhist believers. Monks and nuns as a group are considered "refuges" because they vow to live by a set of specific precepts mandating pure conduct, especially celibacy. This is why Huineng designates the Saṅgha-Jewel as "purity," but he specifies that it is the innate purity of one's mind: "In your own mind take refuge in purity; although defilements and delusions are in one's own nature, one's own nature is not stained."[5]

One of the most fascinating aspects of Chan history is the process by which this insistence on the salvific nature of one's own mind was linked to the ideology of an exclusive line of patriarchs who transmitted the Dharma "from mind to mind" all the way from Śākyamuni Buddha to the eighth-century Chinese present and beyond. Not only was this transmission unique and exclusive, the question of who received it revolved around a very concrete talisman: the robe of Bodhidharma, the first Indian patriarch to bring this Dharma transmission to China. In order to understand the stakes invested in the story of Wuzhu's transmission, we need to understand the evolution of the concepts of patriarchal robe and lineage.

BODHIDHARMA'S ROBE

As noted above, the eighth-century monk Shenhui sowed the seeds of a patriarchal mythos that within a few generations became Chan orthodoxy. According to him, transmission of the true Dharma began with Śākyamuni's transmission to his disciple Mahākāśyapa. Shenhui claimed that in China this transmission was verified by a tangible token of authenticity: a robe given by Bodhidharma to his Chinese disciple Huike in order to signify that the Dharma had passed from India to new ground. Shenhui wrote, "The robe serves as verification of the Dharma and the Dharma is the robe lineage. Robe and Dharma are transferred from one [patriarch] to another and are handed down without alteration. Without the robe one does not spread forth the Dharma, without the Dharma one does not receive the robe."[6]

Shenhui compared the transmission of the "robe of verification" to the transmission of the regalia of a Cakravartin, a universal monarch, to the next reigning prince. This reflects the long-standing Buddhist association between the consecration of a king and Buddhist ordination rituals. The notion of sacred talismans signifying legitimate rule also made sense in the Chinese context: sacred heirlooms were thought to validate the reigning dynasty's mandate. These objects were supposed to protect the dynasty until the time had come for a new cycle and a new dynastic succession.

Buddhist scriptural and anecdotal sources also provided material for the notion of a special robe as a symbol of transmission. In a well-known work, the *Da Tang xiyu ji* (The Tang Dynasty Account of the Western Regions), the famous pilgrim-monk Xuanzang relates a version of the transmission of a robe from the Buddha to his disciple Mahākāśyapa. The Buddha, about to enter nirvāṇa, entrusts his gold-embroidered robe to Mahākāśyapa and publicly invests him with authority as leader of the Saṅgha and successor to the transmission of the true Dharma. The Buddha then predicts that twenty years after the first assembly, when Mahākāśyapa is on the point of entering nirvāṇa, he will enter the sacred Mount Kukkuṭapāda and stand there holding the Buddha's robe in his arms. The mountain will enclose him and he will wait eons for the advent of the future Buddha Maitreya. When Maitreya finally arrives, the mountain will open and Mahākāśyapa will transmit the robe to Maitreya in view of the assembled crowd. Mahākāśyapa will then ascend into the air and self-combust, entering nirvāṇa.[7] Here, a robe serves as a token of continuity between the Buddha of our age, Śākyamuni, and the Buddha of the coming age, spanning uncountable years.

There were magical properties associated even with ordinary monks' robes. Thus, the notion of a special robe, the robe of the Buddha or the robe of

Bodhidharma, had a powerful appeal in a time of transition for Buddhism and for Chinese culture as a whole. Placing such importance on a robe may seem materialistic for a teaching based on realization of one's own buddha nature, just as the idea of patriarchy seems to run counter to the emphasis on one's own nonmediated access to the truth. Yet it has a symbolic force that resonates across cultures. Throughout the world, "inalienable possessions," often textiles, were passed down through the generations as representations of the continuity and authority of the family who held them.[8]

The robe's function as an actual token of transmission, authorizing a monk to claim the title of patriarch, quickly became obsolete. Two generations after Shenhui, possession of "Bodhidharma's robe" was no longer an issue. Yet it captured the mystique of transmission in a way that no subsequent device was able to do. The passing of the robe from Hongren to the Sixth Patriarch Huineng remains the heart of the *Platform Sūtra* for contemporary readers. Clearly, the *Lidai fabao ji* authors had it in mind when they created their own robe drama centered on Wuzhu and the Korean master Wuxiang.

CONSTRUCTING PATRIARCHAL LINEAGES

The story of a master passing what he knows to a single disciple, who endures much hardship to prove himself, may be perennial. However, it is noteworthy that contemporary popular culture associates this motif with East Asia. Films and graphic media draw on Asian images of powerful masters, perplexed disciples, and the fate that binds them together. Vaguely East Asian fashion statements are associated with many of these productions. Robes continue to play important roles.

China has an indigenous tradition of master-disciple relations that goes back at least as far as the anecdotes about Confucius and his disciples found in the *Lunyu* (Analects). However, the blending of Buddhist stories from India with Chinese notions of sympathetic resonance between fated individuals gave rise to the compelling master-disciple narratives that became a Chan specialty.

There are long lists of names, evidently lineages of Indian masters and disciples, appended to certain sūtra translations made in China in the fifth century. It seems clear that Indian Buddhists developed some form of genealogical record fairly early, tracing the first few generations after the Buddha's death.

Later exegetical traditions recorded the names of recent masters associated with the transmission of a particular text. Narratives of master-disciple interactions became increasingly detailed and dramatic in both India and China.

In eighth-century China, Buddhist groups besides the nascent Chan school were also in the process of formulating specialized concepts of lineage, most importantly the Tiantai school, which claimed Tiantai Zhiyi (538–597) as founder. In a preface to Zhiyi's best-known work, the *Mohe zhiguan* (Great Calming and Insight), Zhiyi's disciple Guanding (561–632) laid the foundations for a distinctive Tiantai lineage and transmission ideology. In this preface he describes both ends of a lineage that does not meet in the middle. The "Western" line moves forward from Śākyamuni Buddha, and the "Eastern" line traces antecedents from Zhiyi to his master Huisi (515–577), then to Huisi's master Huiwen (mid-sixth century).

There was no attempt to craft a "string of pearls" linking the two lines, but Nāgārjuna (ca. second–third century), the thirteenth patriarch in the Western line, is evoked as a "high ancestral teacher." Nāgārjuna becomes a spiritual ancestor not because there is a direct line of transmission, but because Huiwen's insights into a work believed to have been authored by Nāgārjuna were the source of the special method of cultivation passed down and explicated in Zhiyi's work.

As Tiantai scholar Linda Penkower points out, this is a creative solution to the problem of validating both the continuity of transmitted teachings and the innovations of individual insight. Linear time is represented in the Western and Eastern lineages, but spiritual affinities and karmic connections also permit transtemporal relationships. In Guanding's biography of Zhiyi, Huisi is said to have had a karmic connection with Zhiyi due to their having listened to the Buddha preach the *Lotus Sūtra* (*Saddharmapuṇḍarīka-sūtra*) together in a past life. Guanding also refers to the *Lotus Sūtra*'s assurance that Śākyamuni is constantly preaching the *Lotus* in his "Bliss Body" or transcendent manifestation. Thus, Zhiyi's enlightenment experience through meditative study of the *Lotus Sūtra* is linked to a past connection with his teacher and to the continued presence of direct transmission from the Buddha.[9]

The Tiantai notion of dual diachronic and synchronic transmission and the Chan ideology of strictly linear transmission drew on a common source. The *Fu fazang zhuan* (Account of the Transmission of the Dharma Treasury), a text of uncertain origins, tells the stories of a succession of Indian patriarchs. It includes dramatic and amusing episodes, but it ends with a decisive act of violence—Siṃha Bhikṣu, the twenty-fourth patriarch, is beheaded by a king in Kashmir and bleeds white milk instead of blood. This is the end of the line of Dharma transmission.

In the early centuries of the Common Era, the notion that Śākyamuni's Dharma was also subject to impermanence began to generate various eschatological narratives and theories. Concern that the world had entered the "final age" of the decline of the Dharma, when kings and monks were corrupt and true teachings difficult to encounter, took hold in China in the sixth century. The compiler of the *Fu fazang zhuan* was clearly influenced by some form of the "final age" doctrine.

The *Fu fazang zhuan* stories were a useful foundation for the version of the patriarchal lineage adopted in Chan genealogies, but someone had to rework the abrupt ending in order to link the lineage to Bodhidharma and the Chinese patriarchs. The *Platform Sūtra* uses most of the *Fu fazang zhuan* lineage and adds more names. The *Lidai fabao ji* authors went further and concocted a story in which Siṃha Bhikṣu, after having transmitted the Dharma to his successor, allows himself to be martyred. He bleeds white milk to demonstrate the falseness of the followers of Mani and Jesus, who are then slaughtered by the king. Siṃha Bhikṣu's disciple continues the transmission. Finally, after five more Indian patriarchs, seven Chinese patriarchs, and many twists of fate, the Dharma is invested in Wuzhu.

The *Fu fazang zhuan* and the *Lidai fabao ji* both stress that Dharma transmission is always imperiled. On the one hand, transmission stories give reassuring evidence of the temporal extension of the Buddha's power. On the other hand, these stories underline the vulnerability of the Dharma's human vessels. In the *Lidai fabao ji* and the other Chan works that promoted rival versions of the tales of the patriarchs, the message is that Chan is a special transmission and one is extremely lucky to have access to it.

A SPECIAL TRANSMISSION

Tales of the patriarchs became a way to establish particular soteriological brands, and each Chan transmission history launched a distinctive critique of the practices of rivals. Contestation became a means to maintain the orthodoxy of no-thought, creating a perpetually polemical context for Chan practice. Chan scholar Bernard Faure has called this the "rhetoric of immediacy."

Professionalization of the clergy in the eighth century was one of the pressures that contributed to the development of a competitive mystique. The idea of a mysterious patriarchy, a hidden line of teachers distinct from ordinary monks and nuns, was one means to address the problems of routinization and mass production of clerics. However, in order to create the mythos of a lineage of masters separate from the merely ordained, it was necessary to create a sense of privileged transmission that was impossible to reproduce through mundane monastic rules and rituals, images, and texts.

Eventually, polemic itself became routinized and ritualized. In the eleventh and twelfth centuries, Chan developed its own monastic institutions and networks, its own "brand." In this context, Chan as "a special transmission outside the scriptures" became a catchy slogan attributed to Bodhidharma. Chan monks established lineages and textual patterns that could be elaborated and adapted, leading to the production of massive hagiographical genealogies like the *Jingde chuandeng lu* (Transmission of the Lamp Compiled in the Jingde Era).

The precision and detail of the branching Chan genealogies of the Song dynasty and beyond must be juxtaposed against the unreliability of transmission accounts in texts of the period that these genealogies claim to represent. The period in which Wuzhu lived and taught was later considered the golden age of Chan, but the dynamics of the spread of Chan-style teachings are far from clear. The fact that Chan transmission narratives of the late eighth century tend to be vague about subsequent transmission points to a kind of built-in obsolescence in the ideology of Chan patriarchy itself. "One patriarch per generation" was an effective way of bringing the Dharma forward from the past, but it was untenable as a map of the future.

As Chan historian John Jorgenson has pointed out, the notion of a Chan patriarchy mirrors the Chinese notion of dynastic succession, in which seven generations are necessary in order to establish a fully fledged dynasty.[10] However, while a dynasty must restrict itself to one emperor per generation, a flourishing school of Buddhism need not be so constrained. Once the "trunk" of six Chinese patriarchs had been established, the fact that there were competing claimants to the title of Seventh Patriarch was nothing less than an indication that the school had begun to be. There was no "Chan school" in existence during the time of the six Chinese patriarchs—it cannot even be said to have begun with Shenhui, the one who yoked six names to a powerfully generative idea. However, once the imaginary line had been drawn in the sands of the past, it began to sprout real branches. It continues to put forth new shoots even today.

WUZHU'S LIFE AND THE TRANSMISSION CONTROVERSY

The *Lidai fabao ji* tale of Wuzhu's life and transmission was probably based on the master's own account, as told to his immediate disciples. There are no other sources on his early life, and comments on his community and teachings appear, with one notable exception, to have been based on the *Lidai fabao ji* itself. The exception is the work of the influential scholar-monk Guifeng Zongmi (780–841), who is considered the Fifth Patriarch of the Huayan school and also claimed transmission in Shenhui's Chan lineage. He wrote extensive assessments of the Chan groups of his day, and he was most critical of the Bao Tang and Hongzhou schools.

The *Lidai fabao ji* story of Wuzhu's early wanderings and his transmission from Wuxiang unfolds in considerable detail, a compelling narrative. Wuzhu was originally from the north, from a district in what is now Shaanxi province. His father is said to have had a distinguished career in the army during the Kaiyuan era (713–741), in the early decades of the reign of Emperor Xuanzong (r. 712–756).

At twenty, it is said, Wuzhu's physical strength and martial prowess attract the attention of an imperial prince and military commissioner, who gives him a post as Patrolling Grand Lance Officer for the *yamen,* a local administrative headquarters combining the functions of district court, police station, jail, and military outpost. Truth be told, Wuzhu's office was not very high-ranking, but it does seem to have called for physical bravery and initiative. For someone not born into the elite, any kind of imperial position would have been a coveted sinecure. Thus, his decision to leave the military in order to seek the Way is presented as proof of his sincerity and determination.

The *Lidai fabao ji* and Zongmi both claim that Wuzhu first studied the Dharma under an enlightened layman named Chen Chuzang. The *Lidai fabao ji* says that when Chen Chuzang met Wuzhu there was an immediate affinity between them, and the lay master "silently transmitted the mind-Dharma."[11] This points to the mystique of mind-to-mind transmission, but it is not transmission of the patriarchy.

Once Wuzhu obtains the Dharma of the sudden teaching, he continues to practice as a layman for some time. In his early thirties he goes to practice with one of Huineng's Dharma heirs, Chan Master Zizai of Taiyuan (Shanxi). Zizai persuades him to renounce lay status, and Wuzhu finally decides to take full vows and become a monk in 749, at the age of thirty-five. It is important to note that ordination would have been difficult (and expensive) without the sponsorship of an established cleric, which Wuzhu's first teacher was not.

Wuzhu then spends a summer or two at Qingliang monastery on Mount Wutai, a renowned Buddhist site. There he hears the discourses of two of Huineng's Dharma heirs, including the famous Shenhui. Wuzhu quickly grasps Shenhui's teachings but declines to go and pay his respects.

The *Lidai fabao ji* authors clearly had an ambivalent attitude toward the controversial proponent of the Southern School. Shenhui is put to use, however; his teachings are introduced immediately before Wuzhu's, and the *Lidai fabao ji* authors make him hint mysteriously that the true Dharma heir is yet to appear. Interestingly, Shenhui is also made to voice an ambivalent assessment of Wuxiang's teachings: "Kim of Yizhou is a Chan Master, but he also did not manage to expound the ultimate teaching. Although he did not expound the ultimate teaching, the Buddha-Dharma is only at his place."[12] In this and other ways, the *Lidai fabao ji* authors claim that Wuzhu is the one who fully manifests the transmission of Bodhidharma even though he has received it through a line of worthy but lesser masters.

After his sojourn at Mount Wutai, Wuzhu spends a couple of years at two different monasteries in Chang'an, the Tang capital. In 751 he goes to the Helan mountains (Ningxia), bordering what is now Inner Mongolia. He spends two years there, and sometime during this period a merchant named Cao Gui comes to pay his respects.

Cao Gui tells him that he looks exactly like the Korean Chan Master Wuxiang (the Venerable Kim) in Sichuan. Cao Gui also conveys some of Wuxiang's words, which Cao Gui says he himself does not understand. Wuzhu, however, instantly grasps their deep meaning and feels he has met the distant master "face to face." Cao Gui describes the resemblance between Wuxiang and Wuzhu as the manifestation of a "transformation body" (*huashen*), the form that buddhas and bodhisattvas take in order to teach beings. He says, "Your features are exactly like those of the Venerable Kim. You both have a mole above the bridge of your nose, and the shape of your face so resembles that of the

Venerable in our locale that one could even say there is no difference. It must be a transformation body."[13]

A sense of mysterious affinity prompts Wuzhu to leave the mountains and make his way south. His progress is gradual, to say the least. He is detained in Lingzhou (Ningxia), unable to get official traveling papers because of the deep attachment he inspires in an imperial prince and several local monks. He "quietly" leaves Lingzhou in 757 and finally gets travel documents in Fengning (Shaanxi), from an official who also tries to keep him from leaving what was considered (with good cause) to be the center of world civilization. After further peregrinations he finally makes it to Wuxiang's Jingzhong monastery in 759.

Wuzhu arrives at the beginning of a precepts-retreat, where he has his first and only meeting with the Korean master. The scene in which Wuzhu and Wuxiang enact the master-disciple relationship is a compelling one, with at least as much dramatic merit as the better-known story of the meeting between Huineng and Hongren. After being invited to stay at the monastery, Wuzhu attends Wuxiang's bodhisattva-precepts retreat for three days. Cryptically, in the middle of his public lecture, Wuxiang gives instructions that are meant for Wuzhu's ears alone:

> Every day in the midst of the great assembly the Venerable Kim would intone in a loud voice, "Why do you not go into the mountains, what good is it to linger?"
>
> His attendant disciples considered this strange [and said,] "The Venerable Kim has never said anything like this before. Why would he suddenly come out with these words?" But the Venerable Wuzhu quietly entered the mountains.[14]

Wuxiang and Wuzhu's subsequent long-distance relationship can be seen as a creative device to explain away the inconvenient fact that Wuzhu was never really Wuxiang's disciple. At the same time, it is a powerful means of expressing the "sudden" teaching, not bound by physical presence or monastic formalities. Symbolically, the wordless bond between master and disciple, indifferent to space or time, resolves the tension between the exclusiveness of mind-to-mind transmission and the inclusiveness of the teaching of innate buddha nature. It also erases the distinction between sudden enlightenment and gradual development.

The motif of mysterious sympathetic resonance between protagonists who are destined to meet is not unique to Chan or to Buddhism, but it was useful in solving one of the dilemmas of the sudden teaching. Any time spent studying with the master *before* receiving Dharma transmission means that the teaching is gradual, after all. It implies that buddha nature is something learned. In other key Chan transmission narratives, this contradiction is resolved in other ways. The Second Patriarch Huike spends years with Bodhidharma *after* receiving initial transmission. Huineng spends nine months at Hongren's place, but they have only one encounter before Huineng receives transmission. The *Lidai fabao ji* story is certainly the most extreme example, as Wuzhu and Wuxiang meet face-to-face only once.

Though Wuzhu does not see Wuxiang again after the initial encounter, he is shown to be intimately connected with the master and aware of events at the distant Jingzhong monastery. In a subsequent scene, Wuzhu on his faraway mountaintop answers a question that the other monks are asking Wuxiang in his hall. Wuzhu's answer is both a challenge to the monastic community and a striking declaration of his bond with Wuxiang:

> [Later] the Venerable Kim longed for him [and said,] "Why doesn't he come?" Preceptor Kong and Preceptor Qin wanted to be able to recognize [Wuzhu, and so they said,] "We fear that one day we might chance to meet but not know who he is."
>
> [From the mountains] the Venerable [Wuzhu] faced toward them with a keen glance and exclaimed, "Although I am here, the Venerable Kim and I see each other constantly. Even if we wish not to know each other, we are face-to-face across a thousand *li*."[15]

Wuzhu then relates a scriptural episode in which all the Buddha's disciples flock to see him when he returns from preaching to his mother in Heaven. The nun Utpalavarṇā resorts to magical powers to be first in line to greet the Buddha. The Buddha admonishes the pushy nun, "Subhuti is in a stone cell continuously in *samādhi,* and so he was first, being able to see my Dharma-body. You came rushing to see my form-body, and so you are last." Wuzhu concludes his lecture to the far-off Jingzhong monks by saying: "The Buddha has given a clear mandate, and that is why I do not go [to see the Venerable Kim]."[16]

Wuzhu's long-distance challenge segues into the story of how he receives Bodhidharma's robe and transmission of the Chan patriarchy. However, this presents another narrative dilemma. How did Bodhidharma's robe get to Sichuan? The *Lidai fabao ji* authors concoct an entertaining but unlikely account in which the famous imperial patroness of Buddhism, Empress Wu Zetian, receives Bodhidharma's robe as a gift from Huineng and passes it on to Chan Master Zhishen. Zhishen is the grandfather-in-the-Dharma of Wuxiang, who is thus claimed to be the legitimate possessor of the robe of verification.

Wuxiang, knowing he is about to die, sends Bodhidharma's robe and a message to Wuzhu through an intermediary. The *Lidai fabao ji* includes two slightly different versions of Wuxiang's indirect transmission. The first is relatively simple and precedes Wuxiang's death scene: the ailing master secretly sends the robe of verification and a message to Wuzhu, and the passage concludes with the assertion that Dharma transmission was "settled from afar."

In the second version, the *Lidai fabao ji* authors elaborate on the dynamics of this unusual long-distance transmission. Wuzhu, sequestered in the mountains, tells the lay disciple Dong Xuan that he should go to Wuxiang to receive the precepts. Wuzhu sends him off with a gift of tea for Wuxiang, and when Dong Xuan gets to Chengdu and presents the tea, he lies and says he is a personal disciple of Wuzhu's. When Dong Xuan is about to return to the mountains, he is given a private audience with Wuxiang. Wuxiang then entrusts him with Bodhidharma's robe, his own personal effects, and a statement of secret transmission: "This was given to the Venerable Shen by Empress [Wu] Zetian. The Venerable Shen gave it to the Venerable Tang, the Venerable Tang gave it to me, and I transmit it to Chan Master Wuzhu. This robe has long been cherished, don't let anyone know of it."[17]

Later, when his disciples ask him about the robe, Wuxiang presents them with a cryptic pun: "My Dharma has gone to the place of nonabiding (*wuzhu*). The robe is hanging from the top of a tree, no one has got it."[18] Still later it is revealed that the robe made it to Wuzhu (Nonabiding) only after further complications. Some army officers who met Wuzhu in the mountains tell this convoluted story to Wuzhu's patron, the imperial minister Du Hongjian:

> We saw that this Chan Master looked exactly like the Venerable Kim. When we first saw him it was as if he were a transformation body of the Venerable Kim. We ventured to question him and remained for some time, and we learned that the Venerable Kim's robe and bowl had previously been dispatched to him via a messenger. [The messenger] hid them for two years and did not deliver them, and then sold them to a monk. When the monk obtained the robe, that night a spirit appeared who told him to send it back to its original owner, [saying] "If

you do not return it, you are most certainly shortening your life." The buyer exchanged it, giving an account of what had happened. After that [the messenger] couldn't sell it, and he restored it to the original Chan Master's place. As soon as we heard that the robe our previous searching had not discovered was now in the immediate vicinity, we asked to make obeisance. Without reservations, [Wuzhu] carried the robe out aloft and revealed it to all the army officers and soldiers, so we know it is at that place.[19]

The *Lidai fabao ji* authors' subsequent rebuttal of the story that Wuzhu actually stole the robe is the only remaining evidence that there was ever such a story in circulation. It is embedded in the *Lidai fabao ji* account of malicious Vinaya masters who attempt to appropriate Wuxiang's lineage for themselves. They take over Wuxiang's cloister in the Jingzhong monastery, staking their claim through a robe they say was his. In order to discourage the local gentry from following Du Hongjian's endorsement of Wuzhu's status as legitimate heir, they circulate a story about the robe in his possession. They claim that Wuzhu got an expensive monk's robe from a local craftsman who had received it in payment for his work. They accuse Wuzhu of failing to pay for the robe and then using it as proof of spurious transmission. These crimes, capped by his refusal to "practice the forms of worship," make him a shady character who should not be allowed to influence other monks.

In this fable of virtue vindicated, the Vinaya masters' accusations are eventually exposed as lies. However, the story also represents orthodox reactions against the challenge that Wuzhu's nonconformity presented to the clergy as a body. What else is buried in its folds? Wuzhu's self-possession in the face of challenges and difficulties is meant to prove that he truly deserves to possess the robe and establish his own place of practice, his own *wuzhu*. The *Lidai fabao ji* tale of indirect and contested transmission is a fabric of imagination and unspeakable truths, but what is unspeakable excludes neither the true resonance of mind-to-mind connection nor the silencing of inconvenient truths.

CHAPTER

3

RADICAL ASPECTS OF WUZHU'S TEACHINGS

FROM BODHISATTVA PRECEPTS TO FORMLESS PRECEPTS

Chan rhetorical rejection of merit practice was captured in the aforementioned emblematic dialogue between Bodhidharma and Emperor Wu of the Liang. The exchange presents merit practice in its shallowest, most self-serving form: Emperor Wu is portrayed as using his superior wealth and power to pile up merit for himself. Yet merit practice was not merely a kind of spiritual materialism aimed at improving one's own conditions. Such practices were also methods of self-purification intended as foundations of the bodhisattva path. This is particularly true of repentance, taking the bodhisattva precepts, and calling on and visualizing the buddhas.

We can see that these salvation-oriented practices were important by the sheer number of texts dedicated to them in the fifth through eighth centuries. Working with Indian models, Chinese Buddhists developed many new rituals for taking the bodhisattva precepts, and these usually began with repentance. Repentance and precepts were soteriologically linked as vows. Taking the bodhisattva precepts meant vowing to become a buddha in order to save other beings and vowing to cultivate the practices that would enable one to realize this goal, a process of innumerable lifetimes. Recognizing past negative actions and praying to the buddhas to aid in removing karmic residue was an important initial stage. In some contexts repentance practice was even thought to remove *kleśa* (defilements), which are deeply ingrained habitual afflictive patterns, what we might call addictions or compulsions.

Images, liturgies, and texts were produced to aid in the practice of visualizing and calling on the buddhas and bodhisattvas so that they might witness vows and repentance, guarantee merit, answer prayers, and responsively effect transformation in the devotee. Even if not all practitioners attempted to visualize buddhas, this practice can be seen in all types of medieval Buddhist lore: scriptures, biographies of monks and nuns, collections of miracle tales, and popular anecdotes. Visualization and evocation of the names of buddhas were integral to the cults of the bodhisattva Avalokiteśvara, the future Buddha Maitreya, and the Buddha of the Western Pure Land, Amitābha.

In order to understand the force of Wuzhu's rejection of such practices, it is important to understand the evolution of precepts practice as it was received and transformed in China. I describe this evolution in three stages, using representative texts as examples: first a seminal Mahāyāna scripture, then an influential apocryphal precepts text claiming Indian origins but written in China, and finally, early Chan liturgical reinterpretations of the precepts.

INDIAN MAHĀYĀNA BODHISATTVA PRECEPTS

In classic Mahāyāna conceptions of the path, receiving the bodhisattva precepts (Skt. *bodhisattvaprātimokṡa*) was one of the early steps, usually the second of ten stages, on the way to becoming a buddha. The *Avataṃsaka-sūtra* (Flower Garland Scripture) was one of the main sources for the formalization of the bodhisattva precepts. In the *Avataṃsaka,* the second or "purity" stage of the bodhisattva path is divided into three levels: 1) precepts against the ten evil actions; 2) practice of the antidotes to the ten evil acts (i.e., the positive cultivation of right action, word, thought); and 3) compassion and altruistic acts toward all beings.[1] The *Avataṃsaka* reinterprets the basic acts of Buddhist practice in terms of universal compassion and the cosmological significance of the bodhisattva path, reinforcing this path with visions of buddhas, bodhisattvas, and divinities. It is likely that the visual detail in this sūtra provided inspiration for the image-maker's art.

Texts that included specific rituals for the bodhisattva precepts often took the *Avataṃsaka* structure as a basis. Of these, the *Bodhisattvabhūmi* (Bodhisattva Stages) was perhaps most influential source for the content and form of bodhisattva precepts ceremonies in China. The ceremony in the *Bodhisattvabhūmi* became a template for later Chinese bodhisattva precepts texts.

The *Bodhisattvabhūmi* translation opens with an assertion of the superiority of the bodhisattva precepts and then explains the Three Groups of Pure Precepts, which correspond to the three levels of the purity stage in the *Avataṃsaka-sūtra,* described above. In the *Bodhisattvabhūmi* precepts ceremony, the petitioner prostrates before the master and states her request to receive the precepts. She pays homage to the buddhas and bodhisattvas and obtains the benefit of their merit in order to be purified. Prostrate before an image of the Buddha, she repeats the request to receive the precepts and concentrates on the merit that is produced by doing so. She is asked to repeat three times that she is a bodhisattva, follows the path of awakening, and desires to receive the Three Groups of Pure Precepts. The monk serving as Preceptor requests administration of the precepts from the buddhas and bodhisattvas on behalf of the petitioner, and the ceremony is concluded. The text has a list of the standard categories of transgressions and the levels of confession and contrition necessary to dissipate their effects. Finally, it is said that in the absence of a qualified member of the clergy, one can administer the precepts to oneself according to the formula given in the text.[2]

PRECEPTS TEXTS WRITTEN IN CHINA

A number of new scriptures appeared during the decades following the Northern Wei Buddhist persecution (444–452). Although some were translations, many were "indigenous scriptures" or apocrypha, compilations that may have elaborated on earlier translations of authentically Indian scriptures but introduced new features that made them more relevant in the Chinese milieu. As these compilations became more widely circulated, they acquired translation and transmission histories.

One of the best-known apocryphal bodhisattva precepts texts was the *Brahmajāla-sūtra* (Scripture of Brahma's Net).[3] It drew from the *Avataṃsaka-sūtra* and *Bodhisattvabhūmi* as well as the *Nirvāṇa-sūtra.* However, it also has characteristics that distinguish it from earlier Mahāyāna precepts texts. It became the most commonly used precepts text in East Asia, eventually supplanting the Vinaya as the basis of monastic ordination in the Tendai sect in Japan. It gave rulers a significant role in the maintenance of Buddhism and promised worldly peace and prosperity as well as liberation. The *Brahmajāla-*

sūtra's ten major and forty-eight minor precepts proved so popular that they circulated as an independent text by the end of the fifth century. Most importantly, the sūtra attempted to resolve incompatibilities between canonical Buddhist monastic practices and Chinese core values, especially filial piety. This is stressed in the *Brahmajāla-sūtra* introduction: "Filial submission is the Dharma of the ultimate path. Filial piety is called *śīla* (discipline), also called restraint."[4]

Notably, the *Brahmajāla-sūtra* formalized procedures for repentance and reception of the precepts that could be validated by the penitent's reception of visionary signs, without the presence of a member of the clergy. The incorporation of such self-administered vows into many of the apocryphal bodhisattva precepts texts suggests that self-directed practices became widespread. It is likely that they were meant to supplement, not replace, practice in an assembly led by ordained monks. However, these ritual scripts gave greater scope and legitimacy both to individual practice and to the collective practices of lay groups without regular access to clerical direction.

CHAN REINTERPRETATION OF THE PRECEPTS

Various forms of repentance and bodhisattva vows developed in the fifth through seventh centuries and continue to flourish in contemporary Chinese Buddhism. In the eighth century, however, Chan groups began to redefine the meaning of precepts practice and devotionalism.

Chan can be said to have been born on the bodhisattva precepts platform. Mass bodhisattva precepts ceremonies enjoyed a boom after the Tang dynasty was shattered in 755, and money raised at such events helped fund the Tang restoration war effort. The importance of bodhisattva precepts retreats is reflected in Chan texts of the period: the *Platform Sūtra* is set on the platform of a precepts assembly, and the crucial meeting between Wuzhu and Wuxiang takes place at a precepts retreat.

The Tiantai school played an important role in developing Buddhist rituals tailored to Chinese cultural life. Buddhist scholar Paul Groner notes a trend that he calls the "professionalization" of bodhisattva ordination rituals, which were used to attain good luck in marriage, birth, and travel, and were also used in funerals and the dedication of new buildings.[5] Hand in hand with ritual specialization was a polarizing tendency toward interiorization and self-validation of the precepts. "Outer" forms of taking the precepts were retained, but there was increasing interest in articulating "inner" precepts as the realization of the nature of one's own mind.

We see this in a pivotal Chan text associated with the "Northern School," the *Dasheng wusheng fangbian men* (The Expedient Means of Attaining Birthlessness in the Mahāyāna). It opens with a precepts ritual and a script for audience responses. Traditional forms are retained; the liturgy includes taking the buddhas and bodhisattvas as preceptors, repeating the precepts, and uttering a formula of repentance. However, at the end the practitioner ritually repeats that the true nature of one's own mind is the same as the nature of the precepts: "To maintain the bodhisattva precepts is to maintain the precepts of the mind, because the Buddha nature is the 'nature of the precepts' (*jiexing*). To activate the mind (*qixin*) for the briefest instant is to go counter to the Buddha nature, to break the bodhisattva precepts."[6]

In the *Dasheng wusheng fangbian men,* conventional and ultimate meanings of the precepts are maintained together. Shenhui's critique of the Northern School, however, targeted practices aimed at purification, claiming that they contributed to misrecognition of the nature of the mind. As this critique gained force, true practice was redefined as the nonobjectification of practice. Any accommodation of conventional practice thus became problematic.

Once again, the *Platform Sūtra* provided a platform for reassessment. In the Dharma talk following the story of his reception of the robe, Huineng goes through all the elements of a typical bodhisattva precepts ceremony. Each element is reinterpreted as formless: taking refuge in the three bodies of the Buddha, the four vows, repentance, and taking refuge in the Three Jewels.[7] The point is that the only effective practice is "sudden," emptying the forms of practice of their purposive presumptions. (You can't get there from here, you are always t/here.) Instead of telling his audience "do not practice the precepts" (which would itself be a precept and a misconception), Huineng transmits the "precepts of formlessness." The following passage is the *Platform Sūtra* version of refuge in the three bodies of the Buddha:

> Good friends, you must all with your own bodies receive the precepts of formlessness and recite in unison what I am about to say. It will make you see the threefold body of the Buddha in your own selves. 'I take refuge in the pure

Dharmakāya Buddha in my own physical body. I take refuge in the ten thousand hundred billion *Nirmāṇakāya* Buddhas in my own physical body. I take refuge in the future perfect *Sambhogakāya* Buddha in my own physical body. (Recite the above three times).[8]

When he has completed this ritual of nonritual, Huineng emphasizes the nonduality of good and evil: "The ten thousand things are all in self-nature. Although you see all men and non-men, evil and good, evil things and good things, you must not throw them aside, nor must you cling to them, nor must you be stained by them, but you must regard them as being like the empty sky."[9]

Though the nonduality of good and evil on the absolute level was a long-standing Buddhist teaching, a formative rhetorical strategy for the Chan school was to critique separation of conventional and absolute on the level of practice. In most Buddhist contexts, basic practices of moral discipline (*śīla*) were foundational for both lay and ordained. With the development of Chan-style critique, the question of how to practice even the ordinary precepts against wrongdoing became controversial.

The Chan/Zen emphasis on immanent (rather than transcendent) nonduality has earned it a reputation as a form of antinomianism. The term "antinomian," literally "against law," derives from a Christian context, namely Paul's contention that Christ's grace made the need to observe moral precepts redundant. A key point argued in Christian and Buddhist debates was that grace—in Chan contexts, enlightenment—does not mean that you are no longer bound by moral laws. It means that your natural disposition is to do what is right in any given situation. In later Chan, key teachings were designed to counter the delusion that the enlightened person is no longer bound by the laws of cause and effect.[10]

It is important to keep in mind that mass precepts assemblies were the public vehicle for the self-conscious antinomianism found in Southern School Chan texts. It was primarily within the well-defined time and space of such an assembly, in a ritual context, that the precepts of formlessness and the emptiness of good and evil could be put into practice.

WUZHU'S TEACHINGS ON THE PRECEPTS

The uniqueness of Wuzhu and his disciples was that they were willing to let the formless precepts go out of the bounds of public ritual and into the temple, there to inform the daily practice of monks, nuns, and even lay devotees. The first of Wuzhu's sermons in the *Lidai fabao ji* makes this point, through a redefinition of the "place of practice," the *bodhimaṇḍa* (Chinese, *daochang;* Japanese, *dōjō*).

> Whenever the Venerable Wuzhu of the Dali [era] Baotang monastery in Chengdu subprefecture in Jiannan addressed students of the Way of the four assemblies, he would say, "Whether a multitude or a single person, regardless of the time, if you have doubts you may confide your questions to me. I am occupying the seat and explaining the Dharma so that you directly see your own natures. Regard direct mind as the *bodhimaṇḍa.* Regard aspiration to practice as the *bodhimaṇḍa.* Regard the profound mind as the *bodhimaṇḍa.* Regard the unstained as the *bodhimaṇḍa.* Regard not-grasping as the *bodhimaṇḍa.* Regard not-rejecting as the *bodhimaṇḍa.* Regard nonaction as *upāya* (expedient means). Regard the vast as *upāya.* Regard equanimity as *upāya.* Regard transcendence of characteristics as the fire and regard liberation as the incense. Regard nonobstruction as repentance. Regard no-thought as the precepts, nonaction and nothing to attain as meditation, and nonduality as wisdom. Do not regard the constructed ritual arena as the *bodhimaṇḍa.*"[11]

Wuzhu's sermon is similar to the *Platform Sūtra* reworking of the precepts ritual. Moreover, his explication of the *bodhimaṇḍa,* the sacred place of practice, is modeled after one of the most popular Mahāyāna texts, the *Vimalakīrtinirdeśa-sūtra* (Scripture on the Expositions of Vimalakīrti): "The mind that aspires to bodhi is the place of practice, for it is without error or misconception. Almsgiving is the place of practice, because it hopes for no reward. Observance of the precepts is the place of practice, because it brings fulfillment of the vows."[12]

The *Lidai fabao ji* grants us glimpses of the living, breathing audience in the *bodhimaṇḍa,* composed of laypeople quite unlike the lay superbodhisattva Vimalakīrti. The influence of the Bao Tang assembly can be felt in Wuzhu's determined and sometimes playful resistance to their dependence on forms, rituals, and precepts. For their sake, he teaches the precepts and "quotes the paddy-crabs."[13] Through their unspoken pressure, we are able to see that Wuzhu's rhetoric of refuge in "direct mind" has roots in the practice of meritorious rituals of refuge to save oneself, one's family, and all beings.

Chan reformulation of practice, even Wuzhu's radical version, retained within its deep structures the devotional and propitiatory magic of self-salvation. Self-seeking and self-realization, merit and no-merit, codependently gave rise to Chan antinomianism and iconoclasm. In contemporary Western Zen environments, it is the resistance or ambivalence toward Asian forms and rituals that is generally most strongly felt. However, after the Bao Tang experiment with abandoning forms, Chan would settle for a reliable paradox: both dependence on forms and resistance to forms are objectifications of practice. So go practice.

THE "THREE PHRASES" CONTROVERSY

The *Lidai fabao ji* claims that Wuzhu's master Wuxiang encapsulated the Chan teachings in three key phrases that address the challenge of creating a sudden practice from the ground up. Wuxiang is said to have attributed these three phrases to the First Patriarch Bodhidharma. It is implied that they are foundational and also a kind of transmission mantra, supplementing the robe. However, their exact wording was contested by the Bao Tang critic Zongmi.

According to the *Lidai fabao ji*, Bodhidharma/Wuxiang's three phrases were "no-recollection, no-thought, and do not be deluded" (*wuyi wunian mowang* 無憶無念莫妄). These were matched with the traditional "three trainings" of moral discipline, meditation, and wisdom: "No-recollection is *śīla*, no-thought is *samādhi*, and 'do not be deluded' is *prajñā*."[14] As these three trainings defined the basic components of practice undertaken by beginners and maintained by advanced practitioners, reinterpretation of their meanings was no trivial matter.

Instead of "do not be deluded" (*mowang* 莫妄), the rival Jingzhong school apparently maintained that Wuxiang taught the homophonous *mowang* 莫忘, "do not forget." The *Lidai fabao ji* alludes to the contested nature of the term *mowang* and insists that the version Wuzhu taught was the correct one. Zongmi, however, agreed with the Jingzhong version. He describes Wuxiang's teaching as follows:

> The "three phrases" are: no-recollection, no-thought, and "do not forget." The idea is: do not recall past *visayas* (domains); do not anticipate future glorious events; always be yoked to these insights, never darkening, never erring. This is called "do not forget." Sometimes [the three topics run]: no remembering of external *visayas,* no thinking of internal mind, dried up with nothing to rely on. *Śīla, samādhi,* and *prajñā* correspond respectively to the three phrases.[15]

Zongmi asserted that the Bao Tang "do not be deluded" was Wuzhu's idea and not the original:

> [The Bao Tang] also transmit the Venerable Kim's three-phrase oral teaching, but they change the character for "forget" to the character for "delusion." They say that all the fellow students have misconstrued the former master's oral tenets. Their characterization of the meaning is that no-recollection and no-thought are reality, and that recollecting thoughts is delusion; recollecting thoughts is not allowed. Therefore they say "do not be deluded."[16]

To complicate matters further, Wuzhu's interpretation was probably influenced by Shenhui, whose lineage Zongmi claimed. *Wang* 妄 (delusion) is the basis of Shenhui's interpretation of the three trainings:

> Friends, the necessity of undertaking the three trainings has from the beginning distinguished the Buddhist teachings. What are the three trainings? They are *śīla, samādhi,* and *prajñā.* That the deluded mind does not arise is called *śīla,* that there is no deluded mind is called *samādhi,* and knowing that the mind is without delusion is called *prajñā.* These are called the three trainings.[17]

According to the *Lidai fabao ji* authors' classification, Wuxiang's teaching was more advanced than Shenhui's, but it did not match Wuzhu's teaching that *śīla, samādhi,* and *prajñā* are effortlessly manifested in no-thought. The three phrases are the first teachings of Wuxiang's that Wuzhu encounters, as conveyed by the merchant Cao Gui. Wuzhu grasps the intent of the phrases immediately, but it is the mysterious resemblance and unspoken understanding between Wuxiang and Wuzhu that is the real transmission. However, the wrangling over three phrases shows that the nonverbal transmission at the heart of Chan was not the whole body, the whole assembly. This dispute over subtly different forms of a single character reflects a sense of unease and uncertainty about how to give basic teachings to ordinary practitioners.

CRITIQUES OF WUZHU'S STYLE OF PRACTICE

Wuzhu repeatedly makes the assertion that moral and formal distinctions belong to the dualistic discriminating mind that disappears in no-thought. Some of his strongest statements are found in a "dialogue" with a group of Vinaya masters who come to call. He opens his discussion by questioning them about the meaning of host and guest, and then proceeds to critique the Vinaya:

> The significance of the Vinaya is to regulate and subdue, and the precepts are not blue, yellow, red, or white. Not color/desire (*se*) and not mind, this is the substance of precepts, this is the fundamental nature of beings, fundamentally complete, fundamentally pure. When deluded thoughts are produced, then one "turns away from awakening and adheres to dust," and this is precisely "violating the Vinaya precepts." When deluded thoughts are not produced, then one turns away from dust and adheres to awakening, and this is precisely "fulfilling the Vinaya precepts."[18]

Wuzhu's nondual precepts are not meant to undermine rigorous practice, although in another *Lidai fabao ji* dialogue a trio of critics accuse Wuzhu of doing just that. Lax practice was not simply a matter of individual transgression, it endangered the saṅgha as a whole. Visible, reliable daily devotions carried out by the clergy were the basis of an unspoken contract between the ordained and the laity who supported them. Wuzhu's approach called this into question. His attempt to instantiate the emptiness of the precepts highlighted the shocking otherness of true nature's lack of reference to conventional economies and social contracts.

Wuzhu and his followers actually abandoned daily monastic and devotional routines, thereby ceasing to contribute to the circulation of merit. This attitude presented a dilemma even within the context of the self-avowed radicalism of the Southern School. Possession of the true transmission was still a soteriological trust fund, a source of support that was intended to be passed down through the generations.

Wuzhu's independent attitude seems to have been more than rhetorical. According to the *Lidai fabao ji,* during his period of seclusion in the mountains Wuzhu is deserted by his fellow monks. He refuses to carry out any recognizable Buddhist activity and just "sits in idleness/emptiness" (*kongxian zuo*). This upsets the monks, who come in a group to complain. Wuzhu's response implies that what they are really concerned about is the possibility that donations to their remote temple will dwindle.

> Daoyi,[19] accompanied by all the minor masters who were their fellow-inmates, said to the Venerable, "I, together with all our fellow inmates, want you to join us in the six daily periods of worship and repentance. We humbly beg the Venerable to listen and accede."
>
> The Venerable said to Daoyi and the others, "Because here we are altogether cut off from provisions, people carry them on foot deep into the mountains. You can't rely on legalistic practice—you want to get ravings by rote, but this is not the Buddha-Dharma at all." The Venerable quoted the *Śūraṃgama-sūtra,* "'The raving mind is not at rest. At rest, it is bodhi. Peerless pure bright mind fundamentally pervades the Dharmadhātu.'[20] No-thought is none other than seeing the Buddha. The presence of thought is none other than birth-and-death. If you want to practice worship and recitation, then leave the mountains. On the plains there are gracious and easeful temple quarters, and you are free to go. If you want to stay with me, you must utterly devote yourself to no-thought. If you can, then you are free to stay. If you cannot, then you must go down."[21]

Daoyi does leave the mountain to go down to Jingzhong monastery, where he tells tales of Wuzhu to Wuxiang. To the consternation of all the monks, Wuxiang is delighted rather than dismayed by reports of Wuzhu's behavior. He says that he too suffered hunger due to his "sitting in idleness," and recalls that when he was practicing alone in the mountains he had only smelted earth (*liantu*) to eat.

This was how Wuzhu and the *Lidai fabao ji* authors defended their own standards for distinguishing the true "Dharma-Jewel" from the dust of material wealth, distinguishing those who were worthy of offerings from those who were not. The Bao Tang school's survival depended on wider acceptance of these standards. Yet they must have been aware that their manifesto, the *Lidai fabao ji,* would draw even more critical attention. Even sympathizers would have found it difficult to explain the basis of the Bao Tang claim for support as Buddhist clergy.

Wuzhu is shown defending the Bao Tang attitude toward the relationship between precepts and patronage to three different audiences: an eminent Chan master from the capital, the group of visiting Vinaya masters, and a group of lay supporters. Let us look at each of these in turn. The first exchange is with Chan Master Tiwu from Chang'an:

> Tiwu knew that the Venerable was the Venerable Kim's disciple, but his words were malicious: "I wish to observe that the people of Jiannan do not arouse the [true] mind. Chan masters [hereabouts] hit people and call it not-hitting, berate people and call it not-berating, and when they receive donations they say 'not-received.' I am deeply perplexed by these matters."
>
> The Venerable replied, "Practicing Prajñāpāramitā, one does not see the one who is awarded favor and does not see the one who extends favor. It is because already there is nothing to receive that one receives all one receives. The not-yet-complete Buddha-Dharma is also endlessly received. From the time when I first put forth the mind up until the present, I have never received a single hair in donations."
>
> When Tiwu heard this he looked around at the officials and said, "The Chan Master speaks with a big voice."
>
> The Venerable asked Tiwu, "So the Ācārya verbally recognizes a Chan Master! Why would one arousing the mind hit people, arousing the mind berate people, and arousing the mind receive donations?"[22]

Tiwu makes a valid point—the notion of nonduality can be used to whitewash a multitude of sins. The *Lidai fabao ji* authors show Wuzhu responding by reinforcing a key Bao Tang claim that donor-beneficiary relations are nondual in the sense of pivotal (both/and, neither/nor), rather than in the mistaken sense of nondistinct. Wuzhu is then shown turning the tables and suggesting that Tiwu is speaking from a superficial dualism and making subjective judgments, which is no different from a superficial nondualism that claims not to recognize them. He may be implying that this is the manner ("arousing the mind") in which Tiwu receives his donations.

This dialogue gives us a fascinating historical glimpse of another aspect of the emerging Chan style: the ability to take and dish out abuse becomes enshrined as a form of practice-in-action or serious play. Tiwu's objection seems to indicate that physical dust-ups in Chan halls predated their literary iconization in works like the *Linji lu* (Record of Linji) and various kōan anecdotes. These works remain pretexts for ritualized mock-violence—which sometimes enables more problematic behavior—in contemporary practice halls.

Wuzhu's second exchange about receiving donations is his dialogue with the Vinaya masters. Here he also challenges his challengers, implying that they are the ones guilty of lax practice. Their attention to form, he asserts, is really due to greed for worldly benefits:

> These days Vinaya masters preach about [sense] "contact" and preach about "purity," preach about "upholding" and preach about "violating." They make forms for receiving the precepts, they make forms for decorum, and even for eating food—everything is made into forms. . . . Nowadays Vinaya masters are only motivated by fame and benefits. Like cats stalking mice, they take mincing steps and creep along, seeing "true" and seeing "false" with their self-styled precepts practice. This is really the extinction of the Buddha-Dharma, it is not the practice of the *śramaṇa* (mendicant).[23]

In the context of the times it was clear that monks with a reputation for rectitude were most likely to be supported. Those who carefully enacted the forms of discipline were most likely to be able to continue consuming their meals with proper discipline. Making precepts practice visible through exacting forms of etiquette and devotion made the merit-field itself visible. It assured the laity that their investments were secure.

Thus, in order to gain support for Wuzhu's no-Way it was not sufficient to defend it against fellow clerics' accusations of laxity or even to mount a counteroffensive against current monastic practice. It was critical to convert lay supporters to the Bao Tang point of view. In a final discourse about donations, Wuzhu tells his lay supporters, "confessing and repenting and intoning prayers, all this is empty delusion." This sermon occupies a pivotal place in the *Lidai fabao ji,* for it is the last of Wuzhu's teachings before the scene of his death. Wuzhu concludes:

> "Who repays the Buddha's kindness? One who practices according to the Dharma. Who is worthy to receive offerings? One who is not involved in worldly affairs. Who consumes offerings? In the Dharma there is nothing that is taken."[24] . . . How about if you *dānapati* (lay donors) root out the source of delusory views and awaken to your unborn substance? Like the roiling of thick clouds and the sun of bright wisdom, the veil of karma will suddenly roll back. Cut delusory conceptualization by emptying the mind, tranquilly not moving.[25]

Wuzhu's practice orientation is consistent. He is shown interpreting precepts and patronage in terms of no-thought to the elite monk, the Vinaya masters, and the laypeople, sometimes even using the same phrases. Nevertheless, there are differences in style and content showing that someone had a keen sensitivity to the responses of different audiences. With the Chan master Wuzhu is shown engaging in Dharma debate. With the Vinaya masters he speaks of the emptiness of the notions of hell and nirvāṇa. With the laity he preaches against dependence on notions of good fortune, repentance, and prayers.

Wuzhu also gives his lay followers concrete advice on how to practice in a more advanced manner. He tells them to "empty the mind." He advises them, "If you want to confess and repent, sit properly and contemplate the characteristic of actuality."[26] However, this is a phrase from the type of contemplation scripture that he criticizes in other contexts.

It is not clear how Wuzhu's teachings were received by the laity, though the fact that his school did not long survive his death is an indication that without his charisma, the style of practice he advocated was not sustainable. There are, however, several surviving indications of disapproval from fellow monks. As noted, the most specific criticisms came from Zongmi, who confirmed and depreciated the Bao Tang school's unconventional manner of practicing and receiving offerings. The following passage is from his *Yuanjue jing dashu chao* (Subcommentary to the Scripture of Perfect Enlightenment), in which he describes the Bao Tang followers:

> Even though the Dharma idea of [Wuzhu's] instruction was just about the same as that of Kim's [Jingzhong] school, [Wuzhu's] teaching of ritual was completely different. The difference lies in the fact that [Wuzhu's school] practices none of the phenomenal marks (*shixiang*) of Buddhism. Having cut their hair and donned robes, they do not receive the precepts. When it comes to doing obeisance and confession, turning and reading [the scriptures], making paintings of Buddha figures, copying sūtras, they revile all such things as delusions (*abhūtaparikalpa, wangxiang*). In the cloister where they dwell they set up no Buddhist artifacts (*foshi*). This is why [I say the Bao Tang idea is] "bound by neither teaching nor praxes" (*jiaoxing buju*). As to "extinguishing consciousness" (*mieshi*), this is the path that the Bao Tang practices. The meaning is: all samsaric wheel-turning is caused by the arising of mind (*qixin*). Arising of mind is the unreal (*wang*). They do not discuss good and bad; non-arising is the real. [Their practice] shows no resemblance whatsoever to practice in terms of phenomenal marks. They take discrimination (*vikalpa, fenbie*) as the enemy and non-discrimination (*avikalpa, wufenbie*) as the wondrous path. . . . Moreover, their idea in reviling all the marks of the teachings (*jiaoxiang*) lies in extinguishing consciousness and [manifesting] the completely real. Therefore, in their dwellings they do not discuss food and clothing, but leave it to people to send offerings. If sent, then they have warm clothing and food enough to eat. If not sent, then they leave matters to hunger and cold. They do not seek to convert, nor do they beg for food. If someone enters their cloister, it does not matter whether he is highborn or lowly, in no case do they welcome him—they do not even stand up. As to singing hymns and praises, making offerings, reprimanding abuses, in all such things they leave it to the other. Indeed, because the purport of their thesis speaks of non-discrimination, their gate of practice has neither right nor wrong. They just value no-mind (*wuxin*) as the wondrous ultimate. Therefore, I have called it "extinguishing consciousness."[27]

The term *mieshi,* "extinguishing consciousness" was Zongmi's way of expressing the problem with the Bao Tang interpretation of Shenhui's *wunian,* no-thought. For Zongmi, Bao Tang antinomianism was similar to the laissez-faire spontaneity advocated by another Sichuan Chan school, the Hongzhou line of Mazu (709–788). Zongmi argued that the "sudden enlightenment" (*dunwu*) experience of direct perception of one's own true nature should be the basis of subsequent "gradual cultivation" (*jianxiu*) and integration of insight. He claimed that the Hongzhou followers' emphasis on all activity as the expression of true nature did not accommodate the particular (personal) transformative aspects of direct experience and gradual cultivation. Zongmi scholar Peter Gregory characterizes his views as follows: "This means, for Tsung-mi, that followers of the Hung-chou line have no clear assurance that their insight is true and, accordingly, their practice of 'simply allowing the mind to act spontaneously' can become a rationalization for deluded activity."[28]

Though there are excellent reasons it died out, I suggest that Bao Tang practice was perhaps closer to a sudden enlightenment–gradual cultivation model than Zongmi was willing to credit. Wuzhu and the *Lidai fabao ji* authors were just as wary of reifying mere function as Zongmi was. Wuzhu's practice of "sitting in idleness" was not spontaneous function. In the earthy words put into Wuxiang's mouth, it was forgetting to eat and shit and piss. The incantations of *wunian* repeated over and over again throughout Wuzhu's Dharma talks are like mantras of continual direct sudden experience. For the Bao Tang, antiformalism itself became a kind of gradual cultivation. Zongmi may have been justified in seeing this as objectifying and nihilistic, a negative attachment to form. However, as attested by Zongmi's own words, the Bao Tang inversion of institutional norms did not promote carefree spontaneity or a free lunch. It necessitated the hard, gradual training of relinquishing expectations moment by moment, becoming indifferent to the fluctuations of abundance and privation.

CHAPTER 4

WUZHU'S FEMALE DISCIPLES

The best-known Mahāyāna scriptural images of female realization are the Dragon King's daughter in the *Lotus Sūtra* and the Goddess in the *Vimalakīrti.* In the *Lotus Sūtra,* the Dragon Princess's ability to achieve enlightenment proves the universal efficacy of the Buddha vehicle. However, she has to turn into a male in order to teach as a buddha. In the *Vimalakīrti,* the Goddess teaches the monk Śariputra about the nonduality of practice and enlightenment by turning him into a woman. These resonant images reverberated throughout Buddhist writings on gender, but what did they mean for those who were neither dragon princesses nor goddesses, but real women practicing in Buddhist temples and assemblies?

THE BACKGROUND OF THE NUN'S ORDER

The first Buddhist nun was the Buddha's aunt and foster mother, Mahāprajāpatī Gotamī. One could say that the Buddha himself created the conditions that made her persist in trying to establish an order of nuns in the face of his opposition. Her elder male clan members were dead, and the son and nephews on whom she might have relied in old age had followed the Buddha into homelessness. Many of her followers were female members of the Buddha's former household or the former wives of men who had become Buddhist monks. In other words, they were abandoned women.

The Buddha refused his cousin Ānanda's pleas on behalf of the would-be nuns several times before finally allowing the order to be formed. Scholars have argued that the Buddha's attitude does not necessarily indicate misogyny but rather a reasonable concern that the fledgling Buddhist order could not afford the appearance of immorality. Allowing nuns to travel with monks could alienate lay donors; however, homeless women on their own were vulnerable to sexual assault.

In any event, the Buddha stipulated eight special rules subordinating nuns to monks and even to male novices. This in turn led to significantly more rules in the *prātimokṣa* (code of behavior) required for a nun's ordination. These special rules maintained an institutional and ritual imbalance between the two orders. Monks could instruct nuns, but not the other way around. An assembly of monks could ordain monks, but a nun's ordination required both senior nuns and monks. As related in the sixth-century *Biqiuni zhuan* (Biographies of Nuns), this created difficulties for the first Chinese female aspirants to ordination, for there were no senior Indian nuns in China.[1]

While the presence of women in the ordained saṅgha was often a source of tension and ambivalence, much of the saṅgha's day-to-day existence was indebted to pious laywomen. Lay devotional practice and support of the saṅgha were seen as the proper spheres of women's practice. Women who renounced householder life were thought to transgress against Brāhmanical Dharma (duty), but males did not.

The Chinese nuns' saṅgha managed to flourish despite its institutional and economic dependence on the monks' saṅgha. Yet after the sixth-century *Biqiuni zhuan,* there is no collection of biographies of Chinese nuns until the twentieth century. Information on seventh- and eighth-century nuns is drawn from scattered inscriptions, tales of the miraculous, and depictions in cave temples.[2]

WOMEN IN THE *LIDAI FABAO JI*

The *Lidai fabao ji* makes a significant contribution to the records of women's practice. It not only provides brief but significant reflections on women's practice in the Tang but is also the first text to feature Chan nuns. However, given Wuzhu's fondness for challenging norms, we might suspect that the inclusion of women in the *Lidai fabao ji* fulfills a familiar didactic and symbolic function. Are the women in the *Lidai fabao ji* pious fictions, like the Dragon Princess and the Goddess, Layman Pang's enlightened daughter, and the feisty old women in later Chan literature?

Let us examine the relevant *Lidai fabao ji* episodes more closely. First, Wuzhu seems to have felt that it was more acceptable to bring female dependents to the monastery than to abandon them. This is a further extension of the ramifications of the "sudden teaching" voiced in the *Platform Sūtra,* where Huineng says, "Good friends, if you wish to practice, it is all right to do so as laymen; you don't have to be in a temple."[3] In the *Lidai fabao ji,* Wuzhu sharply criticizes a group of old laymen for wanting to leave their families and become Wuzhu's disciples:

> There were some old men who told the Venerable, "We, your disciples, have wives and children, and young male and female household dependents. We wish to give them up entirely and submit to the Venerable and study the Way."
>
> The Venerable said, "The Way does not have any particular form that can be cultivated, the Dharma does not have any particular form that can be validated. Just unrestricted no-recollection and no-thought, at all times everything is the Way." He asked the old men, "Do you get it?"
>
> The old men were silent and did not answer, because they didn't understand. The Venerable expounded a verse: "Your wife is an earless shackle, your young are rattling manacles. You are a worthless slave, you have reached old age and cannot escape."[4]

Wuzhu throws the laymen's fears back in their faces, mocking their fettered state to show them that they are bound by ignorance, not by family life. In contrast, a monk named Fayuan, who appears to have been one of Wuzhu's earliest and closest followers, brings his mother along when he seeks to become Wuzhu's disciple. Wuzhu gives them a teaching, ending with his favorite phrase: "At the time of true no-thought, no-thought itself is not." The passage concludes:

> When Master Fayuan heard this, he joined his palms and said to the Venerable, "I am exceedingly glad that I have been able to meet the Venerable. Fayuan and his

aged relative (i.e., my mother and I) humbly beg you to compassionately accept us." And so they stayed in the mountains and never left [the Venerable's] side.[5]

From glimpses of daily life provided by the invaluable Dunhuang social documents that record prayers, dedications, and financial transactions, it is clear that the line between family life and monastic life was not so sharp as Buddhist literature would have us believe. The normative view is that "leaving home" (*chujia*), the term connoting taking monastic vows, really means cutting family ties. In reality there were dependents attached to monasteries as well as monks and nuns supported by their natal families, but the *Lidai fabao ji* authors are unusual in showing their teacher sanctioning such practices.

There are a number of other brief but striking inclusions of women in the *Lidai fabao ji* version of Chan history. First is the introduction of the nun Zongchi into the group of Bodhidharma's close disciples. The *Lidai fabao ji* appears to be the original source for this story, claiming that Bodhidharma classifies his disciples' levels of insight according to who received his marrow, bones, and skin. In a famously provocative line, Bodhidharma says that Zongchi is "the one who got my flesh."

As noted, Empress Wu Zetian plays a pivotal role in the *Lidai fabao ji* story of the patriarchy. She receives Bodhidharma's robe from Huineng and gives it to the Bao Tang ancestral teacher Zhishen. Not only does a a woman who was later cast as a violent usurper of the Tang throne become a kind of interregnum transmission holder, she is portrayed in an unusually sympathetic manner.

Furthermore, in the biography of Wuxiang it is claimed that his sister's example motivated him to become a monk. This account of Wuxiang's vocation is found only in the *Lidai fabao ji:*

> Chan Master Wuxiang of the Jingzhong monastery in Chengdu City Prefecture in Jiannan had the lay surname Kim and was from a clan of Silla princes; his family went back for generations East-of-the-Sea (Korea). Formerly, when he was in his homeland, his youngest sister, hearing of her betrothal ceremony, picked up a knife, slashed her face, and vowed her determination to "return to the true." The Venerable [Wuxiang] saw this and cried, "Girls are pliant and weak, yet she knows the meaning of sticking to chastity. Fellows are hard and strong—how can I be so lacking in spirit?"[6]

Finally, the most significant passage concerns two of Wuzhu's female disciples, Changjingjin and Liaojianxing. This is the earliest portrayal of Chan nuns in a known practice community. Here it is in full:

> The wife and daughter of Administrator Murong of Qingzhou (Gansu) were determined to seek the Mahāyāna. Accompanied by the entire family, young and old, they came to pay obeisance to the Venerable. The Venerable asked the wife, "Where did you come from?"
>
> She replied, "Your disciple heard from afar that the Venerable had great compassion, so we came to pay obeisance."
>
> The Venerable then expounded various essentials of the Dharma for them. When the daughter had heard his talk, she knelt on one knee with her palms joined and explained to the Venerable, "Your disciple is a woman with the three obstructions and five difficulties, and a body that is not free. That is why I have come now to submit to the Venerable; I am determined to cut off the source of birth and death. I humbly beg the Venerable to point out the essentials of the Dharma."
>
> The Venerable said, "If you are capable of such [resolution], then you are a great hero (*dazhangfu er*), why are you 'a woman'?" The Venerable expounded the essentials of the Dharma for her: "No-thought is thus no 'male,' no-thought is thus no 'female.' No-thought is thus no-obstruction, no-thought is thus no-hindrance. No-thought is thus no-birth, no-thought is thus no-death. At the time of true no-thought, no-thought itself is not. This is none other than cutting off the source of birth and death."
>
> When the daughter heard his talk, her eyes did not blink and she stood absolutely still. In an instant, the Venerable knew that this woman had a resolute mind. He gave her the Dharma name Changjingjin (Ever-Pure Progress), and her mother was named Zhengbianzhi (Right Knowledge). They took the tonsure and practiced, and became leaders among nuns.
>
> Later, they brought a younger female cousin with the surname Wei, who was the granddaughter of Grand Councillor Su. She was quick-witted and clever, extensively learned and knowledgeable, and when asked a question she was never without an answer. She came to pay obeisance to the Venerable, and when the Venerable saw that she was obdurate and determined on chastity he expounded the Dharma for her: "This Dharma is not caused and conditioned,

it has neither false nor not-false, and has neither truth nor not-truth. Transcending all characteristics is thus all Dharmas. 'The Dharma is beyond eye, ear, nose, tongue, body, and mind, the Dharma transcends all contemplation practices.' No-thought is thus no-practice, no-thought is thus no-contemplation. No-thought is thus no-body, no-thought is thus no-mind. No-thought is thus no-nobility, no-thought is thus no-lowliness. No-thought is thus no-high, no-thought is thus no-low. At the time of true no-thought, no-thought itself is not."

When the woman heard his talk, she joined her palms together and told the Venerable, "Your disciple is a woman whose obstructions from transgressions are very weighty, but now that I have heard the Dharma, stain and obstruction are completely eliminated." So saying, she wept grievously, a rain of tears. She then requested a Dharma name, and she was named Liaojianxing (Completely Seeing the Nature). When she had been named, she tonsured herself and donned robes, and became a leader among nuns.[7]

Among the accounts of Wuzhu's disciples, the three that stand out are the stories of Changjingjin, Liaojianxing, and Master Fayuan who brought his mother to the monastery. These are the only disciple accounts that include details about family background, and they also include naturalistic dialogue and personal and emotional shadings. In the passage above, Wuzhu calls Changjingjin a "*dazhangfu er*," a great hero male/son. Changjingjin, Liaojianxing, and Master Fayuan emerge as the heros, the *dazhangfu*, among Wuzhu's followers. Perhaps they were also his *er*, his "sons."

Because of the ways that women are represented in the *Lidai fabao ji*, I have suggested that perhaps Liaojianxing, Changjingjin, and Fayuan either wrote or helped write the *Lidai fabao ji*. Elsewhere in the *Lidai fabao ji* (and in Chan literature), literary and intellectual skills are devalued, but in the passage on Liaojianxing these attributes are praised in a way that may betray some degree of anxious self-justification. Female contributions to the text may be the reason female figures play small but significant roles in the *Lidai fabao ji* history of Chan, roles not seen in any other sectarian history of the period.

The female figures validated in the *Lidai fabao ji* stories are telling: a young girl who refuses marriage (Wuxiang's sister), a nun who surfaces inexplicably amid the better-known male disciples of a famous master (Bodhidharma's disciple Zongchi), and a powerful woman who secretly holds the true Dharma robe in trust (Empress Wu). The pair of well-connected young women who became Wuzhu's disciples could conceivably have seen themselves in all these roles.

Furthermore, the tone of the *Lidai fabao ji* reveals an exclusive, even devotional commitment to the master and the Bao Tang group. This would be consistent with the attitude of an educated layperson who decided to bind her or his fate to an unorthodox community. Such a disciple could have no hope of any recognized place within the monastic system.

I am not suggesting that Bao Tang antinomianism included disregarding the rule of chastity, though that might improve sales of this book. In fact, the high tone of devotion in the *Lidai fabao ji* precludes the mundane, while allowing glimpses of the Bao Tang as a small and close-knit family. In between the repetitive passages that represent Wuzhu's Dharma talks we are shown loving snapshots of Wuzhu that reveal the wit, self-importance, and occasional ill humor of a living master rather than a living buddha. These brief encounters have a more personal quality than the stylized patriarchal antics and outbursts in later discourse records and kōans.

One can imagine the special appeal that Wuzhu's formless practice might have had for female Buddhist practitioners. Liaojianxing's account is the only disciple story in the *Lidai fabao ji* that features self-tonsuring. Without benefit of ritual or clergy, she cuts her own hair, dons robes, and becomes a nun immediately. She is represented as a valued member of a demanding community. This was an application of directness that had no currency in the ideological battle for Chan legitimacy. It was, however, a logical and startling consequence of the sudden teaching: any woman could become a *dazhangfu*. The name Wuzhu gave to Liaojianxing, "Completely Seeing the Nature," may reveal an additional facet of his commitment to "practice what he preached." Buddha nature is traceless, neither male nor female, but there are very few traces in early Chan lore that validate an ordinary young woman's ability to see this.

CHAPTER

5

WUZHU'S LEGACY

Criticism of Chan and Zen has a long history. Jesuits encountering Chan in the eighteenth century called it antinomian and quietistic—in other words, amoral and self-indulgently passive in contrast to Western progressive vigor. These charges were repeated and extended to Buddhism in general as more and more missionaries and explorers traveled and lived in Asia, often supported by Western colonial powers.

Partly in reaction, Japanese writers, particularly D. T. Suzuki, celebrated Chan/Zen spontaneity and iconoclasm and caught the imaginations of a generation of disaffected Westerners. More recently, scholars have shown that Chan's iconoclastic, anti-institutional, antinomian, and subitist rhetoric developed in tandem with distinctive Chan iconographies, rituals, institutional settings, disciplines, and esotericism. The radicalism and the ritualism are not antithetical but codependent.

Nevertheless, if we take the claims in the *Lidai fabao ji* seriously, we could say that this Chan group was indeed antinomian and quietistic. Wuzhu interpreted the precepts in a way that his contemporaries considered amoral, and he advocated a practice of no-thought that could be called quietist, celebrating "sitting in idleness/emptiness" and forgetting to eat. I have attempted to show how Wuzhu's moment arrived; now we will look at how it passed away.

LATER REFERENCES TO THE BAO TANG SCHOOL

It is impossible to tell how long the Bao Tang school survived as an independent Chan line, for few clues remain. It is likely that other texts, particularly the *Baolin zhuan* (Transmission of the Baolin Temple), were composed in part to refute the claims of the *Lidai fabao ji.* Aside from Zongmi's critical comments, the most significant reactions came from the monk Shenqing of Huiyi monastery, also in Sichuan. In 806 he produced the *Beishan lu* (Record of North Mountain), in which he condemned both the *Lidai fabao ji* and the *Baolin zhuan* without mentioning them by name. Like Zongmi, Shenqing felt that precepts and scriptural study were essential to Chan practice, and he advocated "unity of the three teachings" (Buddhism, Daoism, and Confucianism).

In the course of presenting his own history of the transmission of Buddhism to China, Shenqing launches a critique of claims made in the *Lidai fabao ji* and *Baolin zhuan.* He uses the language of a legal case, and his judgments are based on both moral arguments and analyses of factual errors. In Shenqing's view, morality and historiography are linked. He argues that the fabrications in the *Lidai fabao ji* and the *Baolin zhuan* show that their teachings are worthless, because the Dharma practice of liars must be flawed.

For Shenqing, moral character was the most important manifestation of practice, and it included Confucian virtues and observances, Buddhist precepts and meditation, and Daoist purification and concentration of energy. One of his objections to the dramatic "perils of the patriarchs" style of hagiography favored by the *Lidai fabao ji* was that it was damaging to the Dharma to portray masters as "only human" rather than as Holy Ones (*shengren*). It is notable that he voiced this objection at a time when teachings like Mazu's "everyday mind is buddha mind" were beginning to spread.

In a passage discussing "lies about transmission," Shenqing takes a passing swipe at the idea of a robe of transmission: "The one who attains the Way loses the self, and to lose the self is to lose the myriad things—how could a robe remain?"[1] He then embarks on an extended critique of iconoclasm and antinomianism, and it is quite clear that he had Wuzhu and his followers in mind:

> Another account says that the source of fault and merit is only the mind, and that is all. [According to these people] extinguishing of the mind is nonactivity (*wuwei*), and the Way resides in nonphenomenality (*wushi*). They don't do ritu-

> als or liturgy, nor do they lecture or recite the scriptures, and they claim this is true nonactivity. They don't request the precepts or guard against transgressions, and they claim this is true transcendence of characteristics. They teach that when there is the mind of practicing [the Dharma] or when there is something that one knows [about the Dharma] then this is the Dharma of the Śrāvakas. Therefore, [they think that] only when the arrangement of [Buddhist] images is discarded and the methods of scriptural [study] are abandoned can one call it the sudden teaching. [They say that] if anything is expounded one should consult one's own feelings, and in approaching texts one should consider and decide [for oneself]—why depend on exegesis and commentary?[2]

Shenqing, as "the prosecutor," then comments on the approach he has described:

> One who [realizes] nonactivity is fused with the void and anchored in tranquility. There is no good that he does not do. Improperly taking ritual, recitation, copying [of scripture], and carving [of images] as obstacles—there we see "activity" (*youwei*), not "nonactivity" (*wuwei*). As for "transcending characteristics"—when illumination penetrates the mind of desires, there are no characteristics that can be obtained. Nonobtaining is then obtaining; abandoning attachment is called transcendence [of characteristics]. However, if one considers not receiving the precepts and giving up maintaining them as transcendence of characteristics, this is assuredly grasping at characteristics. How is this "transcendence of characteristics"?[3]

Shenqing's objections would later be echoed by Zongmi, though the latter assumes a tone of objective assessment rather than judgment. Shenqing cites the practice of "extinguishing of the mind" (*xinmie*) as the key characteristic of the unnamed problematic group. This foreshadows Zongmi's well-known claim that the Bao Tang practiced "extinguishing consciousness" (*mieshi*).

From the passages in which *xinmie* and related concepts appear in the *Lidai fabao ji* (*mieshi* is not used), one can understand why Wuzhu would be accused of equating the practice of no-thought, *wunian*, with extinguishing the mind. One of the subtitles of the *Lidai fabao ji* is "destroying all mind [consciousnesses]."[4] This appearance of nihilism is largely due to the way that Wuzhu associates "mind" with the mind of sense-consciousnesses and characteristics.

For example, *xinmie* appears in a quotation that is used several times: "When the mind is produced then the various dharmas are produced; when the mind is extinguished then the various dharmas are extinguished."[5]

However, taken in context, "mind" is seen to be the mind of delusion or dependence on cycles of birth and death. Wuzhu asserts that true no-thought is the realization that phenomena—most significantly, the karmic burden of past sins—come into being and are extinguished along with delusory mind activity. "Mind" here is *manas* in Yogācāra terms, the activity that identifies with itself as subject in relation to sensations and thoughts. As noted, Wuzhu also emphasizes that all the precepts and the meaning of all the scriptures are realized in true no-thought. These are antinomian views expressed in an apophatic manner ("at the time of true no-thought, no-thought itself is not"), but it is difficult to determine the degree to which they are dualistic or nihilistic.

Moreover, contrary to Shenqing's accusation, nowhere in the *Lidai fabao ji* is "consulting ones' own feelings" recommended as an interpretive standard. In their critiques of the Bao Tang approach, both Shenqing and Zongmi ignore Wuzhu's claim that no-thought perfects rather than precludes study of the scriptures and practice of the precepts. Both critics focus on Bao Tang abandonment of recognized forms of practice as a form of antipractice. They view this as grasping and manipulative (*youwei*). Wuzhu's repeated teachings that one should not depend on forms was certainly carried out by Bao Tang followers "not-doing" recitation and devotional rituals. However, in his sermons this abandonment of form is embedded in the nonduality of no-thought: in doing/not-doing, neither doing nor not-doing, and both doing and not-doing.

Whatever his reasons for doing so, Shenqing at least appears to have read the *Lidai fabao ji* carefully, which we cannot assert with confidence in the case of Zongmi. Indeed, Shenqing provides the only concrete evidence that the *Lidai fabao ji* was ever taken seriously by fellow clergy in Sichuan. Vestiges of respect still clung to Wuzhu's name a generation after his death, and he was included in the authoritative Chan genealogy, the *Jingde chuandeng lu* (Transmission of the Lamp Compiled in the Jingde Era). The *Lidai fabao ji* itself, however, was fated to be seen but not named. It was copied and borrowed from, but not quoted or cited like the *Platform Sūtra,* the *Baolin zhuan,* and other eighth-century Chan texts.

Tibet also played a role in the fate of the *Lidai fabao ji.* The rise and fall of the Tibetan Yarlung dynasty influenced the course of events in Sichuan, which was the staging area for Tang military campaigns against the Nanzhao kingdom (Yunnan) and the Tibetans. Nanzhao allied itself with Tibet against the Tang from 749 until 793, and Tang campaigns into Yunnan in the early 750s led to disastrous troop losses. This contributed to the military weakness that made the Tang so vulnerable when An Lushan rebelled.[6] If Wuzhu had remained in the military, it is quite possible he would have been sent into Yunnan in the early 750s. In that case, the *Lidai fabao ji* would not have been written.

The military officers who became Wuzhu's followers were part of the Tang campaign against the Tibetans in northwest Sichuan. Tang-era Sino-Tibetan hostilities lasted from 737 until the 860s, when the empire created by the Yarlung dynasty collapsed.[7] The rapidly expanding Tibetan empire was a serious threat; the Tibetan army occupied Chang'an in 763, and Dunhuang was part of Tibetan territory from 786 to 848. In the period between the composition of the *Lidai fabao ji* and its entombment in Dunhuang in the eleventh century, there was a complex pattern of military, commercial, and religious interaction among the cultural centers of western Sichuan, Nanzhao, Tibet, and Gansu. This is attested by Tibetan manuscripts in the Dunhuang cache and reflected in Tibetan appropriations of early Chan literature. At least four Tibetan Dunhuang manuscripts show the influence of the *Lidai fabao ji* stories of the patriarchs.[8]

One of the most interesting intersections between Tibet and the world of the *Lidai fabao ji* is a Tibetan account of Wuxiang. According to the *Sba-bzhed* (The Testament of Ba), the Tibetan envoy Ba Sangshi[9] met Wuxiang ("Kim Heshang") in Sichuan and received a prophecy from him.[10]

> On the road along which the five emissaries were traveling to Tibet was a rock outcropping around which no one could move. Whoever saw it died in landslides. The powerful Kim Hwa-shang of the city of Eg-chu,[11] who was able to harness a tiger[12] and who was clairvoyant, entered into meditation for three days at the order of his preceptor.[13] In this way he shattered the rock and then built a temple in the tamed space that was left. He also then had that region

put under plow. Separating [some of the fields] as temple-lands, he came back to Eg-chu, whereupon the Tibetan emissaries received a meditation transmission [from him]. When they asked for prognostications about what would then happen, asking whether the Buddha's doctrine would be established in Tibet, or if the life-threatening demons of Tibet might not act up if the Buddha's scriptures were proclaimed, and whether or not the Tsenpo (emperor) and his son were at ease, the Hwa-shang investigated [these matters] clairvoyantly.[14]

"Kim Heshang" is said to have correctly predicted to the emissaries that the Tibetan emperor Trhi Detsuktsen had died in their absence, and that evil ministers destroyed the Buddhist temple he established. Furthermore, they were told that if the prince survived he would convert to Buddhism—and this prince did indeed become the great Buddhist ruler Trhi Songdetsen (r. 755–797).[15] According to the chronicle, Buddhism was suppressed by pro-Bon ministers until 761, after which Ba Sangshi brought out the three Chinese Dharma texts he had received from Wuxiang and hidden until conditions became favorable. He translated these texts into Tibetan and became the abbot of Samye monastery, where he may have been regarded as a master in Wuxiang's lineage.[16]

Along with stories in the *Sba-bzhed* and fragments of accounts of the masters of the Bao Tang lineage, Wuxiang's and Wuzhu's teachings were known in Tibet in some form. Traces are preserved in texts stemming from the short-lived Tibetan interest in Chan. The fate of Chan in Tibet was said to have been decided in a debate at Samye monastery near Lhasa at the end of the eighth century. The putative debate was between the Chinese Chan master Moheyan and the Indian Mādhyamika master Kamalaśīla, who was said to have won the endorsement of Emperor Trhi Songdetsen. The two debaters were considered representatives of the sudden and gradual approaches to practice, but the "positions" of Moheyan and Kamalaśīla were probably renditions of a more extended controversy not limited to one event or debate.

Moheyan's version of the sudden teachings is portrayed as antinomian, and this was said to be the reason that Trhi Songdetsen decided in favor of "gradualist" Indian Mahāyāna teachings. Though Chan was subsequently suppressed in Tibet, a few Tibetan works showing its influences remain. In connection with Wuzhu's teachings, the most important of these is the Dunhuang manuscript Pelliot Tibetan 116, a collection of excerpts from Chinese Chan texts and other works related to Chan topics.[17]

Passages showing direct and indirect connections with Wuxiang and Wuzhu are found in various sections of this work. For example, there are two quotations attributed to a master called Kim-hun-shen-shi, who may or may not be Wuxiang. They do not strikingly resemble Wuxiang's teachings as represented in the *Lidai fabao ji*, but the basic Chan themes are recognizable: if there is awareness of fundamental nondual mind then there is no objectification of true nature, and afflictions do not arise. This liberation is realized in the practice of nonconceptualization.[18]

Furthermore, P. Tib. 116 replicates the first part of Wuzhu's sermon on regarding the mind as the place of practice. The manuscript also includes a work entitled *Sudden Awakening to the Fundamental Reality* that resembles the *Lidai fabao ji* in tone and teachings.[19] The text consists of questions posed by the disciple Yem and answered by the master Unimpeded Wisdom.[20] It displays the same blend of Northern School meditation techniques and Southern School iconoclasm seen in Moheyan's teachings. One of the responses of Chan Master Unimpeded Wisdom sounds as if it could have come directly from Wuzhu: "What's the use of you giving me gifts, of making vows, and of bowing and burning incense?"[21]

Possible threads linking eighth-century Sichuan Chan and the later Dzogchen and Nyingma schools have become the focus of both scholarly and unscholarly speculation. There is clearly a resemblance between Chan and Dzogchen teachings, but it is difficult to trace concrete connections. Suffice it to say that the *Lidai fabao ji* may have acted as a carrier for elements of Chan that later reappeared in different forms.

SICHUAN CHAN AND THE HONGZHOU SCHOOL

The Hongzhou lineage was the Chan school that best survived the persecution of Buddhism carried out by Emperor Wuzong in 845. Mazu Daoyi (709–788), the progenitor of that lineage, became the common patriarch of the Linji and Guiyang schools, two of the "Five Houses" of Sung Chan. The Linji (Rinzai) lineage was and remains one of the most important of the Chan/Zen traditions, so the question of Mazu's antecedents is not insignificant.

Zongmi asserts that Mazu was once Wuxiang's disciple. Mazu was also a native of Sichuan, and there is some controversy over whether he was more influenced by Wuxiang or by his acknowledged master, Huairang (677–744).[22] The biographies of Korean monks included in the tenth-century *Zutang ji* (Anthology from the Patriarchal Hall) show that they believed Mazu's lineage stemmed from Wuxiang, who was Korean.[23]

The image of Mazu presented in his biography and the style of his "recorded sayings" reflect, like the *Lidai fabao ji,* the need to find an appropriate form for the formless teaching. The Mazu material mediates between conventional and radical approaches that are less extreme than Wuzhu's. However, Mazu is also more clearly and confidently on the side of the new.

Mazu was known for his emphasis on immanence and spontaneous function, famously claiming that buddha nature is fully manifest in everyday activities like eating and wearing clothes. This has an antinomian aspect, as Zongmi points out in his characterization of the Hongzhou teaching: "This means that one should not rouse the mind to cut off bad or practice good. One does not even cultivate the path. The path is mind."[24] According to Zongmi, the Bao Tang and Hongzhou schools were both guilty of misinterpreting the sudden teaching.

Scholars argue about the degree to which Mazu's iconoclastic teachings influenced the actual practices of monks in the meditation hall. No matter how we imagine the behavior of Mazu and his disciples, it is clear that taking immanence ("everyday mind") rather than formlessness as a foundation made the Hongzhou approach more flexible than the Bao Tang approach. Unlike Wuzhu's denial of formal precepts and practices, the notion of "everyday mind" neither privileged nor precluded monastic ordination. It allowed for adaptation of existing monastic institutions and allowed teachers to rework conventional practices. Wuzhu's insistence on abandoning forms was bound to fall back to dualism, because it depended on rejecting symbolic practices.

It is noteworthy that the development of a Chan monastic code is associated with Mazu's line. Mazu's disciple Baizhang (749–814) is said to be the founder of the first independent Chan monastery and the first Chan monastic code, the *Baizhang qinggui* (Baizhang's Pure Rules). Baizhang's biography in the *Song gaoseng zhuan* (Song Dynasty Biographies of Eminent Monks) says that he decided to draw from both the Vinaya and bodhisattva precepts texts in order to create regulations for a separate monastic institution that would not take the Vinaya as the basis of practice.[25] Although the existence of such a text is doubtful, it was claimed as the basis of the authoritative *Chanyuan qinggui* (Rules of Purity for Chan Monasteries) of the twelfth century.

Whether or not Baizhang can be credited with creating a distinctive Chan monasticism, both Mazu and Zongmi contributed to the development of a more inclusive notion of Chan transmission. Hongzhou immanence provided the foundation for a new "Middle Way." It avoided the old formalism of the Vinaya and the bodhisattva precepts, but it also avoided the groundlessness of the formless precepts.

Through the work of many innovators and critics, the emerging Chan school found more subtle means of negotiating authority than robes and rebellion. An important aspect of Chan identity formation was the creation of transmission lineages. Competition between different Chan lineages was subordinated to the representation of the Chan school as a powerful clan made up of many families.

This is how the *Jingde chuandeng lu* works, and it became the authoritative account of Chan transmission. It represents an alliance among the main Chan "houses" and the absorption of patriarchal lineages into a many-limbed genealogy. Tensions inherent in the "kingship" model, the linear master-disciple model of early Chan, were resolved into a more traditional "kinship" model. The power of the mystique of transmission was invested in the branching structure of a widespread gnostic community, rather than an anointed line of charismatic individuals.

CONCLUSION

Elements discussed in this book—the soteriology of the "sudden," transmission of the robe and patriarchy of no-thought, mass precepts retreats and antinomianism, the forms of formlessness, iconoclasm and Chan masters as icons—all contributed to the unique character of Chan/Zen Buddhism. Eighth-century Sichuan Chan was an important source for the styles, traditions, and practices of mainstream Chan in the Song dynasty. Attaining widespread social and cultural influence, Chan underwent further transformations in Japan and Korea. Zen has become a brand, a style, in contemporary global culture. Serious Chan practice continues, adapting to new conditions all over the world.

The imprint of Master Wuzhu's teachings on the world of Chan was not negligible. What, in the end, is his transmission?

The huge repository of Chan lore owes much to the disciples who created the written portrait of their master in the *Lidai fabao ji*. This text modified received genres and introduced new features in ways that would shape Song Chan literature. Stories originating in the *Lidai fabao ji* found their way into the official annals of Chan. Yet the *Lidai fabao ji* itself was repudiated and all but forgotten.

Wuzhu's doctrine of formlessness was not new, but his place of practice was. In order to see both the derivative and the innovative aspects of Wuzhu's experiment, it helps to see him as part of a tradition—not the tradition of meditation, but the tradition of sacred performance. And not just any performance: he appears and disappears in the middle of the audience-participation performance of bodhisattva vows.

In a traditional ordination context, senior monks functioned as preceptors and confirmed the ordination of select members, the monks and nuns. In a bodhisattva precepts ritual, a practitioner could take the buddhas and bodhisattvas as preceptors and take his or her own visualization experience as confirmation of the efficacy of the rite. Visualization ritual was geared toward purification rather than attaining clerical status, but it still served to undermine the exclusivity of clerical privilege. As Chan developed, masters became living buddhas who bestowed the precepts of formlessness. In the *Lidai fabao ji*, a female practitioner tonsures herself and becomes a nun, functioning as the preceptor, the essence of the precepts, and the audience-recipient all in one.

The precepts were the heart of the roles of monk and nun, the empowerment that "painted the eyes" on living icons. The Chan teaching of the formless precepts expressed what had been true all along, that there was no abiding identity to the role of a member of the saṅgha. In the sudden teaching, one becomes a buddha because one *is* a buddha. So far so good, but how does one become a monk or nun? In traditional Buddhism, it was by vowing to act like a monk or nun, but in Chan, what is that acting "like"? There is a kind of catch-22 at work. One can only bring life to the role by practicing it, rehearsing it, and getting it right, but one can only get it right by living it fully all at once. In Chan the art of the role, empowered by ritual, became a living source of likeness.

On the third day of the sixth month of the ninth year of the Dali era (774), [the Venerable] told his disciples, "Bring me a fresh, clean robe, I wish to bathe." When he had bathed and put on the robe, he asked his disciples, "Is it the time of abstinence (i.e., noon) yet?"

They answered, "Yes."

He bound all his disciples to a promise: "If you are filial, obedient children you will not disobey my teachings. I am at the point of the great practice. After I am gone you are not to knit your brows [in distress], you are not to act like worldly and untrained persons. Those who weep, wear mourning garments, and knit their brows shall not be called my disciples. Weeping is precisely the way of the world; the Buddha-Dharma is not thus. 'Transcending all characteristics; this is precisely seeing the Buddha.'"

When he finished speaking, he passed away while remaining in a seated position. The Great Master's springs and autumns amounted to sixty-one.[26]

When Wuzhu tells his disciples to act like adherents of the Buddha-Dharma, not "worldly and untrained persons," he assumes the time-honored role of the Buddha, who also admonished his followers not to weep at his deathbed. This is a scriptural trope, yet it is a trope in service of the unrepeatable. It signals not that Wuzhu is the Buddha, but that Wuzhu is portrayed enacting the role of the Buddha for the last time and forever. The notion of "internalization" of a role is post-Cartesian. In the experience of the world that Wuzhu's teachings convey, there is no abiding internal psyche that is the source of the role, no reified experience that confirms the reality of "being." The stereotypical portrayal of Wuzhu's death is like the final ritual of painting the eyes on a sacred image. The art and the role, empowered by rituals and tropes, become a living source of power.

It was precisely within well-defined ritual time and space, replicable and impermanent, that the precepts of formlessness and the emptiness of good and evil could be practiced and expounded. This was the context in which merit practice, the mainstay of Chinese Buddhism, could be criticized. Yet this ritual enclosure does not mean that either the practice or the critique was meaningless.

Contemporary Zen Buddhists are wary of talking about the *power* of buddhas and bodhisattvas. Yet in the late twentieth century individual teachers, often male, were invested with power to a degree that caused significant problems. I suggest that in traditional East Asian contexts, unquestionably "patriarchal" and far from perfect, the web of devotional practices and the spaces of ritual consecration and deconstruction served to distribute power in important ways. Both group authority and self-actualization of practice were validated in ways that are not clearly visible if we only study lineage charts and antinomian kōan stories.

It is probably fair to say that most contemporary Zen groups practice some form of devotion and vows. Though the idea of "religion without religion" is popular, in each practice community there is disagreement over the degree to which one should jettison particular forms of practice. Questions about how much to use Asian forms will no doubt continue to be debated, but the focus has shifted toward creative adaptation rather than symbolic opposition between "keep" and "reject." The antinomianism and iconoclasm in Chan stories is not seized on as uncritically as it was in the sixties or even the eighties. Contemporary Zen Buddhists tend to assume that meditation is the main practice, and have gotten more sophisticated about dealing with the showy criticisms of meditation acted out by Chan and Zen masters through the ages.

However, there is still a tendency to accept Zen-style mockery of devotional and merit-oriented practices unreflectively, without examining the interdependence of buddha image and buddha nature, merit and no-merit. Western Buddhists are generally open to the notion of karma, yet remain resistant to the notion of merit. Moderns seem able to accept the idea of "consequences" better than we can accept the efficacy of deliberately trying to create beneficial consequences through acting beneficially. The latter seems naïve and self-serving to us. Was Wuzhu's rejection of merit and forms any less naïve and self-serving? What about ours?

In a study of contemporary ritual performers in Taiwan, Donald Sutton examines the evolution of a performance troupe's transmitted forms. After describing the Jiajiang performance and its contexts, Sutton reiterates the questions that informed his study and proposes some answers:

> Why does change keep within fixed bounds, even when in myth, iconographic interpretation, ritual, and choreography, innovation and fluidity are the rule? What, in other words, keeps innovation consistent with the underlying logic of the Jiajiang described above? The deliberate traditionalism of local religion,

> asserting old ways in spite of modernity, is only part of the answer; after all, participating alongside the Jiajiang at festivals are comic troupes that show heavy influence from modern commercial and industrial values (Liu 1986, Sutton 1990a). What is specifically traditionalist about the Jiajiang is that they are not just performers before the gods but also escorts and exorcisers on their behalf. As divine agents they must keep their actions and appearance ritualized in order to convey the requisite weight and importance. To persuade, ritual has to remind us of what we already know in our bones.[27]

He goes on to say that the agent of both standardization and innovation in creating the "requisite weight and importance" of the ritual performance is plural. It is a web of relationships: among community temples, troupe leaders as performance masters and purveyors of ritual services, and festival marketplaces.[28] I would suggest that late eighth-century Chan standardization and innovation developed out of an analogous relationship among established local religious institutions, Chan masters and their troupes of disciples, and the marketplace for religious performance.

This is not meant to be reductive. As Sutton says, ritual reminds us of what we already know in our bones. And what is that? The performance master reminds us not to forget no-recollection and no-thought. Performance connects the gods to the costumes and masks of the actors, the Dharma to the portrait, the flesh to bones.

Wuzhu's contested robe is a costume for being possessed by no-thought. Originally, Shenhui meant to fuse the robe with mind-to-mind transmission so that the two were like emptiness and form, nondual. Stitching together narratives from many sources, the *Lidai fabao ji* authors give us a patchwork of emerging Chan attitudes toward practice. The seams holding the patches together show the internal pressures of Southern School ideology more clearly. Through the *Lidai fabao ji* we see the tension between subitism—the unmediated identity of self-nature and Dharma—and the continued need to negotiate all kinds of relationships, between master and disciple, lay and ordained, sons and mothers, women and men.

The *Lidai fabao ji*'s imperfect seams give us a different view of the "golden age" of Chan. The unmatched edges between the soteriological and political patches of Bodhidharma's costume are revealed. Do the gaps expose lack of integrity or lack of sophistication? We could see Wuzhu and his disciples as engaged in Buddhist business as usual, wearing the cloak of disinterestedness in order to attract secular elites, the consumers in the religious marketplace. However, Wuzhu truly went into this marketplace with empty hands, offering no sin and repentance, no merit, and no-thought.

At this distance it is impossible to distinguish transparent rhetoric from formless practice, and it is also impossible to know what is hidden and revealed. If Wuzhu and his followers practiced no-thought to the extent of dispensing with costumes, masks, and scripts, so that their privileged status as clergy disappeared, this should win them a special place in the history of Buddhist monasticism. Instead, Wuzhu's teachings were lost in the mainstream of Chan. He seems to be not-recollected, but reappears in surprising guises. He left a subtle trace, perhaps a warning about the necessary limits of the ultimate teaching.

Wuzhu's contested robe of verification is the *Lidai fabao ji* itself, the emperor's new clothes. It reveals vanity and courage, the ridiculous and the radical, the deluded and the denuded. The unthinkable became the costume of wisdom, and unlike other robes of the gods, this one could not be removed. It shows that it is impossible to separate the Three Jewels from flesh and bone: "At the time of true no-thought, no-thought itself is not."

PART II

TRANSLATION OF THE *LIDAI FABAO JI*

(RECORD OF THE DHARMA-JEWEL THROUGH THE GENERATIONS)

This translation is based on two Dunhuang manuscripts, S. 516 as the base text and P. 2125 as a supplement for portions illegible in S. 516. Division of the text into sections is based on Yanagida Seizan's Shoki no Zenshi II, *which follows logical divisions in the narrative. Corresponding* Taishō *page and line numbers are given for each section, but the* Taishō *transcription based on P. 2125 has numerous errors. Readers interested in the Chinese text and detailed notes should refer to my earlier work,* The Mystique of Transmission *(Columbia University Press, 2007).*

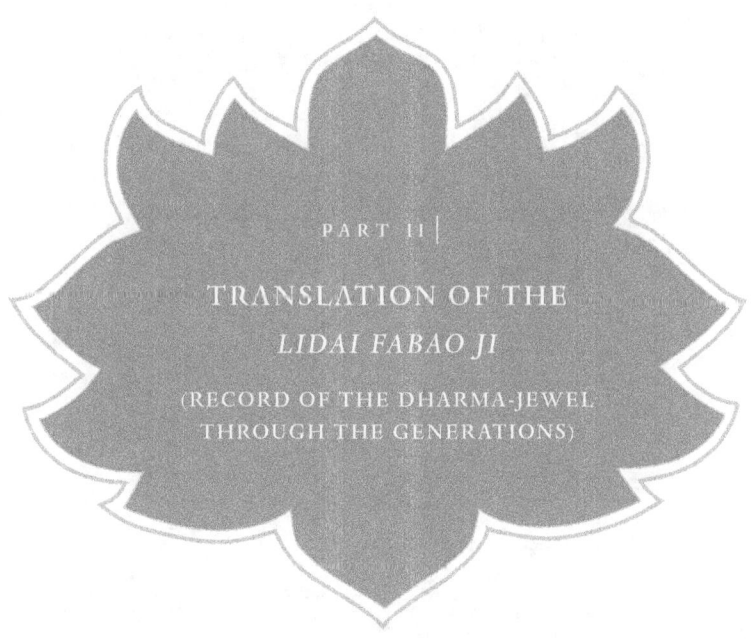

SECTION 1. SOURCES AND THE LEGEND OF EMPEROR MING OF THE HAN (*T.* 51:179A1–179C4)

Record of the Dharma-Jewel Through the Generations. Also called: *The Transmission of the Masters and Disciples of the [True] Lineage.* Also called: *The Transmission Determining True and False, Annihilating Wrong and Displaying Right, and Destroying All Mind [Consciousnesses].* Also called: *The Supreme Vehicle, the Dharma-Gate of Sudden Awakening.*

Based on the authority of the *Abhiniṣkramaṇa-sūtra* (Scripture of the Initial Steps on the Path), *Saṃyuktāgama-sūtra* (Miscellaneous Discourses), *Lalitavistara-sūtra* (Scripture of the Unfolding of the Divine Play [of the Buddha]), *Kumārakuśalaphalanidāna-sūtra* (Scripture of Auspicious Signs), *Manjuśrī-parinirvāṇa-sūtra* (Scripture of the Final Nirvāṇa of Manjuśrī), *Qingjing faxing jing* (Scripture of the Practice of the Pure Dharma), *Strīvivartavyākaraṇa-sūtra* (Scripture of the Unstained Radiant Transformation of the Female Body), *Vinayaviniścaya-Upālipariprcchā-sūtra* (Scripture of the Inquiry of Upāli Regarding Determination of the Vinaya), *Śūraṃgama-sūtra* (Scripture of the Crown of the Buddha's Head), *Vajrasamādhi-sūtra* (Scripture of Adamantine Concentration), *Faju jing* (Verses on Dharma), *Buddhapiṭakaduḥśīlanirgraha-sūtra* (Scripture in Which the Admonitions of the Buddha-Treasury Are Understood), *Yingluo jing* (Gem-Necklace Scripture), *Avataṃsaka-sūtra* (Flower Garland Scripture), *Mahāprajñāpāramitā-sūtra* (Scripture of the Great Perfection of Wisdom), *Chanmen jing* (Scripture of the Chan Teachings), *Nirvāṇa-sūtra* (Scripture of the [Buddha's Final] Nirvāṇa), *Laṅkāvatāra-sūtra* (Scripture of the Appearance of the Dharma in Laṅkā), *Viśeṣacintabrahmaparipṛcchā-sūtra* (Scripture of the Inquiry of the Deity of Thinking), *Saddharmapuṇḍarīka-sūtra* (Scripture of the Lotus of the True Dharma), *Vimalakīrtinirdeśa-sūtra* (Scripture on the Expositions of Vimalakīrti), *Bhaiṣajyaguruvaiḍūryaprabhāsapūrvapraṇidhānaviśeṣa vistara-sūtra* (Elaboration on the Merit of the Previous Vows of the Medicine Master Who Shines Like an Emerald), *Vajracchedikā-sūtra* (Diamond Scripture), *Fufazang jing* (Scripture of the Transmission of the Dharma Treasury), *Daojiao xisheng jing* (Scripture of the Ascension to the West of the Daoist Teachings), *Shi Falin zhuan* (Biography of Shi Falin), *Shi Xushi ji* (Record of the Monk Shi Xushi), *Kaiyuan shijiao mu* (Catalogue of Buddhism in the Kaiyuan Era), *Zhou shu yiji* (Supplement to the Zhou History), *Hanfa neizhuan* (Inner Commentary on the Dharma in the Han), *Yin Xi neizhuan* (Yin Xi's Inner Commentary), *Mouzi* (The Book of Master Mou), *Liezi* (The Book of Master Lie), *Fuzi* (The Book of Master Fu), *Wu shu* (The Wu History), *Bing gu lu*,[1] *Yang Lengqie Yedu gushi* (Laṅkā Yang's Stories of Ye), etc.[2]

According to the *Hanfa neizhuan* (Inner Commentary on the Dharma in the Han),[3] in the third year of the Yongping era (60 C.E.), Emperor Ming of the Later Han dreamed one night that he saw a nine-foot golden man with a halo, flying around the palace. The next morning he asked his court officials, "What sort of auspicious sign was this?"

Grand Astrologer Fu Yi[4] addressed the emperor, saying, "In the West there is a great Holy One called the Buddha—it was his image."

Emperor Ming asked, "How do you know?"

Grand Astrologer Fu Yi replied, "In the *Zhoushu yiji* it says; 'The Buddha was born in the *jiayin* year (958 B.C.E.) of the reign of King Zhao and passed into extinction in the *renshen* year (878 B.C.E.) of King Mu.[5] A thousand years later, his teachings will spread to the Han (China).' Now that time has come."

Emperor Ming dispatched the Gentleman of the Interior Cai Yin and the Erudite Qin Jing and others as envoys to India. They made requests, and the Buddhist image they obtained was a statue of a bodhisattva, the scripture they obtained was the *Scripture in Forty-two Sections*,[6] and the two Dharma masters they obtained were Kāśyapamātaṅga and Dharmaratna.[7] Emperor Ming invited [the monks] to ascend to the audience hall and made offerings to them. Consequently, he established White Horse monastery west of Luoyang city.

On the first day of the first month of the fourteenth year of the Yongping era (71 C.E.), Daoists from Mount Huo of the Five Marchmounts and Mount

Bailu, Chu Shanxin and Fei Shucai and six hundred and ninety others, submitted a memorial:

> We, your servants, have heard that the Ultimate is without form, empty and spontaneous. From remotest antiquity it has been venerated by all alike, and this has not changed in the reigns of a hundred rulers. Yet Your Majesty has given up the root for the branches and has sought teachings in the Western Regions. You have been converted by the preachings of a barbarian divinity and neglect China. We, your servants, are sagacious men, and have read extensively in the classics. We beg that You allow us to compare [our Way with that of the Buddhists]. If there is a victor, we desire that You abolish the one that is specious and false. We know that they will not prove our equals, and will abide by Your Majesty's decision.

The emperor said, "Very well." He ordered that those in charge should see to the preparation of implements. Together with the inner and outer palace officials, civil and military, of the fifth rank and above, on the fifteenth at dawn all were assembled at the White Horse monastery.

Outside the gate of the monastery the Daoists set up three altars and opened twenty-four pickets.[8] Outside the southern gate of the monastery the emperor placed a relic [of the Buddha] as well as Buddhist scriptures and images, and he set up a pavilion adorned with the seven precious gems.

Chu Shanxin and Fei Shucai and the others placed Daoist scriptures, treatises, and talismans on the altars. Then they set fire to them to verify their efficacy and, lamenting and wailing, they incanted: "A barbarian divinity disturbs our China, we beg the Highest Celestial Venerables to enlighten all beings to the difference between true and false." But as soon as the Daoist scriptures, treatises, and talismans were put in the fire they were instantly burned to ashes. The Daoists were greatly surprised. Those who formerly ascended to Heaven now could not, those who formerly rendered themselves invisible now could not, those who formerly entered fire and water now dared not, and those who formerly cast spells and those who did divinations could not get any response. Of all their various abilities there was not one that was efficacious. Chu Shanxin, Fei Shucai, and the others took it to heart so much that they died.

Then the Buddha relic radiated five-colored light and linked jewels covered the entire assembly like a canopy, outshining the disk of the sun. Dharma Master Kāśyapamātaṅga assumed seated and reclining postures in empty space and freely manifested supramundane transformations. The heavens rained jeweled flowers and there was celestial music. Dharmaratna chanted hymns in the Brāhmanical Voice,[9] and Kāśyapamātaṅga spoke the following verse:

> A fox is not in the same class with a lion,
> a lamp is not as brilliant as the sun and moon.
> A pond is not as capacious as the vast ocean,
> and a hillock is not as lofty as Mount Song.

Emperor Ming was greatly pleased, and he permitted the children and the concubines of nobles of the fifth rank and above to become renunciants. Six hundred Daoists submitted to the Buddha and became renunciants. Dharmaratna chanted the *Chujia gongde jing* (Scripture on the Merit of Renunciation), the *Abhiniṣkramaṇa-sūtra,* and other scriptures. Emperor Ming was overjoyed, and the entire realm took refuge in Buddhism.

Emperor Ming asked the two masters, "The Buddha is called the King of the Dharma. Why was he not born in China?"

The Dharma Master Kāśyapamātaṅga replied, "The city of Kapilavastu is the center of a hundred thousand suns and moons, it is the sovereign of the trichilio-megachiliocosms. All *nāgas,* gods, and those who are fortunate are born there. That is why the King of the Dharma was born in India."

Emperor Ming further questioned the Dharma Master, "What was the Buddha's clan? When was he born and when did he die?"

Dharma Master Kāśyapamātaṅga replied, "The Buddha was the descendent of a thousand generations of Golden Cakravartins (Wheel-Turning Kings) and the son of King Śuddhodana. His surname was Gautama; he is also identified as a member the Śākya clan. On the fifteenth day of the seventh month of the *guichou* year (957 B.C.E.), he descended from his palace in Tuṣita Heaven and was incarnated in the womb of the Lady Māyā. On the eighth day of the fourth month of the *jiayin* year (958 B.C.E.), in Lumbini Park, Lady Māyā gave birth to him from her right side. Five hundred men of the Śākya clan, five hundred white horses, and Kaṇṭhaka and Chandaka[10] were born with the Buddha at the same time on the eighth day of the fourth month. On the eighth day of the second month of the *renshen* year (940 B.C.E.) he left the city and became a renunciant, and on the fifteenth day of the second month of the *guiwei* year he entered *parinirvāṇa.* Although the Buddha was not born in the land of the Han, [it was predestined that] one thousand years later, or five hundred years later, when the many beings' conditions [were ripe], he would have his holy disciples go there and make conversions."

SECTION 2. BUDDHISM IN CHINA (*T.* 51:179C4–180A2)

The *Qingjing faxing jing* (Scripture of the Pure Practice of the Dharma) says: "To the northeast of India is the kingdom of China. Few of the people are devout and evildoers are legion. For the present I will dispatch three holy disciples, all bodhisattvas, to appear there and make conversions. Mahākāśyapa will be styled Laozi, Kumara will be called Confucius, and Sumedha will be called Yanhui.[11] They will expound on the five classics: the *Classic of Poetry, Classic of Documents, Classic of Rites,* and *Classic of Music.* By setting august standards they will gradually bring about a transformation. Only after that will the Buddhist scriptures proceed [to China]."[12]

According to the *Mouzi,*[13] long ago Emperor Xiaoming of the Han dreamed one night of a divine person. His body radiated light and he flew about in front of the palace. [The emperor] experienced inner joy and his heart was deeply gladdened. The next day he related [his dream] and asked his ministers, "What was this?"

There was a man of penetration, Fu Yi, who said, "I have heard that in India there was a man who attained the Way who is called Buddha. He can levitate and is able to fly, and his body radiates light. It was probably his divine [manifestation]."

Realizing that this was the case, [the emperor] dispatched the emissary Zhang Qian, the Gentleman of the Palace Guard Qin, the Erudite disciple Wang Zun, and others, twelve people in all. From the Great Yuezhi kingdom[14] they copied and brought back the Buddhist *Scripture in Forty-two Sections,* which was placed in the fourteenth stone chamber of the Orchid Pavilion (i.e., the archives). Then the emperor had a Buddhist monastery erected outside of the Xiyong gate of Luoyang city. He had a court painted on the walls with one thousand chariots and ten thousand cavalrymen encircling it thirteen deep [to welcome the Buddha]. He also had images of the Buddha made at Qingliang Pavilion of the Southern Palace and above the Kaiyang Gate.

The time came when Emperor Ming knew his life was impermanent, and he prepared his tomb. The tomb was called "Displaying Temperance," and he also had Buddhist images made for it. While he was alive the country was prosperous and the people were at peace. Distant barbarian tribes emulated righteousness and all came to "take refuge in virtue." Those who desired to be his subjects numbered in the hundreds of thousands. This was why he was posthumously styled "Ming" (Brilliant). From that time on there were Buddhist monasteries in the vicinity of the capital as well in all the counties and districts, and the students [of Buddhism] accordingly multiplied.

According to the *Jin shu* (Jin History), at the time of Emperor Huan of the Jin (Huan Xuan, 369–404), [the emperor] wanted to cut back the Buddha-Dharma, so he summoned Dharma Master Yuan of Mount Lu (Huiyuan, 334–416). The emperor said, "We have been observing lately that monks and nuns are not sincere in their practice of the precepts; there have been many transgressions. We wish to weed out [the saṅgha]. Shall We at once carry out this culling process?"

Lord Yuan responded, "The jade that is extracted from Mount Kun is covered with dirt and grit. The Li river is rich with gold, yet it is also full of gravel. Your Majesty must respect the Dharma and value its representatives; you must not scorn its representatives or treat the Dharma with contempt." The Jin emperor then issued a general amnesty.[15]

The *Hui sanjiao* (Encountering the Three Teachings) by Emperor Wu of the Xiao Liang (r. 502–549) says: "When I was a child I studied the *Zhou Li* (Rites of Zhou). When I was a youth I thoroughly investigated the six classics. In my middle years I repeatedly examined Daoist books and the 'named and nameless.' In my later years I opened the Buddhist scrolls, and it is like the sun outshining the myriad stars."[16]

SECTION 3. TRANSMISSION FROM INDIA TO CHINA (THE *FU FAZANG ZHUAN*) (*T.* 51:180A2–180C2)

The *Avataṃsaka-sūtra* says: "All buddhas abdicate their status; some become bodhisattvas, some become śrāvakas (disciples), some become cakravartins, some become demon kings, some become princes of kingdoms or great ministers, or lay elders, or palace women and officials, some become powerful ghosts and spirits, or mountain spirits or stream spirits, or river spirits or sea spirits, or spirits that rule the sun or spirits that rule the moon, or morning spirits or evening spirits, or spirits that rule fire or spirits that rule water, or all the spirits of sprouting and ripe grain, or spirits of the trees, and they even become non-Buddhists. They perform various kinds of expedient means in order to assist our Śākyamuni Tathāgata to convert and guide all sentient beings."[17]

The "Dharāṇī" section of the *Mahāprajñāpāramitā-sūtra* says: "At that time, Śāriputra addressed the Buddha, saying, 'World-Honored One, after you enter into nirvāṇa, how will this most profound scripture, the *Prajñāpāramitā,* flourish and prosper?' The Buddha said, 'Śāriputra, after I enter into nirvāṇa, this most profound [scripture], the *Prajñāpāramitā,* will go from the north to the northeast where it will gradually flourish and prosper. In that place there will be many monks, nuns, laymen, and laywomen grounded in the Greater Vehicle who will be able to rely on this most profound [scripture], the *Prajñāpāramitā,* and will have deep faith and delight in it.' He further told Śāriputra, 'After I enter into nirvāṇa, in the latter five hundred years of the latter period of the Dharma, this most profound [scripture], the *Prajñāpāramitā,* will greatly further Buddhism in the northeast.'"[18]

According to the *Fu fazang jing* (Scripture of the Transmission of the Dharma Treasury),[19] after Śākya Tathāgata passed into nirvāṇa, the Dharma Eye was entrusted to Mahākāśyapa. Mahākāśyapa entrusted it to Ānanda, Ānanda entrusted it to Madhyāntika, Madhyāntika entrusted it to Śaṇavāsin, Śaṇavāsin entrusted it to Upagupta, Upagupta entrusted it to Dhṛtaka, Dhṛtaka entrusted it to Miccaka, Miccaka entrusted it to Buddhanandi, Buddhanandi entrusted it to Buddhamitra, Buddhamitra entrusted it to Pārśva Bhikṣu, Pārśva Bhikṣu entrusted it to Puṇyayaśas, Puṇyayaśas entrusted it to Aśvaghoṣa, Aśvaghoṣa entrusted it to Kapimala, Kapimala entrusted it to Nāgārjuna, Nāgārjuna entrusted it to Kāṇadeva, Kāṇadeva entrusted it to Rāhula, Rāhula entrusted it to Saṅghānandi, Saṅghānandi entrusted it to Saṅghāyaśas, Saṅghāyaśas entrusted it to Kumārata, Kumārata entrusted it to Jayata, Jayata entrusted it to Vasubandhu, Vasubandhu entrusted it to Manora, Manora entrusted it to Haklena, Haklena entrusted it to Siṁha Bhikṣu, Siṁha Bhikṣu entrusted it to Śaṇavāsa.

When Siṁha Bhikṣu had transmitted [the Dharma] to Śaṇavāsa, he then went from central India to Kashmir. The king there was named Mihirakula.[20] This king did not believe in the Buddha-Dharma—he destroyed stūpas, demolished monasteries, slaughtered sentient beings, and honored the two heretics Momanni (Mani) and Mishihe (Messiah, i.e., Jesus).

At that time Siṁha Bhikṣu purposely came to convert this kingdom, and the pathless king with his own hands took up a sharp double-edged sword and swore an oath: "If you are a Holy One, the [other] masters must suffer punishment." Siṁha Bhikṣu then manifested a form whereby his body bled white milk. Momanni and Mishihe were executed, and like ordinary men their blood spattered the ground. The king was inspired to take refuge in the Buddha, and he ordered the disciple of Siṁha Bhikṣu (the Dharma had already been transmitted to Śaṇavāsa) to enter South India to preach extensively and liberate beings.

The king then sought out and captured the disciples of the heretics Moman and Mishihe. When he had captured them he set up stocks at court and suspended them by their necks, and the people of the entire country shot arrows at them. The king of Kashmir ordered that if there were [followers] of these creeds in any of the kingdoms, they should be driven from the kingdom.

Owing to Siṁha Bhikṣu, the Buddha-Dharma flourished again. Śaṇavāsa entrusted it to Upagupta, Upagupta entrusted it to Śubhamitra, Śubhamitra entrusted it to Saṅgharakṣa, Saṅgharakṣa entrusted it to Bodhidharmatrāta.[21] Thus, in the Western Kingdoms there were twenty-nine generations; excepting Dharmatrāta, there were twenty-eight generations.

There was a śramaṇa of the Eastern Capital (Luoyang), Master Jingjue, who was the disciple of Chan Master Shenxiu of Yuquan [monastery] and compiled the *Lengqie shizi xuemo ji* (Record of the Lineage of the Masters and Disciples of the *Laṅkāvatāra-sūtra*) in one fascicle. He falsely alleged that the Liu Song dynasty Trepiṭaka[22] Guṇabhadra was the first patriarch. I do not know his source, but he deluded and confused later students by saying [Guṇabhadra] was Patriarchal Master [Bodhi]dharma's master. Guṇabhadra was from the beginning a scripture-translating Trepiṭaka, a student of the Lesser Vehicle, not a Chan Master. He translated the *Laṅkāvatāra-sūtra* in four fascicles, but he did not give an explanation of the *Laṅkāvatāra-sūtra* or transmit it to the Patriarchal Master Dharma. The Patriarchal Master Dharma, from the continuous line of direct transmission of the twenty-eight generations, inherited it from Saṅgharakṣa. Later at Shaolin monastery on Mount Songgao, Great Master Huike personally asked Patriarchal Master Dharma about the succession of the direct transmission, and because there is this record [the matter] is clear. When this Master Jingjue falsely alleged that Guṇabhadra was the first patriarch he profoundly confused the study of the Dharma.

The *Lotus Sūtra* says: "Don't allow intimacy with Trepiṭakas, students of the Lesser Vehicle."[23] Trepiṭaka Guṇabhadra translated the *Laṅkāvatāra-sūtra* in four fascicles and called it the *Abatoubao Lengqie jing*.[24] In the Wei dynasty,

Trepiṭaka Bodhiruci translated it in ten fascicles and called it the *Ru Lengqie jing*.[25] In the Tang dynasty, during the time of [Empress Wu] Zetian, Śikṣānanda translated the *Lengqie jing* in seven fascicles.[26] All of the above were translator Trepiṭakas and not Chan Masters. All of them transmitted the teachings of the written word. Patriarchal Master Dharma was in the lineage of the Chan Dharma. He did not bring a single word, just silently transmitted the mind seal.

SECTION 4. THE FIRST PATRIARCH BODHIDHARMATRĀTA (*T*. 51:180C3–181A18)

LIANG DYNASTY, THE FIRST PATRIARCH

Chan Master Bodhidharmatrāta was the third son of a South Indian king. He became a monk while still young, and as soon as he received instruction from his master he was immediately awakened. He preached in South India and greatly furthered Buddhism.

At one point, he ascertained that the beings of the land of the Han were possessed of the Great Chan nature. So he dispatched two of his disciples, Buddha and Yaśas, to go to the land of the Qin (the Later Qin dynasty, 385–417) and explain the teaching of immediate awakening. When the worthies of the Qin first heard, they were doubtful and none would believe. [The disciples] were cast out and driven to Donglin monastery on Mount Lu.

At that time, Dharma Master Lord Yuan (Huiyuan) was there, and he asked them, "Worthies, what Dharma have you brought, that you were thus cast out?"

Thereupon, the two Brahmins put out their hands and said to Lord Yuan, "The hand changes to a fist and the fist changes to a hand. Does this happen quickly or not?"

Lord Yuan responded, "Very quickly."

The two Brahmins said, "This is not quick. Defilements (*kleśa*) are none other than awakening (*bodhi*). *This* is quick." Lord Yuan was deeply impressed, and thereupon realized that awakening and defilements are one and the same.

Then he asked, "In that other country, from whom did you learn this Dharma?"

The two Brahmins replied, "From our teacher Dharmatrāta." Lord Yuan thereafter had a profound faith [in this Dharma].

[The two disciples] translated the *Chanmen jing* (Scripture of the Chan Teachings) in one fascicle, which completely elucidates the Greater and Lesser Vehicles and the Chan Dharma. Those who transmitted the Dharma in the Western Kingdoms are also included in the preface to the *Chan Scripture.* When the two Brahmins completed the translation, they both passed into extinction on the same day and were buried on Mount Lu, where their stūpa even now remains.

When Dharmatrāta heard that his two disciples had gone to the land of Han to spread the Dharma but none would believe, he sailed across the sea and reached the Liang court. Emperor Wu came out of the city to welcome him personally. He had him ascend to the audience hall and asked the Venerable, "What teachings to convert beings have you brought from the other country?"

Great Master Dharma replied, "I have not brought a single word."

The emperor asked, "What merit have We gained in having monasteries built and people saved, scriptures copied and statues cast?"

The Great Master responded, "No merit whatsoever." He added, "This is contrived goodness, not true merit."

Emperor Wu was a man of ordinary nature and did not understand, so [Bodhidharmatrāta] left that country. Northward there was an atmosphere [more favorable] to the Great Vehicle. He came to the Wei, where he lived at Mount Songgao and received people of all degrees for instruction for six years. Students gathered like hastening clouds and like torrents of rain; the crowds [were thick as] rice, hemp, bamboo, or reeds. But only the Great Master Ke obtained the marrow [of Bodhidharmatrāta's teachings].

Now it happened that in the Wei the Trepiṭaka Bodhiruci and the Vinaya Master Guangtong put poison in some food that they offered [to Bodhidharmatrāta]. When the Great Master finished eating he asked for a dish and vomited up a pint of snakes. Once again they offered him poisoned food. When the Great Master had taken the food and eaten it he sat atop a massive boulder, and when the poison came out the boulder cracked. Altogether they tried to poison him six times.

The Great Master informed his disciples, "I originally came in order to pass on the Dharma. Now that I've gotten someone, what's the good of lingering?" Then he transmitted a *kāṣāya* robe as a verification of the Dharma transmission. He said to Huike, "My destiny is this poison; you also will not escape these tribulations. In the sixth generation, the life of the Dharma heir will be as a dangling thread." He finished speaking and immediately died of the poison. He himself used to say, "I am one hundred and fifty years old," but it was not known how old he actually was.

The Great Master said, "In the land of the Tang there are three people who have gotten my Dharma. One has gotten my marrow, one has gotten my bones, and one has gotten my flesh. The one who got my marrow is Huike, the one who got my bones is Daoyu, and the one who got my flesh is the nun Zongchi." He was buried on Mount Xionger in the Luo region (Henan).

At that time, the Wei emissary Song Yun met the Great Master in the Pamirs. The Great Master was carrying one shoe in his hand. Yun asked, "Great Master, where are you going?"

[Bodhidharmatrāta] replied, "I am returning to my native country. Your king died today."

Yun recorded this. Yun asked the Great Master, "Great Master, once you are gone, to whom has the Buddha-Dharma been entrusted?"

[Bodhidharmatrāta] replied, "Forty years after I've gone there will be a Chinese man of the Way, you can count on it."[27]

When Song Yun returned to court, the old emperor had indeed died and the new emperor was already established. Yun told the court officials, "The Great Master was carrying a single shoe, returning home to the Western Kingdoms. He said, 'The old king of your country has died,' and it is just as he said." The court officials would not believe him, so they opened the Great Master's tomb—and there was only a single shoe.

Emperor Wu of the Xiao Liang wrote a memorial inscription: "His disciple in the Western Kingdoms was Prajñāparamitara. In the Tang Kingdom there are three people, Daoyu, the nun Zongchi, and Huike, who alone received the robe and got the Dharma."

SECTION 5. THE SECOND PATRIARCH HUIKE (*T.* 51:181A19–181B18)

NORTHERN QI DYNASTY, THE SECOND PATRIARCH

Chan Master Huike had the lay surname Ji, and he was from Wulao (Henan). When he was forty, he had served the Great Master [Bodhidharmatrāta] for six years. He was previously called Shenguang. When he first came to serve the Great Master, he stood before the Great Master in the night. That night there was a heavy snowfall and the snow rose up to his waist, but he did not stir.

The Great Master said, "He who would seek the Dharma must spare neither life nor limb." [Huike] then chopped off one of his arms, whereupon his blood flowed as white milk. The Great Master then silently transmitted the mind pledge and passed on to him the *kāṣāya* robe.

The Great Master said, "My destiny is this poison. You also will not escape [troubles], take good care of yourself."

Great Master Ke asked, "Venerable—about this Dharma of yours that has been passed down through the generations in your native country, and those to whom the Dharma was entrusted—please explain it again."

[Bodhidharmatrāta] replied, "All the particulars are explained in the preface to the *Chan Scripture.*"

[Huike] further questioned the Great Master, "In the Western Kingdoms, to whom did you pass the succession, and did you also transmit the *kāṣāya* robe of verification to him or not?"

The Great Master replied, "The people of the Western Kingdoms are devout, they are not devious. My successor there is Prajñāpāramitāra, and I have passed the succession to him without transmitting the robe. In the Tang Kingdom beings have the Great Vehicle nature, [yet some] falsely claim to have obtained the Way and the fruit [of enlightenment], and so I transmit the robe for the sake of verification of the teachings. It is like the consecration of the son of a cakravartin when he obtains the seven jewels and inherits his eminent position as king. Possession of the robe represents the true inheritance of the Dharma."

After Great Master Ke obtained succession, for forty years he secluded himself at Mount Huan and in the Luo and Xiang regions (Henan). After that he received people of all degrees for instruction, and the lay and ordained who took refuge with him were innumerable. When he had been teaching for twenty years difficulties arose, again caused by the clique of the followers of the Trepiṭaka Bodhiruci and Vinaya Master Guangtong, who wanted to harm Great Master Ke.

When the Great Master entrusted the Dharma to Sengcan, [Sengcan] went into seclusion at Mount Sikong. Great Master Ke then feigned madness, preaching the Dharma at the crossroads of the city marketplace. People flocked to him in prodigious numbers. The clique of Bodhiruci's followers declared that

Great Master Ke was uncanny and strange. They petitioned an imperial official, who ordered that another official interrogate him. Great Master Ke responded, "I confess that I truly am uncanny."

The official knew that the many beings were suffering, so he ordered that Great Master Ke be given an official hearing. The Great Master incontestably said, "I truly am uncanny." An imperial edict went to the District Magistrate of Cheng'an, Zhai Chongkan, to the effect that [Huike] was to be executed in accordance with the law.

Great Master Ke told the assembled crowd, "When my Dharma reaches the Fourth Patriarch it will become only nominal." When he had spoken, he wept grievously and then manifested a form whereby his body bled white milk, though the color of his flesh was as usual. The official memorialized the emperor. When the emperor heard, he repented his error [and said], "This was a true bodhisattva." Everyone at court conceived the aspiration to attain the Way, and the Buddha-Dharma flourished once again.

At that time the Great Master was one hundred and seven. His tomb was built in Cheng'an district in the Xiang region, five *li* north of the Zimou river at Dongliu canal. One hundred paces beyond the tomb and fifteen *li* southwest is Wuer Caokou. The *Lengqie Yedu gushi* records this. Sengcan was the disciple who succeeded him, received transmission of the robe, and obtained the Dharma. Later, Shi Falin wrote a memorial inscription.

SECTION 6. THE THIRD PATRIARCH SENGCAN (*T.* 51:181B19–181C8)

SUI DYNASTY, THE THIRD PATRIARCH

Chan Master Can's place of origin is unknown. When he first encountered Great Master Ke, Can appeared to have palsy. They met in the midst of a crowd. Great Master Ke asked, "Where are you from? Why are you here?"

Sengcan replied, "Because I want to serve the Venerable."

Great Master Ke said, "For you, a person afflicted with palsy, what good is it to meet with me?"

Can replied, "Although my body is afflicted, between the mind of the afflicted and the Venerable's mind there is no difference."[28]

Great Master Ke realized that Can was no ordinary man and therefore entrusted the Dharma and the *kāṣāya* robe of verification to him. Great Master Ke said, "You must protect yourself well. I am involved in difficulties, but you must escape them." Great Master Can also feigned madness in the marketplace, and later he hid at Mount Sikong in the Shu region (Anhui).

During the time when Emperor Wu of the Zhou was annihilating the Buddha-Dharma, [Sengcan] hid on Mount Huangong for over a decade. The mountain was quite full of fierce wild animals who often preyed upon the people living there, but once Great Master Can arrived they all took themselves off to another area.

After [Sengcan] had entrusted the Dharma and the robe to Daoxin, the Chan Masters Huan, Yue, Ding, and Yan came to Great Master Can's place and said, "[Of those] since Patriarchal Master Dharma passed on the Dharma, this Lord Can is truly a divine gem.[29] In him the simultaneous functioning of *samādhi* and *prajñā* are utterly inconceivable."

Great Master Can subsequently went with the Chan masters to live in seclusion at Mount Loufu (Guangdong). After three years he went to a Great Assembly vegetarian alms feast and came out and told the crowd, "I now wish to eat." His disciples served him food and drink. When the Great Master finished eating he told the crowd, "People sigh and exclaim that dying in a seated posture is a marvel, but I alone am free in birth and death." When he finished speaking, with one hand he grasped the branch of a tree that stood in the midst of the assembly and died instantly in a standing posture. His age was also unknown. His stūpa is beside Mount Huan temple.

His disciples were very numerous, but only Daoxin inherited the robe and got the Dharma as his successor. Xue Daoheng composed a memorial inscription.

SECTION 7. THE FOURTH PATRIARCH DAOXIN (*T.* 51:181C9–182A10)

TANG DYNASTY, THE FOURTH PATRIARCH

Chan Master Xin's lay surname was Sima, and he was from east of the Yellow river. He became a renunciant when very young and entered the service of Great Master Can. Great Master Can knew that he was especially talented.

He sat day and night without lying down; for over sixty years his sides never touched a mat. He had an exceptional spiritual presence. His eyes usually did not gaze out, [but] when he wanted to look at someone, that person would cower in fear.

In this manner, in the year Daye (605) Great Master Xin saw from afar [something that was happening] in the Ji region. Bandits had been besieging a town for over a hundred days and the spring-fed well was completely dried up. The Great Master entered the city and gave counsel and guidance to both lay and ordained. He had them carry out the practice of [chanting] the *Prajñāpāramitā-sūtra.* The bandits withdrew of their own volition, and the town's spring-fed well began to flow again. There were many who [were inspired to] study the Way.

[Another time] Great Master Xin saw from afar that at Mount Potou in Huangmei in the Qi region there was a canopy of purple clouds. Great Master Xin thereupon went to live on this mountain, which was later renamed Mount Shuangfeng.

In the seventeenth year of the Zhenguan era (643), Emperor Wenwu sent a messenger to Mount Shuangfeng to invite Chan Master Xin to enter the imperial presence. Chan Master Xin pleaded old age and did not go. The messenger returned to the emperor and delivered the message, "Chan Master Xin pleads old age and will not come."

The messenger was sent again to repeat the invitation. He went to Chan Master Xin's place and said, "The emperor sends me to invite the Chan Master."

The Chan Master earnestly pleaded old age and would not go, telling the messenger, "If you want my head you are welcome to behead me and take it, but I absolutely will not go."

The messenger returned to the emperor and delivered the message, "He would allow his head to be cut off and taken, but his mind absolutely will not go." The emperor again sent off the messenger, [this time] wearing a sword with which to get Chan Master Xin's head. He ordered him, "Do not harm the Venerable."

The messenger arrived at the Venerable's place and said, "The Emperor orders me to get the Venerable's head. Will the Chan Master go or not?"

The Venerable replied, "I absolutely will not go."

The messenger said, "The emperor orders that if the Chan Master will not come, I am to cut off his head and bring it."

Great Master Xin extended his head and said, "Chop it and take it." The messenger turned the blade and bent [Daoxin's] neck.

Great Master Xin sang out, "Why don't you chop, how much longer must I wait?"

The messenger replied, "The emperor ordered me not to harm the Venerable."

Chan Master Xin gave a great laugh and said, "I've taught you to recognize someone who stays put."

Great Master Xin thereafter greatly furthered Buddhism, extensively opened the Dharma-gates, and guided people of all degrees. All the *hastināga*[30] of the four directions came to receive his teachings and take refuge.

Over thirty years passed, and only Hongren served him and grasped his meaning. When [Daoxin] had transferred the Dharma and the *kāṣāya* robe to Hongren, he ordered his disciple Master Yuanyi, "Build a reliquary niche on the side of my mountain, and it must be done soon." A while later he asked, "Is the reliquary niche completed or not?"

Yuanyi replied, "It has been accomplished."

In the second year of the Yonghui era (651), on the twenty-fourth day of the intercalary ninth month, the Great Master, without ever having suffered from illness, died instantly in a seated posture. He was at that time seventy-two years old. After he had been entombed for a year, the stone door opened of itself for no reason. The Great Master's appearance was as composed and imposing as ever. Hongren and the others repeatedly paid obeisance to his divine appearance, and they could not master their feelings of devotion. Subsequently, lacquered cloth was applied to the honored countenance. From that time forth, no one dared shut [the tomb door].

His disciples were very numerous, but only Hongren inherited the robe and got the Dharma as his successor. The Secretariat-Director Du Zhenglun composed a memorial inscription.

SECTION 8. THE FIFTH PATRIARCH HONGREN (*T.* 51:182A11–182B5)

TANG DYNASTY, THE FIFTH PATRIARCH

Chan Master Hongren's lay surname was Zhou, and he was from Huangmei. At the age of seven he went to serve Master Xin, and at the age of thirteen he entered upon the Way and donned robes. He was by nature taciturn and imperturbable, and when his fellow students joked around he remained silently unresponsive. He was always diligent in performing duties, and toward others he conducted himself with decorous humility. By day he secretly did things for others and by night he practiced sitting meditation until dawn; never was he negligent. For thirty years he never left Master Xin. He was eight feet tall,[31] and his appearance was completely unlike that of ordinary people.

When he obtained transmission of the Dharma he settled on Mount Pingmao. It was not far east of Mount Shuangfeng. What people of the time called "the East Mountain School" referred to Mount Pingmao, not Mount Song.

There was a time when the wild bandit Ke Dahan and his minions heavily besieged a town in the region of Rao (Jiangxi). There was no way in, not even birds on the wing could get through. The Great Master saw this from afar and came to the town. The bandits fled in confusion, calling back and forth to one another, "Innumerable Vajrapāni carrying cudgels are stomping after us with fierce looks and gnashing teeth, so let us flee quickly." Great Master Ren then went back to Mount Pingmao.

In the fifth year of the Xianqing era (660), the Great Emperor [Gaozong] sent a messenger to Mount Pingmao in Huangmei to invite Great Master Ren, but the Great Master did not accept. Again [the emperor] sent a messenger to invite him, but he did not come. [The emperor] then sent a gift of clothing and medicine as offerings to Mount Pingmao.

Afterward, for over forty years [Hongren] received lay and ordained for instruction, and the *hastināga* of the four directions came to take refuge, hastening and gathering [like clouds]. The Great Master entrusted Huineng with the Dharma and the *kāṣāya* robe.

Later, in the fifth year of the Xianheng era, he ordered his disciple Master Xuanze, "Erect a stūpa for me."

On the fourteenth day of the second month, he asked, "Is the stūpa done or not?"

[Xuanze] replied, "It is completed."

The Great Master said, "I can't very well enter *parinirvāṇa* on the fifteenth day of the second month, the same as the Buddha." He continued, "The people I have taught in the course of my life are countless, but besides Huineng there are just these ten: Master Shenxiu, Master Zhishen, Master Zhide, Master Xuanze, Master Laoan, Master Faru, Master Huizang, Master Xuanyue, and Liu Zhubo. Although you never left me, each of you is but one aspect of a master."

Later, on the eleventh day of the second month of the second year of the Shangyuan era (675), he died instantly in a seated posture. At the time, Great Master Ren was seventy-four years old.

His disciples [were numerous], but only Huineng inherited the robe and got the Dharma as his successor. The scholar Lu Qiujun composed a memorial inscription.

SECTION 9. THE SIXTH PATRIARCH HUINENG, PART 1 (*T.* 51:182B6–182C16)

TANG DYNASTY, THE SIXTH PATRIARCH

The lay surname of Chan Master Neng of Caoqi in Shaozhou was Lu, and he was from Fanyang (Hebei). After his father was posted to Lingwai, he lived in Xinzhou (Guangdong).

When he was twenty-two, he came to Mount Pingmao to pay his respects to Great Master Ren. At their first meeting the Great Master asked, "Where did you come from?"

[Huineng] replied, "I have come from Xinzhou. I want nothing else but to become a buddha."

Great Master Ren said, "You people from Xinzhou are Lao barbarians, why would you become a buddha?"

Huineng replied, "Is there any difference between the buddha nature of a Lao barbarian and the Venerable's buddha nature?" The Great Master was deeply impressed by his ability. He wished to speak with him again, but because there were many people with him he ordered Neng to follow after the crowd.

For eight months [Huineng] worked at treading the rice-hulling pestle, and the sounds of the pestle were consistent and unvarying. Great Master Ren went up to the pestle and instructed him secretly, and he directly saw his own nature. In the night he was secretly summoned to [Hongren's] room, and when they had spoken together for three days and three nights, [Hongren] entrusted the Dharma and *kāṣāya* robe to him [and said], "You are the Great Master of this world, and thus I command you to depart quickly."

The Great Master personally saw him off as far as Jiujiang station and watched him cross the Great River (the Yangzi) before turning around and going home. None of the disciples knew that [Hongren] had passed the Dharma and robe to Huineng. After three days the Great Master announced to the disciples, "You can all disperse, there's no Buddha-Dharma in my vicinity. The Buddha-Dharma has flowed to Lingnan."

The crowd was surprised and asked each other, "Who is there in Lingnan?"

Master Faru of Luzhou replied, "Huineng is there."

A crowd gathered. Among the crowd there was one who had been a general of the fourth rank who had given up his position to enter the Way. His cognomen was Huiming. He had long been with the Great Master [Hongren] but he had been unable to verify awakening. No sooner had he heard Great Master Ren's words than by double-marches day and night he hastened in pursuit [of Huineng]. Atop Mount Dayu (Jiangxi) he met up with Chan Master Neng, who was terrified and feared for his life. He took the *kāṣāya* robe [verifying] transmission of the Dharma and passed it over to Chan Master Huiming.

Chan Master Huiming said, "It is not for the sake of the *kāṣāya* robe that I came. On the day Great Master Ren sent you off, what words of teaching [did he give you]? I beg you to explain it for me." Chan Master Neng fully explained the mind-Dharma of directly realizing the nature. When Master Huiming had heard the Dharma, he put his palms together and made obeisance. He then urged Chan Master Neng, "Cross the mountains quickly, there are many people coming after you." This Chan Master Huiming later settled on Mount Meng (Jiangxi), but the disciples who came from there also only "viewed purity."

Chan Master Neng reached Caoqi in Shaozhou. He taught for over forty years, and the ordained and laity came hastening like clouds. Later, in the second year of the Jingyun era (711), he ordered his disciple Xuanjie to build a stūpa on Mount Long in Xinzhou. In the first year of the Xiantian era (712), he asked "Is the stūpa completed or not?"

[Xuanjie] replied, "It is done."

In the ninth month of that year, [Huineng] left Caoqi and went back to Xinzhou. The Caoqi monks Xuanjie, Zhihai, and the others asked, "After you, Venerable, who will get the Dharma succession and receive transmission of the *kāṣāya* robe of verification?"

The Venerable replied, "Do not ask. After this, hardships will arise in great profusion. How often have we faced death on account of this *kāṣāya* robe? At Great Master Xin's place it was stolen three times, at Great Master Ren's place it was stolen three times, and now at my place it has been stolen six times. At last no one will steal this *kāṣāya* robe of mine, for a woman has taken it away.

So don't ask me anymore. If you want to know who gets my Dharma, twenty years after I have passed on, the one who establishes my doctrine will indeed be the one who has gotten the Dharma."

In the second year of the Xiantian era (713), he suddenly told his disciples, "I am at the point of the great undertaking." On the evening of the third day of the eighth month, he died instantaneously in a seated posture. The Great Master's springs and autumns numbered seventy-six. In Caoqi the canals and streams stopped flowing and the springs and ponds dried up. The sun and moon did not shine and the forests turned white. There was an uncanny, fragrant, auspicious vapor that did not cease for three days and nights. That year Guo'en monastery of Xinzhou hosted the Venerable's corpse, and in the eleventh month he was entombed at Caoqi.

At Taichang monastery the Administrative Aide Wei Ju composed a memorial inscription, but in the seventh year of the Kaiyuan era it was effaced by someone and another memorial was made. It was restored recently, and the Gentleman-in-Attendance Song Ding composed a memorial inscription.

SECTION 10. DHARMA MASTER DAOAN AND SCRIPTURE QUOTATIONS (*T.* 51:182C17–183C1)

During the three hundred years after the Buddhist teachings came east, there were no formal standards at all. Later, around the time of Shi Le of the Jin, Fotudeng's disciple Dharma Master Daoan was at Xiangyang. Fujian of the Qin heard of Daoan's fame from afar, and so he dispatched retainers to attack Xiangyang and capture Dharma Master Daoan. The Qin emperor often honored and met with him, and the sons of the nobility of Chang'an all went to him to [learn to] recite poetry. [The saying] "If students don't rely on Dharma Master Daoan, they will not be able to make sense of difficulties" refers to this. He had worldly wisdom and was a brilliant debater.

Later he also established a method of organization for discourses, and made rules for monks and nuns and a set of codes for the Buddha-Dharma. As for the rules for taking the precepts, he classified them into three sets: the first concerns circulating with incense and determining seating, the second concerns the six periods of repetition of the devotions, and the third concerns the monthly confession of transgressions. Formal deportment and the invocations and hymns used in services all originated with this Dharma Master

Daoan. In recent times there was the Shu (Sichuan) monk Dharma Master Sian, who made the *Zhaiwen* (On Vegetarian Feasts) in four fascicles that is now very widely disseminated.

The *Laṅkāvatāra-sūtra* says, "If you have set up something, everything is completely confounded. If you see it is only from your own mind, then there is no contention."[32]

Moreover it says, "If you depend on inferior Dharma then inferior Dharma arises. If you depend on phenomena then the Dharma will be ruined."[33]

Moreover it says, "If you follow after words and grasp meanings then you build on dharmas (constituents of existence), and because of that construction, when you die you fall into hell."[34]

Moreover it says, "To seek the self in doctrines is fantasy, it is 'wrong view.' If you part from the true principle of the holy teachings, then the delusions you want to extinguish will on the contrary increase, and this is heterodox crazy talk and should not be expounded by the wise."[35]

The *Vajracchedikā-sūtra* says, "Transcending all characteristics is called the buddhas."[36]

Moreover it says, "Someone who sees 'I' through form and seeks 'I' through sounds—this is the false path trodden by men, and [this person] is unable to see the Tathāgata."[37]

The *Viśeṣacintibrahma-paripṛcchā-sūtra* says, "[Viśeṣacintibrahma asked the Buddha,] 'How do the monks follow the Buddha's teachings, how do they follow the Buddha's words?' [The Buddha replied,] 'One whose mind does not move whether praised or censured is following the Buddha's teachings.' He went on, 'Not relying on texts, characters, and words is called following the Buddha's words.'[38] [Viśeṣacintibrahma asked the Buddha,] 'How ought the monks receive offerings?' [The Buddha] replied, 'In the Dharma there is nothing that is taken.' [Viśeṣacintibrahma asked,] 'How does one use the offerings?' [The Buddha replied,] 'One is not involved in worldly dharmas.' [Viśeṣacintibrahma asked,] 'Who repays the Buddha's kindness?' [The Buddha replied,] 'One who practices according to the Dharma.'"[39]

The various Hīnayāna *dhyānas* (absorptions) and the various *samādhi* teachings are not the tenets of the school of the Patriarchal Master Dharma. Examples of their names are as follows: white bones contemplation (*vidagdhaka-samjñā*), counting breaths contemplation, nine visualizations contemplation,[40] five cessations of the mind contemplation,[41] sun contemplation, moon contemplation, tower contemplation, pond contemplation, Buddha contemplation.[42]

The *Chan miyao jing* (Scripture of the Secret Essential Methods of Dhyāna) says, "A person who contracts a fever [does] the contemplation visualizing cold. One who has chills does the contemplation visualizing heat. One with thoughts of carnal desire does the contemplation of poisonous snakes and the contemplation of impurity. One who loves food and drink does the contemplation of snakes and maggots. One who loves clothes does the contemplation of his body wrapped in hot iron."[43] There are various other *samādhi* contemplations.

The *Chan men jing* says, "'In the midst of contemplation in seated meditation, [if] one sees an image of the Buddha's form with the thirty-two characteristics, of variegated radiance, soaring in the air and manifesting transformations at will—is this real or not?' The Buddha said, 'In seated meditation one sees emptiness, there are no things. If one sees the Buddha with thirty-two characteristics, of variegated radiance, soaring in the air and manifesting transformations at will, all these are the distortions of one's own mind, bound up in a demon's net. In empty nirvāṇa, you see that such things are empty delusions.'"[44]

The *Laṅkāvatāra-sūtra* says, "These various characteristics [cause one] to fall into heterodox views."[45]

The "*Dhammapada*" says, "If one studies the various *samādhi* [techniques], this is activity and not the practice of seated meditation. If the mind follows the flow of the realm of sense objects, how can this be called concentration?"[46]

The *Vajrasamādhi-sūtra* says, "[The Buddha said,] 'I do not enter *samādhi* and do not abide in seated meditation. No-birth and no-practice, neither activity nor meditation; this is birthless meditation.'"[47]

The *Viśeṣacintibrahma-paripṛcchā-sūtra* says, "Not dependent on the realm of desire, not abiding in the realms of form or nonform—if one practices *samādhi* in this way, this is the universal practice of the bodhisattvas."[48]

The *Vimalakīrtinirdeśa-sūtra* says that Vimalakīrti rebuked Śāriputra for tranquil sitting in the forest, and he rebuked Subhūti and Mahākāśyapa for nonequanimity.[49]

The *Strīvivarta-vyākaraṇa-sūtra* says, "The Unstained Radiant Woman rebuked Indra, 'You are one of the śrāvakas (disciples), fearing birth and death and delighting in nirvāṇa.'"[50]

The *Vinayaviniścaya-Upāliparipṛcchā-sūtra* says, "The bodhisattvas keep the all-inclusive precepts bestowed on them, whereas the śrāvakas keep each and every precept of convention and each and every precept protecting [the Dharma]."[51]

The *Bhaiṣajyaguruvaiḍūryaprabharāja-sūtra* says, "The Buddha rebuked Ānanda, 'You śrāvakas are as if blind and deaf, not recognizing the truth of unsurpassed emptiness.'"[52]

The *Śūraṃgama-sūtra* says, "[The Tathāgata] rebuked the śrāvakas for having gotten only a little, but taking it as fully sufficient."[53]

The *Buddhapiṭakaduḥśīlanirgraha-sūtra* says, "[The Buddha said,] 'Śāriputra, while the Tathāgata is still alive the Three Jewels are as one taste, but after I have crossed over to extinction it will split into five parts. Śāriputra, for the time being the demons conceal themselves and assist Devadatta's [efforts to] destroy myself, the Dharma, and the saṅgha. Because the Tathāgata's great omniscience yet remains in the world, the loathsome demons are unable to accomplish great evils; in the coming age, however, demons will transform themselves and take the shapes of *śramaṇas* (renunciants). Entering into the saṅgha, they will preach various heresies and will cause many beings to enter into heterodox views due to having been taught false Dharma.[54] At that time evil people led astray by demons will each cling to their own views, [asserting] 'I am right and others are wrong.' Śāriputra, the Tathāgata presciently sees in the world to come such efforts to destroy the Dharma, and so teaches this profound scripture that will completely cut through that to which demons cling.[55]

'Ānanda, take the example of an evil thief who dares not show himself before the king's ministers; though he steals the things of others, he does not call himself a thief. Likewise, Ānanda, are those monks who break the precepts and establish a false *śramaṇa* Dharma yet do not say to themselves, 'I am an evil person,' much less face others and admit to being sinners. Ānanda, such is the worth of this scripture that precept-breaking monks when they hear it will of their own accord give way and become ashamed, and precept-keeping monks will find themselves reaffirmed.'"[56]

The *Śūraṃgama-sūtra* says, "Then the Tathāgata advanced and addressed the assembly and Ānanda, saying, 'All you śaikṣas,[57] pratyekabuddhas,[58] and śrāvakas, today you must have a change of heart and hasten toward *mahābodhi,* the supreme mysterious awakening. I have already explained the Dharma of true practice, but you, as if unaware, practice *śamatha* and *vipaśyanā* (cessation and insight). When the subtle works of demons and demon-realms appear before you, you are unable to recognize them. Cleansing the mind is not the point, you fall into wrong views. Sometimes it is the demons of your own *skandhas* (personality factors), sometimes you are turned back by the deva Māra, sometimes ghosts and spirits attach themselves to you, and sometimes you encounter evil demons of the wilds. Your mind is unclear, and you mistake these thieves for your own children. Moreover, if you return to the center and get a little but take it as sufficient, you are like a fourth *dhyāna* unlearned monk[59] who is deluded and says that he has attained *arhatva* (the final stage). When his heavenly reward is exhausted, the signs of decline appear before him. He has blasphemed against the arhats and meets with rebirth, falling into Avīci Hell.'"[60]

This is why Śākya-Tathāgatha transmitted the gold-embroidered robe. He ordered Mahākāśyapa to wait within Mount Kukkuṭapāda until the World-Honored Maitreya descends to be incarnated, and then hand it over to him. In this evil age, students of Chan are many. Our Patriarchal Master Dharma therefore transmitted a robe representing verification of his Dharma, and ordered that later students must have this [token of] inherited authorization.

SECTION 11. HUINENG, PART 2 (*T.* 51:183C1–184A6)

One day at Mount Pingmao in Huangmei, Great Master [Hong]ren was opening the Dharma gates wide, receiving people of all degrees for instruction. At this time his students were exceedingly numerous, but among them the close attendants who never left the side of Great Master Ren numbered only ten. All of them were [disciples who could] "ascend the hall and enter the chamber."[61] [They were] Zhishen, Shenxiu, Xuanze, Yifang, Zhide, Huizang, Faru, Laoan, Xuanyue, and Liu Zhubo.[62] They were one and all from the ranks of the elite and were monks renowned throughout the entire country. Each said of himself that he was a great *hastināga* who had reached the depths, but we know that [they did not get] very deep at all.

There was a certain man from Xinzhou whose lay surname was Lu and whose [Dharma] name was Huineng. When he was twenty-two he went to pay his respects to Great Master Ren. Great Master Ren asked, "Where have you come from, and with what intentions?"

Huineng replied, "I have come from Lingnan, I have no intentions at all, I only seek to become a buddha."

The Great Master knew that this was no ordinary person, yet because there were so many people in attendance the Great Master said, "Are you able to join the crowd [of disciples] and do physical labor?"

Huineng replied, "I would not begrudge even my life, what is mere physical labor to me?" So he joined the crowd and trod the rice-hulling pestle for eight months. When the Great Master knew that Huineng's potential was perfectly ripe, he secretly summoned him and passed on the Dharma, giving him the *kāṣāya* robe of verification that had been transmitted. He then commanded him to leave the area.

After that, for fear of being recognized Huineng often hid in the mountain forests, sometimes in Xinzhou and sometimes in Shaozhou. For sixteen or seventeen years he remained a layman and never expounded on the Dharma. Then [one day] he arrived at Zhizhi monastery in Nanhai, and it happened that Dharma Master Yinzong was expounding on the *Nirvāṇa-sūtra.*

As Huineng sat down, Yinzong asked the audience, "You all perceive the wind blowing the flagstaff—does the flag at the top move or not?"

Everyone said, "We perceive movement."

Some said, "We perceive the wind moving."

Some said, "We perceive the flag moving."

[Others said,] "It is not the flag moving, it is perception that moves." They argued in this manner and could not decide.

Huineng stood up and replied to the Dharma Master, "It is these people's deluded minds that move and do not move, it is not the flag that moves. The Dharma is fundamentally without either movement or nonmovement."

When the Dharma Master heard this speech he was astounded, utterly at a loss to know what words were these. He asked, "Where does the layman come from?"

Huineng replied, "Originally I have not come and also have never yet gone."

The Dharma Master descended from the high seat and invited Huineng to go to his room, where he carefully questioned him. Huineng went into full particulars about the East Mountain Buddha-Dharma and about having received the *kāṣāya* robe of verification. When Dharma Master Yinzong had seen [the robe], he made obeisance with his head to the ground and exclaimed, "How could I have hoped that in my assembly there would be a great bodhisattva!" When he had said this he again made obeisance and begged Huineng to become a Venerable. Dharma Master Yinzong declared himself [Huineng's] disciple. He bestowed on Chan Master Huineng [the ceremony of] tonsuring and robing, and when he was finished he pledged himself [to Huineng] as his disciple.

He addressed his disciples, exclaiming, "How wonderful, how wonderful! I had recently heard that the Dharma of Master Ren of Huangmei had flowed to Lingnan, but who knew that it was now in our midst? Were any of you aware of it?"

Someone said, "We were not aware of it."

Dharma Master Yinzong said, "What I preach is like bits of rubble, but now here is Chan Master Neng, who has inherited the Dharma teachings of Great Master Ren; it is like pure gold, inconceivably profound."

Dharma Master Yingzong led the followers in making obeisance at the feet of Chan Master Neng. Fearing lest the assembly be in doubt, he requested that the transmitted robe of verification be shown to everyone. Together with them he received the bodhisattva precepts [from Huineng]. Dharma Master Yingzong, along with a great crowd, saw Chan Master Neng off when he returned to Caoqi. There he received people of all degrees for instruction and widely opened the Chan Dharma. All under Heaven have heard that the Caoqi Buddha-Dharma was the most inconceivable.

SECTION 12. ZHISHEN AND EMPRESS WU (*T.* 51:184A6–184B17)

Later, the Great Zhou [dynasty] was established and [Empress Wu] Zetian ascended the throne, who greatly revered the Buddha-Dharma.[63] In the first year of the Changshou era (692), she decreed that every region in the empire should establish a Dayun monastery. On the twentieth day of the second month, she sent Zhang Changqi, director of the Ministry of Personnel, to Caoqi in Shaozhou in order to invite Chan Master Neng [to court]. Chan Master Neng pleaded illness and did not go. Later, in the first year of the Wansui Tongtian era (696), Zetian sent a messenger to invite Chan Master Neng again. When Chan Master Neng did not come, she requested the *kāṣāya* robe of verification transmitted by the First Patriarch Dharma, so that she might make offerings to it in the palace chapel.

Chan Master Neng agreed to this request and gave the *kāṣāya* robe of verification transmitted by the Patriarchal Master Dharma to the imperial messenger. The messenger returned with the transmitted *kāṣāya* robe of verification.

When Zetian saw that the transmitted *kāṣāya* robe of verification had arrived she was extremely pleased, and made offerings to it in the palace chapel.

In the seventh month of the second year of the Wansui Tongtian era (697), Zetian sent Zhang Changqi, director of the Ministry of Personnel, to Dechun monastery in Zizhou to invite Chan Master Shen. Chan Master Shen accepted the invitation and went to the capital, and [the empress] made offerings to him in the palace chapel.

In the [first year of the] Jiushi era (700), [the empress] sent [a messenger] to Yuquan monastery in Jingzhou (Hubei) to invite Chan Master Xiu, to Shoushan monastery in Anzhou (Hubei) to invite Chan Master Xuanze, to Dayun monastery in Suizhou (Hubei) to invite Chan Master Xuanyue, and to Huishan monastery on Mount Song in Luozhou (Henan) to invite Chan Master Laoan. Zetian made offerings to them in the palace chapel. Zetian originally invited all these worthies because of a certain Trepiṭaka Brāhmana from the Western Regions, whom Zetian habitually relied upon and greatly revered.

At that time Chan Master Zhishen of Jiannan was ill and thought about returning to his native place. Because it was so far beyond the mountain passes he felt a little melancholy. That heretic magician Brāhmana said to him, "What difference is there between 'here' and 'there'? How can the Chan Master pine for his native place?"

Zhishen replied, "How does the Trepiṭaka know about it?"

[The Trepiṭaka] answered, "The Chan Master has only to try bringing something to mind, there is nothing I do not know."

Shen replied, "Go ahead and try." He imagined himself dressed in layman's garb, looking toward the section office of the western market.

That Trepiṭaka said, "Bhadanta, how can you, a monk, wear layman's clothing and gaze into the midst of the city?"

Shen said, "Good—go ahead and try [again]." He imagined himself going to the Buddha-relic stūpa at Chanding monastery and standing on the highest disk of the spire.

The Trepiṭaka again said, "How can a monk climb so high and stand up there?"

Shen said, "This one will be really good, try again." Then, right where he was, by relying on the Dharma he produced no thoughts at all. That Trepiṭaka searched all through the Three Worlds in vain.

Thereupon Brāhmana Trepiṭaka was filled with reverence. He bowed down his head at Shen's feet and said to the Venerable, "I did not know that in the country of Tang there was Mahāyāna Buddha-Dharma. Now I rebuke myself body and mind and repent."

[Empress Wu] Zetian saw that the Trepiṭaka had taken refuge in Chan Master Shen. Zetian submitted a question to all the *bhadanta:* "Do the Venerables have desires, or not?"

Shenxiu, Xuanye, Laoan, and Xuanze all said, "We have no desires."

Zetian asked Chan Master Shen, "Does the Venerable have desires, or not?"

Chan Master Shen, fearing that he would not be allowed to return home, complied with the will of Zetian and replied, "I have desires."

Zetian responded, "How can the Venerable have desires?"

Shen replied, "That which is born has desire. That which is not born has no desire." At these words Zetian was awakened. Moreover, seeing that the Trepiṭaka took refuge in the Venerable Shen compounded her deep reverence.

Chan Master Shen took the opportunity to petition that he be allowed to return to his native place. [The empress] ordered that he be given the new translation of the *Avataṃsaka-sūtra* in one part, an embroidered image of Maitreya, and fine banners and such things. She also had him take the *kāṣāya* robe of verification of the Patriarchal Master Dharma.

Zetian said, "As Chan Master Neng did not come, I also offer up this robe of the First Patriarch to the Venerable. Take it back to your native place and perpetually make offerings to it."

In the eleventh month of the first year of the Jinglong era (707), Zetian sent a messenger, the Palace Attendant General Xue Jian, to make a proclamation at Chan Master Neng's place in Caoqi. The empress's message was: "We have offered up the First Patriarch's *kāṣāya* robe of verification to Chan Master Shen and he has undertaken to maintain the offerings. We now separately make offerings of one *kāṣāya* robe of fine linen, five hundred rolls of silk, and ample milk-medicine."[64]

SECTION 13. CHAN MASTER ZHISHEN (*T.* 51:184B18–184C2)

Chan Master Zhishen of Dechun monastery in Zizhou had the lay surname Zhou and was from Runan (Henan). He accompanied his grandfather when the latter was posted to Shu (Sichuan). When he was ten years old he was very partial to the Buddhist teachings, did not eat strong and pungent foods, resolutely adhered to a lofty standard, and did not engage in childish play. When he was thirteen he left his family and entered the Way. First he served Dharma Master Xuanzang, with whom he studied the scriptures and treatises.[65] Later, on hearing of Great Master Ren of Mount Shuangfeng, he left Dharma Master Xuanzang, abandoned the scriptures and treatises, and offered himself as disciple to Great Master Ren at Mount Pingmao. The Great Master said, "You both have a literary nature."[66]

Later, [Zhishen] returned to Dechun monastery in Zizhou and taught the Way for the many beings. He composed the *Xurong guan* (Contemplation on Union with Emptiness) in three fascicles, the *Yuanqi* (Dependent Arising) in one fascicle, and the *Banruoxin shu* (Commentary on the Heart Scripture) in one fascicle. Later, in the seventh month of the second year of the Wansui Tongtian era (697), [Empress Wu] Zetian sent Zhang Changqi, director of the Ministry of Personnel, to Dechun monastery to invite him. So he went up to the Western Capital, but later, due to illness, he petitioned the empress and was allowed to return to Dechun monastery. He taught the Way for the many beings for over thirty years.

In the sixth month of the second year of the Chang'an era (702) he ordered Chuji, "Hold me up." He thereupon entrusted him with the robe of verification, saying, "This robe is the *kāṣāya* robe transmitted by the Patriarchal Master Dharma. Zetian bestowed it on me, and I now entrust it to you. You must protect yourself well." On the evening of the sixth day of the seventh month of that year, he died instantly in a seated posture. He was ninety-four years old.

SECTION 14. CHAN MASTER CHUJI (*T.* 51:184C3–184C16)

Chan Master Chuji was from Foucheng district in Mianzhou (Sichuan). His lay surname was Tang, and his family had for generations favored Confucianism. Chuji diligently studied the *Book of Odes* and the *Book of Rites,* and he had moral integrity and filial piety. When he was ten his father died. He lamented, "There is nothing in Heaven and earth! I have heard that the Buddha-Dharma is inconceivable and roots out the suffering of life and death."

So he offered himself as disciple to the Venerable Shen. The Venerable Shen asked, "Where do you come from?"

Chuji replied, "I come in order to offer myself to the Venerable." The Venerable knew he was no ordinary person.

When they went to the capital, [Chuji] carried the Great Master all the way by himself, without switching off with another person. He was over nine feet tall, and his disposition was blessed. In a crowd only his head could be seen [towering above the rest], and whoever saw him looked up to him with respect.

Later he went back to live in Dechun monastery in Zizhou, where he taught the Way for the many beings for twenty years. In the fourth month of the twenty-fourth year of the Kaiyuan era (736) he secretly sent his servant Wang Huang to summon Chan Master Wuxiang from East-of-the-Sea (Korea). He entrusted him with the Dharma and the *kāṣāya* robe of verification, saying, "This robe is the robe of verification of the Patriarchal Master Dharma. Zetian bestowed it on the Venerable Shen, the Venerable Shen gave it to me, and I in turn entrust it to you. You must protect yourself well. Go and find a good mountain and stay there."

Later, on the twenty-seventh day of the fifth month of that year, he told his disciples, "I will not long remain." In the middle of the night during the Hour of the Rat, he died instantly in a seated posture. Great Master Chuji was sixty-eight years old.

SECTION 15. CHAN MASTER WUXIANG (*T.* 51:184C17–185B14)

Chan Master Wuxiang of the Jingzhong monastery in Chengdu city prefecture in Jiannan had the lay surname Kim and was from a clan of Silla princes; his family went back for generations East-of-the-Sea (Korea). Formerly, when he was in his homeland, his youngest sister, hearing of her betrothal ceremony, picked up a knife, slashed her face, and vowed her determination to "return to the true." The Venerable [Wuxiang] saw this and cried, "Girls are pliant and weak, yet she knows the meaning of sticking to chastity. Fellows are hard and strong—how can I be so lacking in spirit?"

He thereupon took the tonsure and left his kin, crossed the sea westward, and arrived in the Kingdom of Tang. He sought out masters and inquired about the Way, he wandered around and passed through each [monastery] in turn until he reached Dechun monastery in Zizhou and made obeisance to the Venerable Tang (Chuji). The Venerable Tang was ill and did not come out to greet him, so Wuxiang burned one of his fingers as a candle and dedicated it as an offering to the Venerable Tang. The Venerable realized that this was no ordinary man and kept him at his side for two years.

Wuxiang later lived in the Tiangu mountains (Sichuan). Meanwhile, back at Dechun monastery, the Venerable Tang sent his servant Wang Huang [to Wuxiang] and secretly entrusted to him the robe of verification, [saying], "This robe is the robe transmitted by the Patriarchal Master Dharma. Zetian bestowed it upon the Venerable Shen, the Venerable Shen gave it to me, and I entrust it to you."

The Venerable Kim, having been entrusted with the Dharma and the robe of verification, lived beneath a cliff in the Tiangu mountains. His clothing was made of grass and his diet sparse, and when there was no food left he ate earth. The wild beasts were moved to protect him. Later, the Grand Master Zhangqiu requested that he open the Chan Dharma.[67] Living at Jingzhong monastery, Wuxiang taught the Way for the many beings for more than twenty years.

On the fifteenth day of the fifth month of the first year of the Baoying era (762), [Wuxiang] suddenly thought of Chan Master Wuzhu of the Baiya mountains, [thinking] "I am ill. Surely he will come to see me." Time and again he asked his attendants, "Why hasn't Chan Master Wuzhu come? I am growing old." He secretly sent the laborer Dong Xuan, [saying], "Take my robe of verification and seventeen other items of clothing, and secretly deliver them to Chan Master Wuzhu. He must protect himself well. It is not yet time for him to come out of the mountains, he should wait three to five more years, and when there is peace throughout the land then he can come out." [Thus] the transmission was settled from afar.

On the nineteenth day of the fifth month, [Wuxiang] ordered his disciples, "Bring me a new, clean robe, I wish to bathe." In the middle of the night during the Hour of the Rat, he died solemnly in a seated posture. On that day, the sun and moon gave no light and heaven and earth turned white. The Dharma banners' [poles] snapped and the Nairañjanā river dried up.[68] All beings were bereft and students of the Way had no one on whom to rely. At that time, the Great Master was seventy-nine years old.

The Venerable Kim, every twelfth and first month, administered the "receiving of conditions" (precepts) for countless numbers of people of the four assemblies. The *bodhimaṇḍa* (place of practice) sanctuary was magnificently arranged, and [Wuxiang] occupied the high seat to expound the Dharma. He would first lead a vocal recollection of the Buddha. As the recitation ended at the end of an exhalation and the cessation of sound, he would expound, "No-recollection, no-thought, and 'do not be deluded': no-recollection is *śila,* no-thought is *samādhi,* and 'do not be deluded' is *prajñā.* These three phrases are the gates of perfectly maintaining [the precepts]."

He also would say, "When thoughts do not arise it is like the mirror's face, able to reflect the myriad images. When thoughts arise it is like the mirror's back, unable to reflect."

He also would say, "In an instant one distinguishes cognition arising, in an instant cognition arises and is extinguished, and if in the instant cognition is extinguished this cognition is not for an instant interrupted, then this is seeing the Buddha.

"To illustrate—two men were fellow travelers, and both arrived in another country. Their fathers sent them letters of instruction and admonition. One received his letter, and once he had read it he obeyed his father's instructions and did not do anything that was against the law. The other man also received his letter, and once he had read it he did not comply with the instructions given but heedlessly did all evil. Among the many beings, those who rely on no-thought are the filial, obedient sons; those who are attached to texts and characters are the unfilial sons."

He also said, "To illustrate—there was a man who was lying in a drunken stupor. His mother came calling for him, wishing to get him to return home. But the son, in his drunken confusion, viciously cursed his mother. Beings are drunk on the wine of ignorance and do not believe that they themselves can see the nature and achieve the Way of the Buddha."

He would also quote the *Awakening of Faith,* saying, "'The mind is the gate of thusness. The mind is the gate of birth and extinction.'[69] No-thought is none other than the gate of thusness. The existence of thought is none other than the gate of birth and extinction."

He also would say, "When the tip of ignorance emerges, the tip of *prajñā* sinks. When the tip of ignorance sinks, the tip of *prajñā* emerges."

He would also quote the *Nirvāṇa-sūtra,* saying, "'The domestic dog and the wild deer'—the domestic dog illustrates delusive thinking, and the wild deer illustrates buddha nature."[70]

He would also say, "Damask is originally silk thread without any 'texts and characters' (i.e., design). Only after a skilled worker has woven it does it have a design. Later, when it is torn up it returns to the original silk thread. The silk thread illustrates buddha nature, the design illustrates delusive thinking."

He would also say, "Water is not separate from waves and waves are not separate from water. The waves illustrate delusive thinking, the water illustrates buddha nature."

He would also say, "A band of men were carrying hemp, and along the way they came across a place where there was silver. One man then threw away his load and picked up the silver. The others said, 'It has already been determined that we carry hemp, we will never discard it.' Farther on they came to a place where there was gold, [and the one man] discarded the silver and picked up the gold. The others said, 'It has already been determined that we carry hemp, we will never throw it away.' The gold illustrates nirvāṇa, the hemp illustrates birth-and-death."[71]

He also would say, "These three phrases of mine are teachings that were originally transmitted by the Patriarchal Master Dharma. I do not say that this is what was taught by the Venerable Shen or the Venerable Tang."

He also said, "It has been permitted that the disciple has understanding surpassing that of his masters. Because the Venerables Shen and Tang did not expound the ultimate teaching, I have by a winding course inherited the robe of verification."

The Venerable Kim thus did not draw from areas that the Venerables Shen and Tang had expounded. Whenever he taught the precepts from the high seat he would say frankly, "These three phrases of mine that were transmitted by the Patriarchal Master Dharma are the gates of completely maintaining [practice]. The nonarising of thought is the gate of *śila,* the nonarising of thought is the gate of *samādhi,* the nonarising of thought is the gate of *prajñā.* No-thought is thus the complete fulfillment of *śila, samādhi,* and *prajñā;* it is the gate through which all the buddhas of the past, future, and present, [countless as] the Ganges sands, have entered. It is not possible that there could be any other gates."

SECTION 16. THE VENERABLE SHENHUI (*T.* 51:185B14–185C26)

The Venerable Shenhui of Heze monastery in the Eastern Capital (Luoyang) would set up a [bodhisattva precepts ordination] platform every month and expound on the Dharma for people. He knocked down "Purity Chan" and upheld "Tathāgata Chan."[72] He upheld direct experience *and* verbal explanation. Regarding precepts, meditation, and wisdom, he did not knock down verbal explanation. He said, "Just as I am speaking now is none other than *śila,* just as I am speaking now is none other than *samādhi,* just as I am speaking now is none other than *prajñā.*" He expounded the Dharma of no-thought and upheld seeing the nature.

In the middle of the Kaiyuan era, at Huatai (Henan),[73] he set forth the cardinal tenets of the school for students of the Way from throughout the land. The Venerable Hui said, "It seems that there will be someone who will explain it more fully. I really cannot presume to explain it." This is because the Venerable Hui did not get the robe of verification.

In the middle of the eighth year of the Tianbao era (749), he also set forth the cardinal tenets of the school at Heze monastery in Luozhou (Luoyang). He was asked by Dharma Master Chongyuan, "Regarding the three virtues and ten holinesses, what level of practice can you testify to?"

Hui replied, "The *Nirvāṇa-sūtra* says, 'Homage to Cunda, homage to Cunda, his body was that of an ordinary mortal, his mind was the same as the Buddha's mind.'"[74]

The Venerable Hui then asked Dharma Master Yuan, "How many times now have you lectured on the *Nirvāṇa-sūtra*?"

Dharma Master Yuan replied, "Over forty times."

[Hui] asked, "Has the Dharma Master perceived buddha nature or not?"

The Dharma Master replied, "I have not perceived it."

The Venerable Hui said, "In the 'Lion's Roar' section [of the *Nirvāṇa-sūtra*] it says, 'If one has not perceived buddha nature, then one is not fit to lecture on the *Nirvāṇa-sūtra.* If one has perceived buddha nature, only then is one fit to lecture on the *Nirvāṇa-sūtra.*'"[75]

Dharma Master Yuan then asked, "Has the Venerable Hui perceived buddha nature or not?"

Hui replied, "I have perceived it."

[Yuan] asked, "In what way do you perceive? Is it by the eyes that you have perceived, or by the ears or the nose, etc., that you have perceived?"

Hui replied, "Perceiving is not so quantifiable, perceiving is simply perceiving."

[Yuan] asked, "Do you perceive the same as Cunda, or not?"

Hui replied, "I perceive by inference (*biliang jian*). Comparison (*bi*) means 'comparable to Cunda.' Estimation/knowing (*liang*) is 'equivalent to Cunda.' I dare not make a final conclusion."[76]

He was further questioned by Dharma Master Yuan, "Chan Master, has the First Patriarch's *kāṣāya* robe been transmitted or not?"

Hui replied, "It has been transmitted. When it is not transmitted, the Dharma will be broken off."

[Yuan] asked, "Has the Chan Master got it or not?"

[Hui] replied, "It is not at my place."

Dharma Master Yuan asked, "Who has got this *kāṣāya* robe?"

Hui replied, "Someone has got it. In due course it should be apparent. When this person expounds on the Dharma, the true Dharma will flow forth, and false Dharmas will perish of themselves. In order to further the great work of the Buddha-Dharma, he is hidden and has not yet come out."

When the Venerable Hui was in Jing subprefecture (Hubei), there were men of the Western Kingdoms, the Bhadra (Elder) Kaśyapa, An Shuti (an astrologer of Parthia), and about twenty others, who went up to the place where the Venerable was expounding on the Dharma and asked, "The First Patriarch's *kāṣāya* robe of verification—has the Venerable got it or not?"

[Hui] replied, "It is not at my place." He then asked the Bhadra and the others, "Where have you come from?"

Kaśyapa replied, "We have come from Jiannan."

[Hui] asked, "Do you know Chan Master Kim?"

Kaśyapa replied, "We are all the Venerable Kim's disciples."

The Venerable Hui asked, "Explain, you who have been taught by Chan Master Kim, how does he teach the Way?"

Kaśyapa replied, "'When the tip of ignorance emerges, the tip of nirvāṇa sinks; when the tip of *prajñā* emerges, the tip of ignorance sinks. When there is thought it is like the face of a mirror.'"

The Venerable Hui shouted at him, "Don't speak such empty prattle! Your name is Kaśyapa, a Brāhmanical sort of name, [so one would think that] surely you had some good roots, but you are nothing but a bed-wetting Brāhman!"

The Venerable Hui said, "Your Chan Master Shen of Jiannan was a Dharma Master who did not expound the ultimate teaching. Chan Master Tang was Chan Master Shen's disciple, and he also did not expound the ultimate teaching. Of Chan Master Tang's disciples, Zhao of Zizhou (Sichuan) is a Dharma

Master, Wang of Lingzhou (Sichuan) is a Vinaya Master, and Biao of Baxi (Sichuan) is a Dharma Master. Kim of Yizhou (Sichuan) is a Chan Master, but he also did not manage to expound the ultimate teaching. Although he did not expound the ultimate teaching, the Buddha-Dharma is only at his place."

Director Ma Xiong was sent to Caoqi to pay respects to the Venerable Neng's stūpa. He asked the old monk who was guarding the stūpa, "Where is the *kāṣāya* robe of verification transmitted by the First Patriarch?"

The old monk replied, "When the Venerable Neng was alive, Master Xuanjie, Master Zhihai, and the others asked the Venerable Neng, 'Has the *kāṣāya* robe of succession been transmitted or not? To whom has the Buddha-Dharma been entrusted?' The Venerable Neng replied, 'A woman has taken my robe away. As for my Dharma, twenty years after my death [the one who] establishes the cardinal tenet of the school is the one who will have gotten my Dharma.'"

SECTION 17. DISCOURSES OF THE VENERABLE WUZHU (*T.* 51:185C26–186A14)

Whenever the Venerable Wuzhu of the Dali-era Bao Tang monastery in Chengdu subprefecture in Jiannan taught for the sake of students of the Way of the four assemblies, [he would say], "Whether a multitude or a single person, regardless of the time, if you have doubts you may confide your questions to me. I am occupying the seat and explaining the Dharma, directly pointing [so that you] see your own natures. Regard direct mind as the *bodhimaṇḍa* (place of practice). Regard aspiration to practice as the *bodhimaṇḍa*. Regard the profound mind as the *bodhimaṇḍa*. Regard the unstained as the *bodhimaṇḍa*. Regard not-grasping as the *bodhimaṇḍa*. Regard not-rejecting as the *bodhimaṇḍa*. Regard nonaction as *upāya*. Regard the vast as *upāya*. Regard equanimity as *upāya*. Regard transcendence of characteristics as the fire and regard liberation as the incense. Regard nonobstruction as repentance. Regard no-thought as the precepts, nonaction and nothing to attain as meditation, and nonduality as wisdom. Do not regard the constructed ritual arena as the *bodhimaṇḍa*."[77]

The Venerable said, "All beings are fundamentally pure and fundamentally complete and can be neither augmented nor reduced. By allowing one thought to defile the mind, in the Three Worlds you will take on the various kinds of bodies. Provisionally, 'Good Friends' point directly to fundamental nature. Seeing the nature is thus the Way of becoming a buddha, and attachment to characteristics is thus sinking into the cycle of birth and death. It is because beings have thought that one provisionally teaches no-thought, but if there is no presence of thought, then no-thought itself is not. Extinguishing the mind of the Three Worlds but not dwelling in stillness, 'not abiding in characteristics but not without efficacy.'[78] Simply separating from empty delusion is called liberation."

He further said, "The presence of mind is 'ocean waves,' but no-mind is heterodoxy. Complying with birth-and-death is the stain of beings, but depending on stillness is the movement of nirvāṇa. Not complying with birth, not depending on stillness, 'not entering *samādhi,* not abiding in seated meditation, there is no-birth and no-practice, and the mind is without loss or gain.'[79] Both intangible and tangible phenomena are negated, and neither nature nor characteristics is set up."

SECTION 18. WUZHU AND WUXIANG (*T.* 51:186A15–187C7)

The Venerable was from the Mei district of Fengxiang (Shaanxi). His family name was Li. His Dharma name was Wuzhu, and his years amounted to five decades.[80] During the Kaiyuan era (713–741), his father distinguished himself serving in the army at Shuofang. When he was twenty, his physical strength surpassed that of other men and he excelled in the arts of war. At the time, the Prince of Xin'an (d. 743) served as the Military Commissioner of the He[bei] and Shuo[fang] circuits. Seeing that the Venerable was brave and ardent, the Prince of Xin'an retained him as the Patrolling Grand Lance Officer of the Yamen. The Venerable always lamented to himself, "Who among men is not delighted by worldly glory? I am a 'real hero,' (*dazhang fu*) but I have yet to meet a 'Good Friend.' One can't frivolously waste one's life."

So he gave up his official position to search for a teacher from whom to inquire about the Way. He chanced to meet the white-robed layman Chen Chuzhang, whose origins are unknown. People then called him an incarnation of Vimalakīrti. He expounded the Dharma of the sudden teaching. From the moment that he met the Venerable [Wuzhu], he privately sealed their mutual understanding and silently transmitted the mind-Dharma. Having obtained the Dharma, the Venerable at once cut through thinking and ceased all restless anxiety, abandoning both phenomena and characteristics. For three or five years, [Wuzhu] practiced as a white-robed [layman].

During the Tianbao era (742–755), [Wuzhu] chanced to hear of the Venerable Ming of Mount Daoci in Fanyang (Hebei), the Venerable Shenhui of the Eastern Capital (Luoyang), and the Venerable Zizai of Taiyuan subprefecture (Shanxi), all of whom were disciples of the sixth Patriarchal Master [Huineng] and taught the Dharma of the sudden teaching. At the time, the Venerable was not yet a renunciant.

Then he went to Taiyuan and made obeisance to the Venerable Zizai. The Venerable Zizai taught, "In the midst of purity to be without the marks of purity, this is the true purity of the buddha nature." As soon as the Venerable heard the Dharma he made up his mind, and he wanted to renounce his former path. The old Venerable and all the Vinaya masters and worthies entreated him to stay and would not let him go, [saying], "This is the ridgepole of the true Dharma." And so he took the tonsure and donned a robe.

In the eighth year of the Tianbao era (749), when he had received the complete precepts, he left the old Venerable and went to Qingliang monastery on Mount Wutai,[81] where he spent one summer. He heard expositions concerning the "traces of the way" from the Venerable Ming of Mount Daoci, and the import of the sayings of the Venerable Shenhui. Because he understood their gist, he did not go to pay his respects to them.

In the ninth year of the Tianbao era (750), at the end of the summer he left the mountains and reached the Western Capital (Chang'an), where he came and went between the Anguo and Chongsheng monasteries.

In the tenth year of the Tianbao era (751), he retraced his steps from the Western Capital to North Lingzhou and lived in the Helan mountains (Ningxia) for two years.[82] It happened that there was a merchant, Cao Gui, who came to pay his respects and asked, "Has the Venerable ever been to Jiannan? Do you know the Venerable Kim?"

[Wuzhu] answered, "I don't know him."

Gui said, "Your features are exactly like those of the Venerable Kim. You [both] have a mole above the bridge of your nose, and the shape of your face so resembles that of the Venerable in our locale that one could even say there is no difference. It must be a transformation-body."

The Venerable asked Cao Gui, "So the layman has come from Jiannan. What doctrine does that Venerable teach?" Cao Gui replied, "'No-recollection, no-thought, and do not forget.' Once, after receiving the bodhisattva precepts [during a retreat], I was leaving and the Venerable Kim asked me, 'Where are you going?' I answered, 'My honored father and mother are still living, so I wish to return home to see them.' The Venerable Kim told me, 'Just not recollecting, not thinking, relinquishing everything, clear and vast—see whether your father and mother are there or not.' That is certainly what I heard at the time, but I do not yet understand it. Now I submit it to you, Venerable."

When the Venerable heard this teaching he understood clearly, and from afar he met the Venerable Kim face to face. Consequently, he left Mount Helan and went to North Lingzhou (Ningxia) to be issued traveling papers to go to Jiannan and pay his respects to the Venerable Kim. Thereupon the Garrison [Military Commissioner] Prince Yaosi would not let him go. The Worthy Venerable Shi, the Vinaya Master Biancai, the Vinaya Master Huizhuang, and the other worthies all refused to let him go.

In the tenth month of the second year of the Zhide era (757) [Wuzhu] quietly left North Lingzhou, and on his way to Dingyuan city he got to Fengning (Shaanxi), where the Military Commander Yang Hanzhang issued his traveling papers. The military commander earnestly tried to keep him. He asked the Venerable, "Is the Buddha-Dharma only in Jiannan, or is it also here? If 'there' and 'here' are one, then why do you go?"

The Venerable replied, "If one knows the mind and sees the nature, then the Buddha-Dharma pervades all places. But I am still at the stage of learning, and my 'Good Friend' is in Jiannan, so I will go far away and submit myself to him."

The military commander further asked the Venerable, "Who is your 'Good Friend'?"

The Venerable replied, "The Venerable Wuxiang; his lay surname is Kim, and these days people call him the Venerable Kim." The military commander prostrated himself and then issued the traveling papers.

The Venerable gradually made his way south to Fengxiang. There also the worthies earnestly tried to keep him from going, but again he did not stay. Then he took the Mount Taibai road (Shanxi), entered Mount Taibai, and stayed the summer there. At the end of the summer he took the Xishui Valley road and came out in Nanliangzhou (Sichuan). The monks and disciples earnestly tried to keep him, but he did not stay.

In the first month of the second year of the Qianyuan era (759), he reached Jingzhong monastery in Chengdu subprefecture. When he first arrived he met

Master Anqian, who led him in to see the Venerable Kim. When the Venerable Kim saw him he was extremely pleased. The Venerable Kim delegated Master Anqian to act as host, and he arranged for Wuzhu to stay in a cloister below the bell tower.[83] This was during a bodhisattva precepts retreat, and that night [Wuzhu] followed the crowd and received the precepts. It lasted only three days and three nights.

Every day in the midst of the great assembly the Venerable Kim would intone in a loud voice, "Why do you not go into the mountains, what good is it to linger?"

His attendant disciples considered this strange [and said], "The Venerable Kim has never said anything like this before. Why would he suddenly come out with these words?" But the Venerable Wuzhu quietly entered the mountains.

[Later] the Venerable Kim longed for him [and said], "Why doesn't he come?" Preceptor Kong and Preceptor Qin wanted to be able to recognize [Wuzhu, and so they said], "We fear that one day we might chance to meet but not know who he is."

[From the mountains] the Venerable [Wuzhu] faced toward them with a keen glance and exclaimed, "Although I am here, the Venerable Kim and I see each other constantly. Even if we wish not to know each other, we are face to face across a thousand *li*. With my regards, I will preach a parable for you.

"Long ago when the Buddha was alive, when he spent three months of the summer retreat in Trāyastriṃśa Heaven expounding the Dharma for [his mother] Mahāmāyā, the sixteen great kings and all beings longed for the Buddha. So they sent Mahāmaudgalyāyana to Trāyastriṃśa Heaven to ask the Buddha [to return]. When the Buddha was to descend to Jambudvīpa, Subhuti was [meditating] in a stone cell. When he heard that the Buddha was to descend he wanted to leave his cell, but then thought to himself, 'I have heard the World-Honored One [say], 'If you are in *samādhi,* then this is seeing me. If you come rushing to see my form body, where is the benefit?' [Subhuti] therefore reentered *samādhi.*

"At that time, the nun Utpalavarṇā,[84] being determined to expunge her evil reputation, desired to be the first to greet the Buddha. All the kings of great kingdoms and the eight divisions of *nāgas* and divinities had completely encircled [the Buddha] in circumambulations, there was no pathway through. [The nun] transformed herself into the thousand sons of a great cakravartin king and surrounded [the company], and the *nāgas,* divinities, and kings opened a path. The nun Utpalavarṇā then returned to her original form, and when she had circumambulated the World-Honored One, she joined her palms and spoke a verse: 'I am the first to greet the Buddha, I am the first to make obeisance to the Buddha.' Having spoken the verse, she made obeisance and stood up. At that, the World-Honored One told the nun, 'In this company, you are last.' The nun said to the World-Honored One, 'In this company there are no arhats, why do you say I am last?' The World-Honored One told the nun, 'Subhuti is in a stone cell continuously in *samādhi,* and so he was first, being able to see my Dharma body. You came rushing to see my form body, and so you are last.'"[85]

[Wuzhu concluded,] "The Buddha has given a clear mandate, and that is why I do not go [to see the Venerable Kim]."

Master Daoyi, [Wuzhu's] fellow inmate [at the mountain hermitage], practiced chanting, worship, and recitation [of the Buddha's name], while the Venerable [Wuzhu] completely cut through thinking and ceased all anxiety, and entered into the field of self-validating [enlightenment]. Daoyi, accompanied by all the minor masters who were their fellow inmates, said to the Venerable, "I, together with all our fellow inmates, want you to join us in the six daily periods of worship and repentance. We humbly beg the Venerable to listen and accede."

The Venerable said to Daoyi and the others, "Because here we are altogether cut off from provisions, people carry them on foot deep into the mountains. You can't rely on legalistic practice—you want to get ravings by rote, but this is not the Buddha-Dharma at all." The Venerable quoted the *Śūraṃgama-sūtra,* "'The raving mind is not at rest. At rest, it is bodhi. Peerless pure bright mind fundamentally pervades the Dharmadhātu.'[86] No-thought is none other than seeing the Buddha. The presence of thought is none other than birth-and-death. If you want to practice worship and recitation, then leave the mountains. On the plains there are gracious and easeful temple quarters, and you are free to go. If you want to stay with me, you must utterly devote yourself to no-thought. If you can, then you are free to stay. If you cannot, then you must go down."

As Master Daoyi's views did not go along with [Wuzhu's] fundamental intent, he took leave of the Venerable and left Mount Tiancang. Arriving at Jingzhong monastery in Yizhou, he met with Preceptor Kong and the others and said, "Chan Master Wuzhu in the mountains doesn't practice worship or recitation, he just sits in idleness (*kongxian zuo*)."

Hekong and the others heard this with manifold amazement, [exclaiming,] "How could this be the Buddha-Dharma?" They took Master Daoyi to see the

Venerable Kim. Before Daoyi had finished making obeisances, Hekong and the others informed the Venerable Kim, "Chan Master Wuzhu of Mount Tiancang just sits in idleness. He is not willing to worship and recite, and neither will he teach his fellow inmates to worship and recite. What is this? How could this be the Buddha-Dharma?"

The Venerable Kim exploded at Hekong, Daoyi, and the others, "You get out! When I was at the stage of learning, I wouldn't get around to eating, I just sat in idleness. I didn't even make an effort to shit or piss. You lot don't realize that when I was at Mount Tiangu, I didn't worship or recite, either. All my fellow students got angry with me and left the mountain. No one sent provisions, and I had only smelted earth as food. But even then I didn't make an effort to leave the mountain, and I devoted myself to sitting in idleness.

"When Abbot Meng heard from my fellow students that I was sitting in idleness, he immediately went to the Venerable Tang to slander me. When the Venerable Tang heard I was sitting in idleness, he was overjoyed. Meanwhile I was at Mount Tiangu and knew nothing of the slander. Hearing that the Venerable Tang was gravely ill, I came from Mount Tiangu to Dechun monastery in Zizhou. Abbot Meng saw me coming and would not let me enter the monastery. The Venerable Tang heard that I had come and sent someone to summon me to appear before his hall. I had not yet completed my obeisance when the Venerable Tang asked me, 'At Mount Tiangu, how do you occupy yourself?' I replied, 'I don't do a thing. I am just immersed and oblivious.' The Venerable Tang retorted, 'You are oblivious, I am also oblivious!' The Venerable Tang knew [about true practice], the others had no inkling."

From the mountains, the Venerable [Wuzhu] knew the Venerable Kim thought of him from afar, and he immediately knew [Wuxiang's] intentions. So the Venerable said to Xuan, "Layman, the direct tributary of the Buddha-Dharma of the Patriarchal Master Dharma has flowed to Jiannan; the Venerable Kim is it. If you do not receive the bodhisattva precepts [from him], it is just like returning from a mountain of treasure empty-handed."

When Xuan heard this, he joined his palms and stood up, [saying], "Then your disciple will go to Chengdu subprefecture to receive the bodhisattva precepts."

The Venerable said, "Here is half a catty of bud tea. If you are going, then take this bud tea as a token of faith and present it to the Venerable Kim. Convey Wuzhu's words and prostrations to the Venerable Kim. If the Venerable

Kim should inquire after me, say that Wuzhu does not yet intend to come out of the mountains."

Xuan then took leave of the Venerable, taking the bud tea to offer [to Wuxiang]. On the thirteenth day of the month designated *si*,[87] he reached Jingzhong monastery in Chengdu subprefecture, but because the Venerable Kim was ill no one was allowed to see him. Dong Xuan chanced on Master Bodhi, who took him to see the Venerable Kim. [Dong Xuan] prepared and set out the bud tea offered by Chan Master Wuzhu and conveyed [Wuzhu's] prostration to the Venerable Kim. When the Venerable Kim heard the message and saw the bud tea, he was very pleased and said to Dong Xuan, "Since Chan Master Wuzhu has sent a token of faith to me, why didn't he come to me himself?"

Dong Xuan replied, "On the day I set out, Chan Master Wuzhu said that he does not yet intend to leave the mountains."

The Venerable Kim asked Dong Xuan, "And who are you?"

Xuan lied to the Venerable Kim and replied, "I am Chan Master Wuzhu's personal disciple."

The Venerable Kim told Xuan, "On the day you go back to the Baiya mountains, I have a token of faith to send, so you must come to see me."

On the fifteenth day, [Dong Xuan] went to see the Venerable Kim. He said, "I wish to return to the Baiya mountains. I am at your command."

[Wuxiang] sent away his personal attendant disciples, [saying], "You must all leave the hall." Then he summoned Dong Xuan to enter. Xuan obeyed and entered the hall and kneeled with his palms joined. The Venerable Kim brought out the *kāṣāya* robe, [the one that] the rarest few among men have had in their keeping. He revealed it [and said], "This was given to the Venerable Shen by Empress [Wu] Zetian. The Venerable Shen gave it to the Venerable Tang, the Venerable Tang gave it to me, and I transmit it to Chan Master Wuzhu. This robe has long been cherished, don't let anyone know of it." When he finished speaking he became choked with sobbing [and said], "This robe has been passed from legitimate heir to legitimate heir, one must make utmost effort, utmost effort!" Then he took from his own person his *kāṣāya*, under and outer robes, and sitting cloth. Altogether there were seventeen things.

[He said], "I am getting on in years. You take these things and convey them secretly to Chan Master Wuzhu, and transmit my words: 'Take good care of yourself, and make utmost effort, utmost effort! It is not yet time to leave the mountains. Wait three to five years longer, and only leave when a person of consequence welcomes you.'" At that he dispatched Dong Xuan, [saying], "Go quickly, and do not let anyone learn of this."

When he had seen Dong Xuan go, the Venerable Kim said to himself, "These things will get there late, but they will get through in the end." When the Venerable Kim was speaking there was no one around. When the disciples outside the hall heard the Venerable's voice they entered the hall at once and asked the Venerable Kim, "Why were you talking all by yourself?"

The Venerable said, "I was just muttering."

Because the Venerable Kim was gravely ill, there were those who when they saw this decided to ask, "Where has the Venerable passed down the robe of verification that was transmitted [to him]? To whom will the Venerable entrust the Buddha-Dharma?"

The Venerable Kim said, "My Dharma has gone to the place of nonabiding (*wuzhu*). The robe is hanging from the top of a tree, no one has got it." The Venerable Kim said to them, "This is not your sphere, you should each get back to your original place."

[Thus] on the fifteenth day of the month designated *si* of the first year, that was changed to the fifteenth day of the fifth month of the first year of the Baoying era (762), the investiture of the Dharma was completed from afar. On the nineteenth day, [Wuxiang] ordered his disciples, "Get me new, fresh clothes. I will bathe now." In the middle of the night in the Hour of the Rat, he died solemnly in a seated posture.

SECTION 19. DU HONGJIAN'S ARRIVAL IN SHU (*T.* 51:187C7–188B21)

As soon as the Lord Minister Du [Hongjian],[88] Vice-Marshal and Vice-Director of the Chancellery, first arrived in Chengdu Superior Prefecture, he heard that the Venerable Kim was inconceivable. As the Venerable Kim had passed on, [Du Hongjian] expected that he had left a successor. So he went to Jingzhong monastery and to Ningguo monastery on Mount Heng to look around, and he saw the Venerable Kim's mortal remains. The Lord Minister took the opportunity to ask the lesser masters, "Surely there is a successor-disciple, a monk who received the robe and bowl?"

The lesser masters replied, "There was no one at all to succeed him. When the Venerable was alive he had two *kāṣāya* robes; one is at Ningguo monastery on Mount Heng and one remains at the Jingzhong monastery receiving dedicatory offerings."

The Lord Minister did not believe them, and further questioned the Vinaya Masters: "I had heard from afar that the Venerable Kim was a great 'Good Friend' who was entrusted with the robe and bowl that have been passed down from master to master. Now that the Venerable Kim has passed on, where is his successor-disciple?"

The Vinaya masters told the Lord Minister, "Chan Master Kim was a foreign barbarian, entirely lacking the Buddha-Dharma. While alive he did not lecture on the Dharma much, and his words were unable to attain the truth. Although while he was alive the offerings and donations were sufficient, [among his disciples] only Kong is a monk with merit. The rest of his disciples are unfamiliar with the Buddha-Dharma."

The Lord Minister was highly perceptive, and he knew that these were no more than jealous words. Thereupon he returned home, and he asked his personal clerks Ma Liang and Kang Ran, "Do you know of any exemplary monks or worthies in Jiannan?"

Ma Liang replied, "At the governmental court I have often heard the military commissioner and commanders say that west of the Canya pass in the Baiya mountains there is Chan Master Wuzhu, who has got the Venerable Kim's robe and bowl and is his successor-disciple. This Chan Master is virtuous and genuine, and he never leaves the mountains."

When the Lord Minister heard this he said to Ma Liang and the others, "I heard from afar that the Venerable Kim was a great 'Good Friend.' Yesterday I went myself to Ningguo monastery of Mount Heng and Jingzhong monastery, and I asked the Venerable Kim's personal disciples. They all said there was no successor-disciple who had the robe and bowl. Then I asked the Vinaya masters, and they all slandered [the Venerable Kim]. Based on this evidence, Chan Master Wuzhu of the Baiya mountains must indeed be a man of the Way."

So when he next went to the district headquarters he asked all the army officers, "In this jurisdiction, do you know of any famous monks or worthies?"

The Military Vice-Commissioners Niu Wangxian, Li Xuying, Gui Chengwang, Dong Jiahui, Zhang Wen, Yin Yu, Zhang Yuguang, Zhang Zhen, Wei Luan, and Qin Ti reported to the Lord Minister, "In the Baiya mountains there is the Chan Master Wuzhu. The Venerable Kim's robe and bowl are at his place, and he is inconceivable."

The Lord Minister asked Niu Wangxian, "How did you come to know this?"

He replied, "The high grand master sends me to serve at the Shibei encampment. Because it is not far from [Wuzhu's] place of practice, I often go to make obeisance, and thus I know he is inconceivable."

The Lord Minister inquired further, "You just spoke of the robe and bowl being there, but who knows if this is really true?"

Qin Ti and Zhang Huang reported together, "We are the acting patrolling inspectors of the left and right. On the day that the Venerable Kim passed into extinction, his personal attendant disciples of both monasteries were all abuzz. They delegated Attendant-in-Ordinary He to tell the grand master, 'Until we know the truth regarding the Venerable Kim's robe of verification, we are unwilling to cremate him.' The high grand master sent us patrolling inspectors of the left and right out to investigate; we were in charge of getting to the truth.

"At first we were only able to get two *kāṣāya;* the two monasteries each had one robe, and we did not know where to search for the robe of verification. At the time, we did not know that west of the Canya pass in the Baiya mountains there is Chan Master Wuzhu. Later, we were appointed file leaders to lead cavalry up into the western mountains. We were about to attack Danggou city (i.e., the Tibetans) but had not yet advanced our troops, and we were quartered at the Shibei encampment. The encampment was close to his place of practice and, accompanied by the other generals, we went there bearing dedicatory offerings. We saw that this Chan Master looked exactly like the Venerable Kim. When we first saw him it was as if he was a transformation-body of the Venerable Kim.

"We ventured to question him and remained for some time, and we learned that the Venerable Kim's robe and bowl had previously been dispatched to him via a messenger. [The messenger] hid them for two years and did not deliver them, then sold them to a monk. When the monk obtained the robe, that night a spirit appeared and told him to send it back to its original owner, [saying], 'If you do not return it, you are most certainly shortening your life.' The buyer exchanged it, giving an account of what had happened. After that [the messenger] couldn't sell it and restored it to the original Chan Master's place. As soon as we heard that the robe our previous searching had not discovered was now in the immediate vicinity, we asked to make obeisance. Without reservations, [Wuzhu] carried the robe out aloft and revealed it to all the army officers and soldiers, so we know it is at that place."

When the Lord Minister heard this he said, "Astounding, quite astounding! Monks would hide the Buddha-Dharma, unlike a layman. A layman, rather, wants the Buddha-Dharma to flow forth." The Military Vice-Commissioners Li Lingying, Zhang Wen, Niu Wangxian, Gui Chengwang, Dong Jiahui, Wei Luan, and Qin Ti collectively signed a petition inviting the Venerable [to come down from the mountains]. The Lord Minister inclined toward [the views of] the army officers who knew Chan Master Wuzhu, and was himself moved to request him to come. The Lord Minister sent the Imperial Entertainments Chief Minister Murong Ding as a special messenger, and ordered that an official document be issued. At each region and district along the way there were to be fine pennants splendidly arranged, and monks and Daoists, elders and the aged would chant together. [He also] sent a highly competent district official to go to the mountains and make the collective invitation.

Before the official document had been issued, Master Xiaojin[89] and Great Master Zhang of the Jingzhong and Ningguo monasteries heard of the invitation to the Venerable Wuzhu, and they were deeply alarmed and utterly at a loss. They consulted all the Vinaya Masters and proposed an evil deed. First, Minister Yan's cousin Vinaya Master Xiao and others got the Grand Mistress to take away the Venerable Kim's Chan cloister and make it a Vinaya cloister, and take the Venerable Kim's Chan hall and make it a Vinaya hall. Master Xiaojin [thus] unethically [made himself] secure. Vinaya Master Xiao and others were in on the plan; they had a stele erected for the Vinaya cloister, and Du Ang wrote the inscription. The Vinaya Masters Zhang Zhizu and Wang Yingyao, as well as Master Xiaojin and Great Master Zhang, got Director Du Ang to do it. Vinaya Master [Wang] Yingyao and the Attendant Censor Wang Jian had the same surname, and they recognized each other as brothers.

They got the official wife of Vice-Director Cui to arrange a vegetarian feast. When they had finished eating, Master Xiaojin held up a fine linen *kāṣāya* that Vice-Director Pei had donated and displayed it to the Vice-Director and his wife. Weeping, Master Xiaojin said, "This is the robe of verification that has been passed down."

The Vice-Director said, "I was not aware of this before, when I invited Chan Master Wuzhu. But the Lord Minister's mind is made up, and he will not heed such as I."

The treacherous clique of Du Ang and Wang Jian, fearing that their Vinaya cloister would be taken away, turned around and asked all the Vinaya Masters,

"This mountain monk 'Chan Master Wuzhu'—what sort of spiritual practice does he have?"

Vinaya Master Yingyao and the others replied, "To rely on this Chan Master Wuzhu would be unwise. Inviting this monk would be profoundly disadvantageous to the clergy as a whole."

Minister [Yan] asked, "Why would it be disadvantageous for the clergy?" [Yingyao] replied, "There is a craftsman on the Min river who is an inlay artisan of average skill. He got a *kāṣāya* [as payment] that had an estimated value of twenty thousand cash. The craftsman's robe was taken away by that Chan Master and was never returned. [Wuzhu] claimed, 'This was bestowed on me by the Venerable Kim.' [Moreover], he does not practice the forms of worship and recitation. Based on this evidence, it would be disadvantageous for the clergy [were he to be invited]."

The Vice-Director said to the Vinaya masters, "Previously, when I was with the cavalry in the western mountains, I learned the whole situation. Why do you Vinaya Masters resort to slander?" So saying, he left his seat. [The faces of] the malicious clique drained of color; they were utterly at a loss. Their evil deed was thus thwarted.

SECTION 20. DU HONGJIAN AND WUZHU MEET (*T.* 51:188B21–189B22)

On the twenty-third day of the ninth month of the second year of the Yongtai era (766), the Imperial Entertainments Chief Minister Murong Ding, acting as special messenger, and the district officials, monks, [lay followers] of the Way, and such, all went to Mount Baiya to invite the Venerable [Wuzhu]. Conveying the invitations and obeisances of the Lord Minister [Du Hongjian], the Vice-Director [Cui Gan], and the army supervisor, they implored the Venerable: "Do not forsake mercy; for the sake of beings of the Three Shu,[90] make a 'Great Bridge,'" they beseeched him fervently.

The Venerable knew that the Lord Minister profoundly defended the Buddha-Dharma and cherished the Mahāyāna, he knew that the Vice-Director was benevolent and generous, and he knew that the army supervisor honored the Buddha, Dharma, and saṅgha. He judged that these were associates of the same karmic destiny and did not turn down the invitation. And so there were "fine pennants and a jeweled parasol" (i.e., a procession befitting a buddha).

All the worthies of the region, fearing that the Venerable would not come out from Mount Baiya, also went to the mountain monastery to join in the invitation. They welcomed the Venerable with a jeweled sedan chair and would have had him sit in it, but the Venerable declined and proceeded step by step in a slow and dignified manner. When he was about to leave, the earth quaked six times in the Mao Zhou area, the mountains and rivers roared, and the insects and birds cried out.

The ordinary people all asked each other, "What good omens are these?" When they saw that official representatives had come to welcome the Venerable, then the local monks, nuns, and lay followers of the Way redoubled their pleas that the Venerable remain. The special messenger told the monks and laypersons and the others, "The Lord Minister and the Vice-Director consider this important for the benefit of the common people of the Three Shu. Of what account is this area, when we have promised not to let him be detained?"

When the Venerable had not yet come out of the mountains, outlaws and thieves were running rampant, not all the regions had been civilized, the cost of grain and rice was rising ever higher, and the masses were very anxious. When the Lord Minister and Vice-Director invited the Venerable to come out of the mountains, wherever he went the cost of grain and rice fell by half, the people were content and happy, and all the territory was refined and civilized. The outlaws and thieves were completely eradicated, and all progressed peacefully and without incident. When the Venerable arrived in a region, officials came to welcome him; when he came to a district, the district magistrate came to guide him along the road. Every household hung out banners, at each doorway they burned incense, and everyone said, "The common people are blessed with good fortune." Lay followers of the Way filled the roads, chanting, "The Venerable Wuxiang has gone, the Venerable Wuzhu has come. Thus it is that buddha upon buddha confers his hand [in blessing], the salvific teachings continue without interruption, lamp lights lamp in succession, and the Dharma-eye is redoubled in clarity. The Dharma banner is established—indeed a great work of the Buddha-Dharma!"

The Lord Minister sent his Chief Warrant Officer Qin Hua to welcome the Venerable from afar. Warrant Officer Qin conveyed the Lord Minister's message, saying [on his behalf], "I have suddenly caught a chill and am unable to come to welcome you from afar. I will pay my obeisances when you arrive."

The Governor of Chengdu, Lord Cui, Military Commissioner of the Jiannan West River Command, and concurrent Vice-Director of the Left and Censor-in-

Chief, ordered Inspector-in-Chief Wang Xuiyan, Director of Imperial Manufactories Li Junzhao, Local Inspector Du Zhang, and others to convey a message. Making obeisances to the Venerable [they said on Lord Cui's behalf], "I, your disciple, am lord of the locality, and it would be proper if I myself were to welcome you from afar. However, owing to the Lord Minister's illness, your disciple and the army supervisor do not dare to go before him. We humbly beg the Venerable to favor us with his gracious understanding." So saying, [the delegates] immediately conducted the Venerable to Konghui monastery and settled him there.

From the twenty-ninth day of the ninth month to the first day of the tenth month, Lord Minister Du, Army Supervisor Wu, all the directors and attendant censors, the East River-Capital Liaison Representative Director Du Ji, Adjutant Du Zang, the Commissioner South of the Qiong [River] and Vice-Censor Xianyu Shuming, Directors Yang Yan, Du Ya, Du Ang, Ma Xiong, and Chen Can, the Surveillance Commissioner's Supernumerary Administrative Assistant Li Bu, Supernumerary Liu Zihua, the "Green Sprouts" Official[91] Wu Yu, Special Supply Commissioner Wei Xiayou, Attendant Censors Di Boji, Cui Kang, Cui Ti, Wang Jian, Su Chang, and Sima Lian, the two Vice-Governors Cheng Ben and Bo Zifang, the two District Magistrates Ban Xun and Li Rong, and the thief-catching officer all came to the gates of Konghui monastery.

Inspector-in-Chief Wang Xuiyan and the Lord Minister's Chief Warrant Officers Qin Hua and Wei Zhejiao came first to tell the Venerable, "The Lord Minister is coming to present himself to the Venerable."

[Wuzhu] replied, "If he's coming then it's up to him."

The warrant officers told the Venerable, "A minister of state is a very important person, you ought to go out and welcome him."

The Venerable said, "It would not be appropriate to welcome him. 'Welcoming' is human feelings. 'Not welcoming' is the Buddha-Dharma."

The warrant officers wanted to say more, but [at that moment] the Lord Minister entered the cloister and saw that the Venerable's demeanor was unmoving, majestically composed. The Lord Minister bowed at the lower level, made obeisance with palms joined, and politely inquired after [Wuzhu's] "rising and resting" (i.e., his health and comfort). None of the directors and attendant censors had ever seen such a thing. When they first saw that the Venerable neither welcomed [the minister] nor rose, they looked at one another and asked, "Why does he neither welcome [the minister] nor rise?"

Directors Yang Yan and Du Ya had long served the Lord Minister; they were very familiar with his will, and moreover learned in the Buddha-Dharma. They said to all the directors and attendant censors, "Observe this Chan Master—he must certainly possess the Way. The Lord Minister can judge for himself, why take this as strange?" When the military vice-commissioner, inspector-in-chief, and thief-catching officer outside the door first heard that the Venerable met the Lord Minister without rising or welcoming him, they trembled with fear and lost color, and were soaked through with perspiration. The attendants listened secretly, waiting for orders [to punish Wuzhu]. [However,] they saw the Lord Minister take a seat, talking and laughing. The Venerable spoke on the Dharma, and the Lord Minister joined his palms and touched his forehead to the ground. All the directors and attendant censors were delighted, and once the people outside the door heard about it they were no longer grieved.

When he was first seated the Lord Minister asked, "Why did the Venerable come here?"

The Venerable said, "I came from afar in order to submit myself to the Venerable Kim."

The Lord Minister further asked, "Where were you before? Since you came from afar to submit yourself to the Venerable Kim, what Dharma did he teach?"

Wuzhu replied, "I have been at Baofu monastery at Mount Tai, as well as Fenzhou and other areas, and I sat at Mount Helan. I heard that the Venerable Kim taught the Dharma of the sudden teaching, and so I came from afar to submit myself to him."

The Lord Minister asked the Venerable, "The Venerable Kim taught 'no-recollection, no-thought, and do not forget,' isn't that so?"

The Venerable replied, "Yes."

The Lord Minister further asked, "These three phrases, are they one or are they three?"

The Venerable replied, "They are one, not three. No-recollection is *śila,* no-thought is *samādhi,* and 'do not be deluded' is *prajñā.*" He spoke further, "The nonarising of thought is the gate of *śila,* the nonarising of thought is the gate of *samādhi,* the nonarising of thought is the gate of *prajñā.* No-thought is thus the complete fulfillment of *śila, samādhi,* and *prajñā.*"

The Lord Minister asked further, "Regarding the character *wang,* is it [the one with] *nu* 女 below *wang* 亡, or with *xin* 心 below *wang*?"

The Venerable replied, "*Nu* below *wang.*"

[The Lord Minister asked,] "Do you have any evidence, or not?"

The Venerable replied, "I have." Then he quoted the "*Dhammapada*": "If you preach about the Dharma of 'good effort', you are preaching out of self-conceit. If you are without self-conceit there is no 'good' and no 'good effort.' If you arouse the mind of 'good effort,' this is delusion and not good effort. If you are able [to experience] mind without delusion, then good effort has no limit."[92]

The Lord Minister heard this teaching, then said to the Venerable, "Do you see the tree in front of the courtyard or not?"

The Venerable replied, "I see it."

The Lord Minister further questioned the Venerable, "Outside the wall behind us there is a tree, can you see it or not?"

The Venerable replied, "I see it. Do not discuss 'in front' and 'behind.' In the world of the ten directions, I see everywhere and hear everything."

Atop the tree in front of the courtyard, a crow called. The Lord Minister again asked the Venerable, "Do you hear the crow call or not?"

The Venerable replied, "This seeing, hearing, perceiving, and knowing is worldly seeing, hearing, perceiving, and knowing. The *Vimalakīrti-sūtra* says, 'If you go about seeing, hearing, perceiving, and knowing, then this is seeing, hearing, perceiving, and knowing. The Dharma transcends seeing, hearing, perceiving, and knowing.'[93] No-thought is thus no-seeing, no-thought is thus no-knowing. It is because beings have thought that one provisionally teaches no-thought, but at the time of true no-thought, no-thought itself is not."

He went on to quote the *Vajrasamādhi-sūtra*, "'The Most Honored Greatly Enlightened One expounded the Dharma of producing no-thought. [Regarding] the mind of no-thought and nonproduction, the mind is constantly produced and never extinguished.'[94] Further, the *Vimalakīrti-sūtra* says, 'Not-practicing is bodhi, because it is without recollection.' 'Always seek no-thought, the wisdom characterized by actuality.'[95] The *Laṅkāvatāra-sūtra* says, 'The Holy One's inner reference point is to constantly abide in no-thought.'[96] The *Śūraṃgama-sūtra* says, 'Ānanda, if you initiate the mind [even] for a short time, the suffering due to defilements will have [already] arisen first.' Further, it says, 'So long as sight is separate from seeing, then seeing cannot be attained.'[97] The *Viśeṣacinta-sūtra* says, 'How is it that all dharmas are true, and how is it that all dharmas are wrong? If one makes distinctions with the mind, then all dharmas are wrong. If one does not make distinctions with the mind, all dharmas are true. In the midst of no-mind dharmas, once one gives rise to distinctions of mind everything is wrong.'[98] The *Laṅkāvatāra-sūtra* says, 'Seeing the Buddha and hearing the Dharma is your own mind making distinctions. One for whom 'seeing' does not arise—this is called seeing the Buddha.'"[99]

When the Lord Minister had listened to this teaching he made obeisance to the Venerable. He said to the Venerable, "I have heard you speak for the first time. When you, Venerable, had not yet descended from the mountains, I went to Jingzhong monastery and Ningguo monastery and viewed the Venerable Kim's mortal remains. He was a great 'Good Friend,' so I knew that somewhere in Jiannan there had to be a 'Good Friend.' I asked every one of the masters and monks in turn about the Venerable Kim's three phrases and the *wang* character, and they all said that *wang* was written with *xin* underneath it, and that the three phrases were separate. They did not settle your disciple's doubts. I asked all the army officers, 'In Jiannan is there really no genuine monk?' There was not a single person who disagreed. The Military Vice-Commissioners and Directors Niu Wangxian and Qin Ti and all the army officers reported unanimously to me that the Venerable was virtuous and genuine. So I have welcomed you from afar, and I humbly beg the Venerable not to forsake mercy; create great 'good causes' for the beings of the Three Shu." He ceased speaking and made obeisance, [then continued,] "Your disciple is constrained by public affairs, and the Vice-Director and all the military vice-commissioners have not yet been able to pay obeisance to the Venerable. So long as I am in Jiannan, I will not fail to attend you daily." So saying, he took his leave.

SECTION 21. CUI GAN'S VISIT (*T.* 51:189B22–190B16)

Vice-Director [Cui][100] learned that the Lord Minister had joyfully declared "The Venerable is unfathomable." He immediately went with his wife, Ren,[101] and the military commissioners and army officers to make obeisances to the Venerable. When they had inquired after [Wuzhu's] "rising and resting," the officers were seated in sections, and [Cui] permitted all the army officers to listen with them to the Venerable expounding the Dharma. At that time Dharma Master Wuying and Dharma Master Qingyuan, eminently sagacious among monks, were seated among the assembly.

The Venerable quoted the *Śūraṃgama-sūtra:* "[The Buddha said], 'Ānanda, all beings since beginningless time experience every kind of reversal; by the kind of deed, [destinies] are self-determined, as numerous as *rudrākṣa* seeds.[102]

Not all those who practice are able to attain unsurpassed bodhi. They may instead become śrāvakas, pratyekas, may become [denizens of] non-Buddhist heavens, or retainers of the Demon King. This is all due to not knowing the two kinds of roots, and practicing in error and confusion. It is like boiling sand and wanting it to become fine viands. Although an eon as long as the number of atoms of a world ground to dust may elapse, it is in the end impossible. What are the two kinds [of roots]? Ānanda, the first is the root of beginningless birth and death. Thus, you, along with all beings, presently take the mind that grasps after conditions as yourself. The second is beginningless bodhi-nirvāṇa, originally pure substance. With you at present the consciousness essence is unilluminated, and thus you are able to be born in various conditions. Those who forget conditions consequently lose their original luminosity. Even though you practice day in and day out, if you are not self-aware, you will vainly enter into every destiny.'"[103]

The Venerable continued, "All beings are fundamentally pure and fundamentally complete. From the buddhas at the upper end down to sentient beings, all are of the same pure nature. However, with a single thought [produced by] the deluded mind of beings, the Three Worlds are dyed. It is because beings have thought that one provisionally teaches no-thought, but if there is no presence of thought, then no-thought itself is not. No-thought is thus no-birth, no-thought is thus no-extinction. No-thought is thus no-love, no-thought is thus no-hate. No-thought is thus no-grasping, no-thought is thus no-abandoning. No-thought is thus no-high, no-thought is thus no-low. No-thought is thus no-male, no-thought is thus no-female. No-thought is thus no-true, no-thought is thus no-false. At the time of true no-thought, no-thought itself is not. 'When the mind is produced then the various dharmas are produced, when the mind is extinguished then the various dharmas are extinguished.'[104] 'As one's mind is, so also are the stains of wrongdoing, so also are all dharmas.'[105] At the time of true no-thought, 'all dharmas are the Buddha-Dharma,'[106] there is not a single dharma separate from bodhi."

[Wuzhu] went on, "Due to delusion there is birth, due to delusion there is extinction. Birth and extinction are called delusion, extinguishing delusion is called true reality. This is designated as the Tathāgatha, unsurpassed bodhi, and the great nirvāṇa."

When the Venerable had expounded the Dharma, he [sat] majestically unmoving. The Vice-Director listened with joined palms, and then he addressed the Venerable, "I am lord of the locality, and it would have been proper if I myself had welcomed you from afar, but due to official matters I was prevented. I beg the Venerable not to blame me. When I was a cavalry officer in the western mountains, the Venerable was in a hermitage in the Baiya mountains, and so from the outset you have been the head of the family. If there is anything you need, I have specially deputed the local inspector to respectfully make offerings to the Venerable."

The Venerable said, "One who cultivates the Prajñāparamitā needs nothing whatsoever." He went on, "If you have only discriminating mind, then Heaven discriminates your offerings. Howsoever the mind discriminates [is determinative]: not-seeking mind and not-coveting mind discriminates not-receiving mind and not-stained mind. If the Brahmaloka is not sought, the Brahmaloka is reached of itself; if karmic reward is not sought, karmic reward is reached of itself.[107] The incomparably precious jewel unsought is reached of itself." He went on, "Knowing satisfaction is great wealth and honor, having few desires is the greatest peace and happiness."[108]

When the Vice-Director heard the Venerable's words, he joined his palms and touched his forehead to the ground in obeisance. Dharma Master Qingyuan made obeisance and said to the Venerable, "Once I heard [your] Dharma, the net of doubt was suddenly removed.[109] I now submit myself to the Venerable, I beg to receive mercy and compassion from the Venerable."

But Dharma Master Wuying succumbed to pride and, shaking, changed color. The Venerable asked Dharma Master Wuying, "Do you recognize host and guest or not?"[110]

Dharma Master Wuying replied, drawing from various forms of Dharma and widely quoting exegetical literature. The Venerable said, "The Dharma Master does not recognize host and guest. Concentrating on sense objects, you take the flowing mind of birth and extinction itself as understanding. It is like boiling sand wishing it to become fine food—however many eons [it boils], it will only become hot sand. It is only deceiving yourself and deceiving others. The *Laṅkāvatāra-sūtra* says: 'If you follow after words and grasp meanings then you build on dharmas, and because of that construction, when you die you fall into hell.'"[111]

When Dharma Master Wuying heard this, his body tilted to one side so that he sat off-kilter. The Venerable asked the Dharma Master, "How many kinds of *avyākṛta* (categories of morally neutral) are there?"

The Dharma Master replied, "*Vipāka-avyākṛta* (morally neutral results from good or evil causes), *pariṇama-avyākṛta* (morally neutral death and rebirth), *śilpa-avyākṛta* (morally neutral arts and skills), and *īryā-patha-avyākṛta* (morally neutral postures and physical movements)."

The Venerable asked, "What is *vyākṛta* (category of morally good or bad)?"

The Dharma Master replied, "The sixth consciousness (*manovijñāna*) is *vyākṛta.*"

The Venerable said, "The sixth consciousness is the *viparyāsa* (delusion) consciousness. [The reason that] the many beings do not exit the Three Worlds is all due to the consciousnesses. When thought is not produced, then the Three Worlds are released. Those who shave their heads and cut their hair are all disciples of the Buddha, they can't [waste time] studying *vyākṛta* and *avyākṛta.* Dharma masters these days all study '*avyākṛta,*' they don't have faith in the Mahāyāna. 'What is the Mahāyāna? Internally self-confirmed and unmoving, this is the unsurpassed Mahāyāna. My unsurpassed Mahāyāna goes beyond names and words, its meaning is [for those of] profound understanding, fools are unable to realize it.'[112] 'Realization' is realization that all feelings and consciousnesses are void, tranquil, and unborn—this is what I call realization."

When Dharma Master Wuying heard this, he shut his mouth wordlessly. The Venerable said, "There are two kinds of *avyākṛta.* One is *nivṛta-avyākṛta* (morally neutral with hindrances preventing realization). The other is *anivṛta-avyākṛta* (morally neutral without hindrances). [From] the sixth consciousness to the five consciousnesses of sight and the other [senses], all belong to the category of *nivṛta-avyākṛta.* From the sixth consciousness to the eighth consciousness, all belong to the category of *anivṛta-avyākṛta.* Both are phrases [arising from] the compulsion to name. Further adding a ninth consciousness that is a pure consciousness is also setting up delusion."[113]

The Venerable quoted from the *Laṅkāvatāra-sūtra:* "'The eighth and ninth and the various consciousnesses are like the ocean's many breaking waves. Habits continually increase, solid and dense as tangled roots. The mind follows the flow of one's conditioned state like iron to a lodestone.'[114] 'As when a cascade of water runs out the waves do not arise, likewise when the consciousnesses are extinguished, the various consciousnesses are not produced.'[115] 'The bodies produced by the various thoughts, I explain as the conditioned mind's apprehensions.'[116] '[One who] attains the nonconceptual Dharma is a disciple of the Buddha and not a śrāvaka.'"[117]

When Dharma Master Wuying heard this teaching, he only said admiringly, "Inconceivable."

The Venerable further inquired, "The *Laṅkāvatāra-sūtra* says, 'Using a wedge to push out a wedge.'[118] What does this mean?"

Dharma Master Wuying replied, "It is like splitting wood—first one drives in a large wedge, then one drives in a small wedge, forcing out the large wedge."

The Venerable responded to the Dharma Master, "When the small wedge pushes out the large wedge, while the large wedge is out, the small wedge is still in. Why does one use a wedge to push out a wedge?"

The Dharma Master didn't dare utter another word. So the Venerable explained, "The [large] wedge illustrates the wedge of the defilements of the many beings, and the [small] wedge is a simile for the buddhas' and tathāgatas' verbal teachings. When there are no defilements, the Dharma does not of itself [remain]. It is like having an illness and receiving a prescription. If the illness is cured, the prescription and the medicine are both discarded. Thus, Dharma masters now who grasp at the Dharma of verbal teachings are like sick people who grasp prescriptions but are unable to swallow the medicine. Not abandoning texts and characters is like a wedge remaining in the wood. The *Laṅkāvatāra-sūtra* says, 'It is like using a finger to point at something. A small child looks at the finger and does not look at the object.'[119] If one follows the pointing of verbal explanation and conceives an attachment to it, then at the end of one's life one is ultimately unable to relinquish the finger of texts and characters and grasp the cardinal meaning."

The Venerable again questioned the Dharma Master, [asking him about] the meaning of the Three Jewels and the Four [Noble] Truths, and he also asked about the meaning of the Three Bodies of the Buddha. The Dharma Master still didn't dare reply, and only said admiringly that the Venerable was inconceivable.

When the Vice-Director heard the Dharma sermon, his delight was redoubled. [He said,] "That day [when you met the Lord Minister] I was afraid lest the Venerable's long sojourn in the mountain monastery should make him overawed by the Lord Minister and unable [to speak]. I was deeply grieved due to these causes. Among the monks of the Three Rivers there was not one who corresponded to the Lord Minister's intent. As soon as the Lord Minister had seen you, Venerable, he said to me that you were a genuine man of the Way, inherently perspicacious, and altogether different from the other monks. He sighed in praise that you were inconceivable. When I heard the Lord Minister's words, my joy was unsurpassed. It was my good fortune, and from that moment my sorrows were no more." The army officers were also moved to joy;

they could not speak, they touched their foreheads to the ground in obeisance and departed.

SECTION 22. DIALOGUE WITH CHAN MASTER TIWU (*T.* 51:190B16–190C18)

At that time there was a Master Tiwu of the Eastern Capital, eminently sagacious among monks. He sought out masters everywhere. [He was notable for] adherence to the precepts and his imposing demeanor, and in all matters of the Dharma he was astute and eloquent. He was also designated a Chan Master, and he was a disciple of Chan Master Hongzheng of Shengshan monastery (Luoyang). Together with Dou Cheng of Jinyuan, Li Qutai of Shifang, Su Cheng of Qingcheng, the Administrative Assistant Zhou Xia, and others, [Tiwu] came seeking to question the Venerable. [They] proceeded directly to the meditation hall, and when they had each greeted the Venerable individually they took their seats.

Tiwu asked the Venerable, "Whose disciple are you, and whose doctrines [do you adhere to]?"

The Venerable replied, "The Buddha's doctrines. I am the Buddha's disciple." The Venerable declared, "Ācārya, you cut your hair and wear robes, and are thus the Buddha's disciple. What use is it to ask about teachers and doctrines? 'Rely on scriptures of the complete meaning, do not rely on scriptures of incomplete meaning.'[120] If you have some doubts, then question as you will."

Tiwu knew that the Venerable was the Venerable Kim's disciple, but his words were malicious: "I wish to observe that the people of Jiannan do not arouse the [true] mind. Chan masters [hereabouts] hit people and call it not-hitting, berate people and call it not-berating, and when they receive donations they say, 'not-received.' I am deeply perplexed by these matters."

The Venerable replied, "Practicing Prajñāpāramitā one does not see the one who is awarded favor and does not see the one who extends favor. It is because already there is nothing to receive that one receives all one receives. The not-yet-complete Buddha-Dharma is also endlessly received. From the time when I first put forth the mind up until the present, I have never received a single hair in donations."

When Tiwu heard this he looked around at the officials and said, "The Chan Master speaks with a big voice."

The Venerable asked Tiwu, "So the Ācārya verbally recognizes a Chan Master! Why would one arousing the mind hit people, arousing the mind berate people, and arousing the mind receive donations?"

Tiwu knew himself that he had lost doctrinal [ground]. He was taken aback and lost color, and for a long while he did not speak. Then he asked the Venerable, "Do you comprehend the *Laṅkāvatāra-sūtra* or not?"

The Venerable replied, "Comprehending is not-comprehending."

The officials exclaimed in concert to the Venerable, "The Chan Master alone should expound [on the Dharma], what point is there in questioning each other?"

The Venerable told the officials, "If I expound [on the Dharma], I am afraid you officials will not believe."

The officials replied, "We believe!"

The Venerable then explained, "If I were to expound completely, anyone who heard it would become disturbed in mind, would fall prey to doubt and not believe."[121] Then he quoted from the *Laṅkāvatāra-sūtra,* saying, "A fool delights in delusive preaching and does not hear true wisdom. 'Verbal explanation is the origin of the Three Worlds, the real extinguishes the cause of suffering. Verbal explanation is flux, the real transcends texts and characters.'[122] 'In a deluded state of mind, the foolish give rise to the two kinds of views. If you do not recognize mind and causes, then you give rise to the two delusions. If you understand mind and the field of conditions, then delusion is not produced.'"[123]

Tiwu, attempting to redeem himself, quoted the *Lotus Sūtra* regarding the Three Vehicles. The Venerable quoted the *Laṅkāvatāra-sūtra,* saying: "'Those idiots teach that there are Three Vehicles, they do not explain that there is only mind, and no field of conditions whatsoever.'[124] 'The mind that is unaware produces active thinking, which is the demons' net.'"[125] He also quoted from the *Viśeṣacintā-sūtra:* "How is it that all dharmas are true, and how is it that all dharmas are wrong? If one makes distinctions with the mind, then all dharmas are wrong. If one does not make distinctions with the mind, all dharmas are true. In the midst of no-mind dharmas, once one gives rise to distinctions of mind everything is wrong."[126]

SECTION 23. DIALOGUE WITH CHAN MASTER HUIYI (*T.* 51:190C18–22)

There was Chan Master Huiyi, whom people in those days called "the monk of Plum Mountain." He asked the Venerable, "As for the Northern Chan masters, how do they go about 'entering'?"

The Venerable replied, "A Chan Master is neither 'Southern' nor 'Northern,' he neither enters nor exits. One has neither gain nor loss; not flowing and not fixed, not sinking and not floating, lively like a fish jumping!"[127] When Huiyi heard this, he joined his palms and knocked his head [on the ground], then sat down.

SECTION 24. DIALOGUE WITH MASTERS YIJING, ZHUMO, AND TANGWEN (*T.* 51:190C22–191A27)

Master Yijing, Master Zhumo, and Master Tangwen were all disciples of Chan Master Huiming. They came wishing to stay with the Venerable. The Venerable asked, "Ācārya, what scriptures and treatises have you explicated?"

Master Tangwen replied, "I have explicated the *Baifa lun* (Treatise on One Hundred Dharmas),[128] I have lectured on it for the monks." The Venerable invited him to expound on it. Tangwen replied, "Inside there are five [kinds of] *asaṃskṛta* (the unconditioned), outside there are five [kinds of] *saṃskṛta* (conditionality); together they encompass all dharmas."

The Venerable quoted the *Laṅkāvatāra-sūtra,* saying: "'Those without wisdom constantly make a distinction between *saṃskṛta* and *asaṃskṛta.*'[129] 'Those who practice must not give rise to distinctions.'[130] 'Scripture after scripture expounds delusory concepts; in the end none departs from [mere] designations. If you transcend verbal explanation then there is nothing to explain.'"[131]

Tangwen said to Master Yijing, "Please, Ācārya, you ask next." So Yijing asked the Venerable, "Chan Master, how do you produce seated meditation (*zuochan*)?"

The Venerable replied, "Not producing, this is 'Chan.'"

Yijing didn't understand it himself, and he asked Zhumo, "What does this mean?" Zhumo didn't understand either. Instead he told Master Yijing to ask something else.

The Venerable knew they didn't understand, and so he asked Yijing, "Ācārya, what scriptures and treatises have you explicated?"

He replied, "I have explicated the *Pusa jie* (Bodhisattva Precepts),[132] I have lectured on it for the monks."

The Venerable asked, "What is the substance of the precepts, and what is their meaning?"

Yijing had no words with which to reply, and then he burst out with invective: "It's not that I don't understand, it was only in order to test you. Your sort of 'Chan'—I despise 'not practicing'!"

Zhumo chimed in, "I despise your dull 'not doing,' I despise your stupefying 'not practicing,' I despise your lazy 'not doing,' I despise your slovenly 'not entering'!"

The Venerable addressed the monks, "'The principle of suchness (*tathātā*) encompasses all wisdom.'[133] 'My unsurpassed Mahāyāna goes beyond names and words. Its meaning is [for those of] profound understanding, fools do not comprehend it.'[134] I will tell the Ācārya an instructive tale. At dawn in a small village there was the sound of a little girl crying. A neighbor heard and went to take a look, and she saw the mother angrily hitting [the child]. The neighbor asked, 'Why are you hitting her?' The mother replied, 'Because she wet the bed.' The neighbor scolded the mother, 'This child is very young, why are you hitting her?' Once again the sound of crying was heard. The neighbor went to inquire, and saw a fine fellow about thirty years old whose mother was beating him with a cudgel. The neighbor asked, 'What are you beating him for?' The mother replied, 'He wet the bed.' The neighbor heard this and said, 'As he is a grown man he probably did it deliberately, so you certainly should beat him severely.' It is this way when the monks are 'like elephants and horses, contentious and uncooperative. It compounds the sharp poisons so that they penetrate to the bone.'"[135]

The Venerable once again expounded for them, "If you seek the bliss of tranquil extinction, you must learn the *śramaṇa* (renunciant) Dharma. 'The no-mind of transcending consciousness, this is precisely the *śramaṇa* Dharma.'[136] You Ācārya shave off your hair and put on robes and say to yourselves, 'I am the Buddha's disciple,' but you are unwilling to learn the *śramaṇa* Dharma. You just say, 'slovenly doing, lazy doing, I despise dull not-entering.' This is not the *śramaṇa* lion, this is a kind of wild dog. The Buddha made a prediction: 'In generations to come there will be those whose bodies wear the *kāṣāya* but delusively preach 'being' and 'nonbeing' and harm my true Dharma.'[137] 'It is like using a finger to point at something. An ignorant common person looks at the finger and doesn't look at the object.'[138] If one follows the pointing of verbal explanation and conceives an attachment to it, then at the end of one's life one is ultimately unable to relinquish the finger of texts and characters. 'If you follow after words and grasp meanings then you build on dharmas, and because of that construction, when you die you fall into hell.'"[139]

When the monks heard this they were confused, lost color, and fled.

SECTION 25. DIALOGUE WITH MASTER JINGZANG (*T.* 51:191A28-B17)

Master Jingzang of Shengguang monastery in the Western Capital heard that the Venerable was inconceivable and came from afar to submit himself to the Venerable. The Venerable asked, "How did you know that I am inconceivable?"

Jingzang replied, "I knew that the Venerable Kim transmitted his robe and bowl to the Venerable."

The Venerable asked, "How did you know this?"

Jingzang replied, "Monk and layman alike say that Venerable was invested with the transmission from legitimate heir to legitimate heir, and has got the Venerable Kim's Dharma. I am blessed with great good fortune to be able to meet the Venerable." When he finished speaking, he made obeisance.

The Venerable asked, "What scriptures and treatises have you studied?" [Jingzang] replied, "I have read a commentary on the *Vimalakīrti-sūtra,* and I also studied seated meditation according to the doctrines of [Mount] Taibai."

The Venerable then expounded the Dharma for him: "Nonintention is the Way, not contemplating is Chan. Neither grasped nor rejected, objects arrive and yet are not caused. If you read commentaries, thus is the clamor of conceptualization set in motion. If you 'study the doctrines of [Mount] Taibai,' you doctrinalize seated meditation, and thus intentions and conceptions climb up like vines. If you want to stay here, let nothing whatsoever of what you have studied so far remain in your mind." He asked Jingzang, "Can you do that or not?"

[Jingzang] replied, "I can. In compassion, Venerable, bestow your guidance on me. I will take you as my model."

The Venerable saw that Jingzang was a truly worthy vessel of the Dharma, and so he once more expounded the Dharma for him: "If there is but one thing in your mind, you will not depart from the Three Worlds. 'The existence of dharmas is conventional truth, and no-nature is the cardinal meaning.'[140] 'Transcending all characteristics is called the buddhas.'[141] No-thought is thus no-characteristics, presence of thought is thus empty delusion. No-thought departs the Three Worlds, thought remains in the Three Worlds. No-thought is thus no-true, no-thought is thus no-false. No-thought is thus no-self, no-thought is thus no-other. If you transcend both self and other, you achieve buddha-awakening. At the time of true no-thought, no-thought itself is not."

When he heard this teaching Jingzang leaped for joy, and then he asked the Venerable to change his Dharma name. He was named Chaozang, and he constantly attended [the Venerable], never leaving his side.

SECTION 26. DIALOGUE WITH MASTER ZHIYI (*T.* 51:191B18–C2)

Master Zhiyi, disciple of Chan Master Jue of Kaiyuan monastery in Longzhou, was designated by his contemporaries as a monk of upstanding character. He came to submit himself to the Venerable. The Venerable asked, "Where did you come from?"

Master Zhiyi replied, "I came from Longzhou."

The Venerable asked, "Whose disciple are you?"

Master Zhiyi replied, "I am the disciple of Master Jue."

"Whose disciple is the Venerable Jue?"

"He is the disciple of the Venerable Old Fu."

The Venerable said, "Tell me about your own stage of practice."

Master Zhiyi revealed the teachings of his original master and said, "Viewing purity."[142]

The Venerable then expounded the Dharma for him: "The Dharma has neither stain nor purity, how does one 'view purity'? Right here purity was never established, why would there be stains? Viewing purity is in fact stains, viewing stains is in fact purity. Delusive thinking is stains, nondelusive thinking is purity. Grasping 'I' is stain, not grasping 'I' is purity. No-thought is thus no-stain, no-thought is thus no-purity. [No-thought is thus no-true,] no-thought is thus no-false. No-thought is thus no-self, no-thought is thus no-other. If you transcend both self and other, you achieve buddha awakening. At the time of true self, self itself is not."

When Master Zhiyi heard this teaching he was enlightened at [the Venerable's] words. He never moved from the place in which he heard the Dharma talk. The Venerable saw that Master Zhiyi had a determined nature and was utterly sincere, and had a loyal and filial heart. Thus he changed his name to Chaoran. [Chaoran] never left [the Venerable's] side, and he served him with delight.

SECTION 27. DIALOGUE WITH MASTER ZHONGXIN (*T.* 51:191C2–15)

Master Zhongxin of Dengzhou (Shandong) was widely read in the *Classic of Poetry* and *Classic of Documents*, and his Buddhist character was learned and refined. He abandoned all worldly affairs and came to submit himself to the Venerable, [saying]: "I am from a frontier region at the edge of the sea, I have come far to submit myself to the Venerable." So saying, he made obeisance.

The Venerable replied, "The Way has neither far nor near, why do you speak of 'far'?"

Zhongxin explained to the Venerable, "The matter of life and death is great. I heard that the Venerable has great compassion and therefore I came to submit myself to the Venerable. It is not for the sake of clothing and food; I humbly beg you to deign to consider me."

The Venerable asked, "Scholars are too full of anxious thought. If you are able to abandon gain, I will allow you to stay here."

Zhongxin replied, "'If one hears of the Way in the morning one can die in the evening.'[143] I don't care about my own life, how could I be concerned about texts and characters?"

The Venerable then expounded the Dharma for him, "'The Most Honored Greatly Enlightened One expounded the Dharma of producing no-thought. [Regarding] the mind of no-thought and non-production, the mind is constantly producing and never extinguished.'[144] At all times self-present, do not retreat and do not turn. Not sinking and not floating, not flowing and not fixed, not moving and not shaking, not coming and not going, lively like a fish jumping! Walking and sitting, everything is meditation."

When Master Zhongxin heard this talk, he sat stern and unmoving. When the Venerable saw this, he knew he had awakened to the Mahāyāna. He changed [Zhongxin's] name to Chaoji. At the mountain (monastery) [Chaoji] would often secretly perform acts of service at night. He didn't let anyone know and when it was light he would come back to his old place.

SECTION 28. DIALOGUE WITH DHARMA MASTER FALUN (*T.* 51:191C15–192A7)

There was a Dharma Master Falun who explicated *Nirvāṇa-sūtra* commentaries and was extensively learned and brilliant. He took account of no one else, and considered himself "number one." So he went to [Wuzhu's] temple to dispute with the Venerable. When he saw the Venerable from a distance, he looked mysterious and unusual, unlike other monks. Master Falun approached and made obeisance, and inquired after the Venerable's health. When the Venerable saw [Falun] from a distance he knew he was a Dharma Master, so he merely had him take a seat. The Venerable asked, "What scriptures and treatises does the Dharma Master explicate?"

[Falun] replied, "I explicate the *Nirvāṇa-sūtra.*"

The Venerable asked, "How do you explicate the *Nirvāṇa-sūtra*?" The Dharma Master then quoted from various commentaries.

The Venerable expounded, saying, "These are not the *Nirvāṇa-sūtra,* these are all just verbal explanations. 'Verbal explanation is the origin of the Three Worlds, the real extinguishes the cause of suffering. Verbal explanation is flux, the real transcends texts and characters.'[145] The Bodhisattva 'King of Lofty Noble Virtue' asked, 'World-Honored One, what is the *mahāparinirvāṇa*?' The Buddha said, 'Exhausting all movement of thought, the mind of conceptualization ceases. Such a Dharma characteristic is called the *mahāparinirvāṇa.*'[146] Why lecture on deluded conceptualization as nirvāṇa? If you expound thus, it is not really explicating. How can you say that you explicate nirvāṇa?" When Falun heard this talk there was not a word he dared utter in reply.

The Venerable said, "'The existence of dharmas is conventional truth, and no-nature is the cardinal meaning.'[147] Verbal explication is thus attachment, and mental brilliance is a demonic device. No-thought is thus no-attachment, no-thought is thus no-bondage. No-thought is nirvāṇa, thinking is birth and death; no-thought is mental brilliance, thinking is dullness. No-thought is thus no 'that,' no-thought is thus no 'this.' No-thought is thus no Buddha, no-thought is no beings. In the great compassionate wisdom of *prajñā,* there are no buddhas and no beings. 'There is neither nirvāṇa-Buddha nor Buddha-nirvāṇa.'[148] Those who understand this explication are the true explicators. If you do not explicate like this, then you are just a common fellow attached to characteristics."

When Master Falun heard [the Venerable's] talk, he knocked his forehead on the ground and [requested] refuge: "I, a petty master, have transmitted deceptions for a long time, but now I have been able to meet the Venerable and my darkened eyes are again illuminated. I humbly beg the Venerable to compassionately accept me."

SECTION 29. DIALOGUE WITH THE BROTHERS YIXING AND HUIMING (*T.* 51:192A7–24)

At the Chanlin monastery in Suizhou (Shaanxi), two monks who were brothers both maintained the *Lotus Sūtra,* such that people at that time called them the chroniclers of the *Lotus.*[149] The elder brother's Dharma name was Master Yixing, and the younger was named Master Huiming. They came to submit to the Venerable. The Venerable asked them, "Where do you come from? What teachings have you studied previously?"

Master Huiming said, "We came from Suizhou. We maintain the *Lotus Sūtra;* every day we recite it three times."

The Venerable asked, "In the 'Peaceful Joyful Practice' section it says, 'All dharmas are empty and without any being, they have no permanent abode and no arising or extinction. This is called the intimate place of the wise.'[150] [What can you say about that?]"

Huiming and his brother heard this and said, "We are sunk in delusion. All we understand is the practice of recitation by relying on the text, we have not yet realized the meaning. We humbly beg the Venerable to guide us in our blindness."

The Venerable then expounded the Dharma for them: "'Dharmas have the characteristic of tranquil extinction and cannot be presented verbally.'[151] 'The Dharma cannot be expressed, the characteristic of words is tranquil extinction.'[152] 'Transcending characteristics and extinguishing characteristics, forever the characteristic of tranquil extinction, finally returning home to emptiness.'[153] 'Always completely enter the practice of empty tranquility.'[154] 'The Buddha Treasury [of scriptures numerous as] the Ganges sands are completely understood in a single thought.'[155] If you want to stay at the mountain (monastery), you can never practice recitation. Always at ease and indifferent; are you able to do this or not?" Huiming and his brother realized that practicing recitation was not the ultimate, therefore they submitted themselves to the Venerable.

The Venerable then expounded for them once more: "No-thought is thus no-birth, no-thought is thus no-death. No-thought is thus no-distance, no-thought is thus no-proximity. No-thought is none other than chronicling the *Lotus*, thought is none other than *Lotus* chronicles. No-thought is none other than revolving the *Lotus*, thought is none other than *Lotus* revolutions.[156] At the time of true no-thought, no-thought itself is not." When Huiming and his brother heard this, their minds were made up instantly. So they stayed at the monastery and delighted in doing service.

SECTION 30. DIALOGUE WITH CHANGJINGJIN AND LIAOJIANXING (FEMALE DISCIPLES) (*T.* 51:192A24–B18)

The wife and daughter of Administrator Murong of Qingzhou (Gansu) were determined to seek the Mahāyāna. Accompanied by the entire family, young and old, they came to pay obeisance to the Venerable. The Venerable asked the wife, "Where did you come from?"

She replied, "Your disciple heard from afar that the Venerable had great compassion, so we came to pay obeisance."

The Venerable then expounded various essentials of the Dharma for them. When the daughter had heard his talk, she knelt on one knee with her palms joined and explained to the Venerable, "Your disciple is a woman with the three obstructions and five difficulties,[157] and a body that is not free. That is why I have come now to submit to the Venerable; I am determined to cut off the source of birth and death. I humbly beg the Venerable to point out the essentials of the Dharma."

The Venerable said, "If you are capable of such [resolution], then you are a great hero (*dazhangfu er*), why are you 'a woman'?" The Venerable expounded the essentials of the Dharma for her: "No-thought is thus no 'male,' no-thought is thus no 'female.' No-thought is thus no-obstruction, no-thought is thus no-hindrance. No-thought is thus no-birth, no-thought is thus no-death. At the time of true no-thought, no-thought itself is not. This is none other than cutting off the source of birth and death."

When the daughter heard his talk, her eyes did not blink and she stood absolutely still. In an instant, the Venerable knew that this woman had a resolute mind. He gave her the Dharma name Changjingjin (Ever-Pure Progress), and her mother was named Zhengbianzhi (Right Knowledge). They took the tonsure and practiced, and became leaders among nuns.

Later, they brought a younger female cousin with the surname Wei, who was the granddaughter of Grand Councillor Su. She was quick-witted and clever, extensively learned and knowledgeable, and when asked a question she was never without an answer. She came to pay obeisance to the Venerable, and when the Venerable saw that she was obdurate and determined on chastity he expounded the Dharma for her: "This Dharma is not caused and conditioned, it has neither false nor not-false, and has neither truth nor not-truth. Transcending all characteristics is thus all dharmas. 'The Dharma is beyond eye, ear, nose, tongue, body, and mind; the Dharma transcends all contemplation practices.'[158] No-thought is thus no-practice, no-thought is thus no-contemplation. No-thought is thus no-body, no-thought is thus no-mind. No-thought is thus no-nobility, no-thought is thus no-lowliness. No-thought is thus no-high, no-thought is thus no-low. At the time of true no-thought, no-thought itself is not."

When the woman heard his talk, she joined her palms together and told the Venerable, "Your disciple is a woman whose obstructions from transgressions are very weighty, but now that I have heard the Dharma, stain and obstruction are completely eliminated." So saying, she wept grievously, a rain of tears. She then requested a Dharma name, and she was named Liaojianxing (Completely Seeing the Nature). When she had been named, she tonsured herself and donned robes, and became a leader among nuns.

SECTION 31. EXCERPTS AND QUOTATIONS, PART 1 (*T.* 51:192B18–193A15)

"Who repays the Buddha's kindness? One who practices according to the Dharma. Who consumes offerings? One who is not involved in worldly affairs. Who is worthy of offerings? In the Dharma there is nothing that is taken."[159] If one is able to practice in this way, one naturally has offerings from Heaven's kitchen.

The Venerable explained to his disciples, "If one restrains oneself and indulges others, the ten thousand things will all be in harmony. If one restrains others and indulges oneself, the ten thousand things are not [as] oneself."

He also spoke verses:

In a hair's-turn instant of thought, one contemplates self-presence.
Do not debate principles of the Way with fellow students.
Seeing the mirror [nature of the field of cognition], one is none other than a great hero,
but if one is unclear then one is just the same as the mass of beings.

Just cultivate your own practice, do not look at the errors or correctness of others.
If you do not assess others by word or thought, then the three categories of action (thought, word, and deed) are naturally pure.
If you want to see the Buddha land of the mind, everywhere revere suchness nature.

Good sons, when the stingy mind is exhausted,
then the mind of the eye of the Way opens, bright as the sun.
If one has even a hair's-turn of stingy mind,
then the eye of the Way will be covered over.
This is the great pit of darkness,
it cannot be completely plumbed and it is truly difficult to exit.

He also spoke this verse:

Now the quality of my intention is very good;
walking, staying still, sitting, and lying down are all complete.
When seeing there is not a thing to be seen;
in the end there is not a word that can be spoken.
Only attain this quality of intention,
and rest on the high wooden pillow until dawn.[160]

What the Venerable quoted was the complete meaning of the scriptures, the tenetless 'Dharma gate of the mind-ground.' At the same time, he broke down verbal explanation. What the Venerable taught was teaching the unteachable. Now I beg my fellow students to rely only on the essential meaning in practicing, do not become attached to verbal explanation. If one is attached to verbal explanation, then one loses for oneself the [fortunate] allotment of [being able to] practice.

The *Vajracchedikā-sūtra* says: "If you grasp at Dharma characteristics, this is attachment to 'I,' 'others,' and 'beings.' If you grasp at what are not Dharma characteristics, this is attachment to 'I,' 'others,' and 'beings.' For this reason, one ought not grasp at the Dharma, and one ought not grasp at what is not the Dharma. It is because of this essential meaning that the Tathāgata often said, 'All you monks, know that my preaching the Dharma is like the simile of the raft—if even the Dharma ought to be abandoned, how much more so what is not the Dharma?'"[161]

The *Avataṃsaka-sūtra* says: "It is like a poor person day and night counting the treasure of others, himself lacking even a single piece of cash. Amid the Dharma but not practicing—the well versed are also like this. It is like a deaf person setting up musical [instruments]; others hear, but he himself does not hear. Amid the Dharma but not practicing—the well versed are also like this. It is like a blind person setting up a collection of images; others see, but he himself does not see. Amid the Dharma but not practicing—the well versed are also like this. It is like a starving person setting out drink and food; others fill up, but his own belly is empty. Amid the Dharma but not practicing—the well versed are also like this. It is like an oceangoing ship master who is able to cross to the other shore; others go, but he himself does not go. Amid the Dharma but not practicing—the well versed are also like this."[162]

The "*Dhammapada-sūtra*" says, "A person who preaches about food will never be satiated by it."[163]

The *Śūraṃgama-sūtra* says: "Although Ānanda was strong in memorization, he did not avoid falling into wrong views. Awakened contemplation departs from conceptualization, body and mind cannot reach it. To be well versed through successive eons is not equal to one day's practice of non-outflow Dharma."[164]

The *Fangguang jing* says, "When a single thought disturbs *samādhi,* it is like destroying three thousand worlds filled with people. When a single thought is in *samādhi,* it is like reviving three thousand worlds filled with people."[165]

The *Vimalakīrti-sūtra* says, "'The mind does not abide inside, and also does not exist outside—this is quiet sitting. Those who are able to [sit] like this, the buddhas will validate.'[166] 'One cannot teach the Dharma characterized by actuality with the mind of birth-and-death.'[167] 'The Dharma is beyond eye, ear, nose, tongue, body and mind, the Dharma transcends all contemplation practices. Dharma of this character—how could one teach it?'[168] This is why the bodhisattva Manjuśrī praised Vimalakīrti's nonverbal exposition, [saying,] 'This is directly entering the gate of the nondual Dharma.'"[169]

The Venerable explained, "The Dharma of no-thought [is that] the Dharma is fundamentally nonsubjective."

He also said, "Cognizance setting up cognition is thus the origin of ignorance. [But if there is] cognizance without seeing, thinking is then nirvāṇa, absolute purity without outflows."

He also broke down the "knowing" illness: "Knowing practice is also tranquil extinction, this is precisely the Way of bodhi."

He also broke down the "wisdom" illness: "Wisdom seeking after wisdom does not attain wisdom. 'No wisdom and also no attainment; because there is nothing to attain, this is in fact a bodhisattva.'"[170]

He also said, "Perfect bodhi is returning to nothing to attain. 'When there is not the least Dharma that can be attained, this is called *anuttara-samyak-saṃbodhi*.'"[171]

He also broke down the "fundamental" illness: "What is 'fundamental'? All beings are fundamentally pure, fundamentally perfect and complete. Where there is origin there is profit, and because there is profit, the mind gathers and collects. The home of consciousness gains conveniences, and conveniences are thus the cycle of birth-and-death. Fundamental transcendence transcends 'other,' thus there is nothing on which to depend. Self and other both profit, you achieve Buddha awakening. The Buddha does not have the characteristic of the roots of the field of sense-cognition; not-seeing is called seeing the Buddha 'in the midst of ultimate emptiness, gloriously established.'"[172]

He also broke down the "purity" illness, "nirvāṇa" illness, "spontaneity" illness, "realization" illness, "contemplation" illness, "dhyāna" illness, and "Dharma" illness: "One who abides in 'this' has the illness of abiding in this. The Dharma is neither stained nor pure; nor is there any nirvāṇa or Buddha; the Dharma transcends contemplation practice. 'Transcendently sitting on dewy ground, the factor of consciousness (*vijñāṇa-skandha*) [attains] final liberation (*parinirvāṇa*).'[173] 'One far transcends realization as something realized.'[174] 'Not entering *samādhi,* not abiding in seated meditation, the mind is without gain or loss.'"[175]

He also broke down the "one" illness: "'Even "one" is not as one, as one it breaks down all numbers.'[176] 'Once "one" root returns to the source, the six roots attain release.'[177] 'If you determine it in "one" place, there is nothing that is not differentiated.'[178] 'Everything around you on up to the ten thousand appearances is imprinted by one Dharma.'[179] '"One" fundamentally does not arise, and the three functions have no actualization.'[180] 'When the mind does not calculate, this is energetic great contemplation.'[181] 'All of you ought to transcend [notions of] self and others; "self" is one's own nature, "other" is deluded thinking.'[182] When deluded thinking does not arise, then this is transcending both self and other, achieving Buddha awakening."

SECTION 32. EXCERPTS AND QUOTATIONS, PART 2 (*T.* 51:193A15–B2)

The Venerable always said, "If there is a karmic cause it will penetrate a thousand *li;* if there is no cause, then even people facing each other will not recognize each other. When one is only conscious of the Dharma, this in none other than 'seeing the Buddha,' and this is all the scriptures of complete meaning."

When the Venerable took his seat, he usually taught the precepts to all those studying the Way. Fearing that they would get attached to verbal explanation, from time to time he would quote the crabs in the paddy field and ask about it, but the assembly didn't understand.

He also quoted Brahmacarya Wang's poem:

The eye of wisdom is close to the mind of emptiness,
not the holes that open into your skull.
You don't recognize what [the person] facing you says,
it doesn't matter that your mother's surname is respectable.[183]

There were some old men who told the Venerable, "We, your disciples, have wives and children, and young male and female household dependents. We wish to give them up entirely and submit to the Venerable and study the Way."

The Venerable said, "The Way does not have any particular form that can be cultivated, the Dharma does not have any particular form that can be validated. Just unrestricted no-recollection and no-thought, at all times everything is the Way." He asked the old men, "Do you get it?" The old men were silent and did not answer, because they didn't understand. The Venerable expounded a verse: "Your wife is an earless shackle, your young are rattling manacles. You are a worthless slave, you have reached old age and cannot escape."

Another time, some masters and monks of Jiannan wanted to go to [Wu]tai shan to pay obeisance, and they took their leave of the Venerable. The Venerable asked, "Worthies, where are you going?"

The monks replied, "To pay our respects to Mañjuśrī."

The Venerable said, "Worthies, the Buddha is in body and mind, Mañjuśrī is not far. When deluded thoughts are not produced, this is none other than 'seeing the Buddha.' Why take the trouble to go so far?" The masters and monks wanted to leave. The Venerable expounded a verse for them: "Lost children restlessly dashing like waves, circling the mountain and paying obeisance to a pile of earth. Mañjuśrī is right here; you are climbing the Buddha's back to search for Amitābha."

SECTION 33. TEA VERSE (*T.* 51:193B2–19)

Once when the Venerable was drinking tea, [a party of] thirty directors and censors of the secretariat came to pay their respects, and when they had done this they took seats and asked, "Venerable, you really love tea, don't you?"

The Venerable said, "Yes." Then he recited a tea verse for them:

The obscure valley produces the mysterious herb
that serves as a medium for entering the Way.
Woodcutters gather its leaves,
the delicious flavor flows into an earthen vessel.
It tranquilizes worries and clarifies void consciousness,
brightens the mind and illuminates the terrace of understanding.
Without wearing down one's vital energy,
it directly moves the Dharma gates to open.[184]

Upon hearing this the directors asked, "Venerable, why do you not teach people to read scriptures, recollect the Buddha, and perform devotions? We, your disciples, do not understand."

The Venerable said, "One validates final nirvāṇa for oneself; I also teach others like this. Do not hold onto the Tathāgata's incomplete teaching. Returning to one's own understanding, self-awakening initiates training. The buddhas validate this person as one who has attained true *samādhi*."

When the Venerable finished speaking, [he sat there] majestic and unmoving. The directors and censors sighed together, "This is something we haven't encountered!" They asked, "Venerable, why do you not teach the phenomenal forms of the Dharma?"

The Venerable replied, "'The subtle principle of the Mahāyāna reaches principle's empty extent. Beings involved in conditionality are unable to enter it.'[185] The teachings of the scriptures point to the fundamental nature of beings. Seeing the nature is thus the Way of becoming a buddha; attachment to characteristics is thus sinking into the cycle [of birth and death]. 'When the mind is produced then the various dharmas are produced, when the mind is extinguished then the various dharmas are extinguished.'[186] Transmitting the scriptures and performing devotions are all arousals of the mind. Arousing the mind is precisely birth and death, not arousing the mind is precisely seeing the Buddha."

They asked further, "If the Venerable teaches by relying on this, do people get it?"

The Venerable said, "They do. Arousing the mind is precisely defilements, movement of thought is precisely the demons' net. 'All dharmas involved in conditionality are like the froth of dream visions, like dew and like lightning. You ought to contemplate them thus.'"[187] When the officials heard his talk, the net of doubt was suddenly removed. All together, they said they would become his disciples.

SECTION 34. DIALOGUE WITH DAOISTS (*T.* 51:193B20–194A20)

Another time [Wuzhu was visited by] scores of Daoist priests and scores of recluses, and also twenty Dharma Masters, Vinaya Masters, and Treatise Masters. They were all "collars and sleeves" (leading figures) in Jiannan.

The Venerable asked the Daoists, "'The Way that can be spoken/trodden is not the constant Way, the names that can be named are not the constant names.'[188] Is this not what Laojun (Laozi) taught?"

The Daoists answered, "It is."

The Venerable said, "Do you, Honored Masters, understand the meaning or not?" The Daoists were silent and did not reply.

The Venerable further asked [about the meaning of]: "'To undertake learning one increases day by day, to undertake the Way one decreases day by day. Decreasing it and further decreasing it, one finally arrives at nondoing. In nondoing, there is nothing that is not done.'"[189]

He also asked, "The *Zhuangzi* (Book of Master Zhuang) says, 'That which produces life is not born, that which destroys life does not die.' [What does this mean?]"[190] None of the Daoists dared reply. The Venerable said, "Among Daoists nowadays, not one studies Laojun, they only study vilification of the Buddha." When the Daoists heard this, they lost color and joined their palms together.

The Venerable then asked the recluses, "Did not Confucius explain the *Yijing* (Book of Changes)?"

The recluses answered, "Yes, he did."

The Venerable further asked, "Did not Confucius teach benevolence, righteousness, propriety, wisdom, and faith?"[191]

They answered, "He did."

The Venerable asked, "What about the [cardinal meaning of] the *Yijing*?" The recluses were all speechless. The Venerable then expounded for them: "The *Yijing* says, 'Nonconceiving and nondoing, tranquil and unmoving; stimulated, the [response] that follows pervades all.'[192] What is the meaning of this?" The recluses dared not reply.

The Venerable explained further, "In the *Yijing*, 'Not transforming, not changing' is the fundamental nature of beings. 'Nonconceiving, nondoing, tranquil and unmoving' is the fundamental nature of beings. If one does not transform and does not change, does not conceptualize and does not imagine, this is the practice of benevolence, righteousness, propriety, wisdom, and faith. These days scholars do not see fundamental nature, they do not recognize host and guest. They concentrate on sense-objects and take this as scholarly inquiry, a great mistake. Confucius explained nonconceiving and nondoing, [he had] great discernment."

The recluses asked the Venerable, "'Stimulated, the [response] that follows pervades all'—what does this mean?"

The Venerable replied, "If the Brahmaloka is not sought, the Brahmaloka is reached of itself; if karmic reward is not sought, karmic reward is reached of itself.[193] The defilements are completely exhausted, the seeds [in the storehouse consciousness] are also removed, and Brahma, Indra, the *nāgas* and *devas* are all moved to do reverence. For this reason, when the Tathāgata entered a town to eat, all the grasses and trees bowed their heads, and all the mountains and rivers leaned toward the Buddha. How much more so the many beings? This is 'stimulated, the [response] that follows pervades all.'" The recluses all made obeisance to the Venerable at once, and all desired to become his disciples.

The Venerable further questioned the Daoists, saying, "'When those of high virtue do not lose virtue, it is because of having virtue. When those of low virtue do not lose virtue, it is because of being without virtue.'[194] What does this mean?"

The Daoists said, "Please, Venerable, explain it for us."

The Venerable explained, "A person of high virtue has a mind of 'nothing to attain.' 'Because there is nothing to attain, this is in fact 'a bodhisattva.' [195] 'When there is not the least Dharma that can be attained, this is called '*anuttara-samyak-saṃbodhi*.'[196] This is the meaning of high virtue. [As for] 'When those of low virtue do not lose virtue, it is because of being without virtue'; a person of low virtue is one who seeks something. If one seeks something then one has defilements. The mind of defilements is precisely 'losing virtue.' This is the meaning of 'losing virtue.'"

He went on, "[Regarding] 'To undertake learning one increases day by day.' If one has the mind of learning this only adds to the defilements of birth-and-death, and this is not 'increase.'

"[Regarding] 'To undertake the Way, one decreases day by day. Decreasing it and further decreasing it, one finally arrives at nondoing. In nondoing, there is nothing that is not done.' The Way is fundamental nature. Reaching the Way cuts off words, deluded thoughts are not produced, and this is precisely 'decreasing it.' When one contemplates the Mind King, one parts with everything altogether, and this is 'further decreasing it.'

"[Regarding] 'One finally arrives at nondoing'—when one experiences the emptiness of the nature in nirvāṇa, this Dharma is at this time seen. 'In nondoing, there is nothing that is not done'—this means not abiding in nondoing. Practicing nonarising, one does not make nonarising into evidence. Practicing in emptiness, one does not make emptiness into evidence, and this is the meaning of 'nothing that is not done.'"

[The Venerable continued,] "Furthermore, [as for] Zhuangzi saying, 'that which produces life is not born.' When deluded thoughts do not arise, this is precisely 'not born.' [Regarding] 'That which destroys life does not die.' The meaning of 'does not die' is precisely 'unborn.'"

[The Venerable] went on, "[Regarding] 'the Way that can be spoken is not the constant Way.' This is precisely the fundamental nature of beings. Verbal explanation does not reach it, thus this is 'not the constant Way.' 'The names that can be named are not the constant names' is also the fundamental nature of beings. 'With only verbal explanation there is no true meaning at all,'[197] 'only names, only characters.'[198] The Dharma cannot be explained, this [is the meaning of] 'not the constant names.'"

When the Daoists had heard his talk, they joined their palms and asked the Venerable, "If one explains it like this, then this means 'Buddhism and Daoism are not two.'"

The Venerable said, "Not so. Zhuangzi and Laozi covered nondoing and no-characteristics, the one, purity, and spontaneity. The Buddha is not like this, he taught that both causation and spontaneity are idle theories. 'All worthies and saints accord with the Dharma of nondoing, yet there are differences.'[199] The Buddha thus does not abide in nondoing and does not abide in no-characteristics. Abiding in no characteristics, one does not see the Mahāyāna. People of the two vehicles are drunk on the wine of *samādhi,* and common people are drunk on the wine of ignorance. Śrāvakas abide in the wisdom of complete [removal of defilements]. Pratyekabuddhas abide in the wisdom of tranquil purity. The Tathāgata's wisdom keeps arising without depletion. Zhuangzi, Laozi, and Confucius's teachings are to be lumped together with those of the śrāvakas. The Buddha rebuked the śrāvakas, [saying they were] as if blind, as if deaf. 'Stream-entrants, once-returners, nonreturners, and arhats are all saints, yet their minds are completely deluded.'[200] The Buddha thus does not sink into the crowd, but transcends all. The Dharma is without stain or purity, the Dharma is without form or feature, the Dharma is without restless disturbance, the Dharma is without a location, the Dharma is without grasping or discarding. Therefore it transcends Confucius, Zhuangzi, and Laozi. 'The Buddha is always in the world, yet is not stained by worldly dharmas. Due to not separating "the world" [from the ultimate], we do reverence without having anything to contemplate.'[201] What Confucius and Laozi taught all had something attached. All of it is the sphere of śrāvakas, the two vehicles." The Daoists did obeisance, and all of them became his disciples. With silent faith they received [the opportunity to] listen to the Dharma.

SECTION 35. DIALOGUE WITH DHARMA MASTERS (*T.* 51:194A20–194B1)

He asked the Dharma Masters, "What is the Buddha-Jewel, what is the Dharma-Jewel, what is the Saṅgha-Jewel?"

The Dharma Masters were silent and did not speak. The Venerable explained, "Knowing the Dharma is precisely the Buddha-Jewel, transcending characteristics is precisely the Dharma-Jewel, and nondoing is precisely the Saṅgha-Jewel."[202]

He also asked the Dharma Masters, "The Dharma is without verbal explanation, how does one explain the Dharma? 'One who explains the Dharma does so without explaining and without manifestation. Those who listen to the Dharma do so without hearing and without obtaining.'[203] 'That there is no Dharma that can be explained is called explaining the Dharma.'[204] 'Those who always know that the Tathāgata does not explain the Dharma are called complete hearers [of the Dharma].'[205] How do the Dharma masters explain the Dharma?"

A Dharma Master replied, "There are three kinds of *prajñā*. One is the *prajñā* of texts and characters, the second is the *prajñā* characterized by actuality, and the third is the *prajñā* of contemplating radiance."[206]

The Venerable replied, "'Texts and characters have nothing actual and nothing on which to depend. Altogether unified in tranquil extinction, fundamentally there is nothing that moves.'[207] 'My Dharma is without actuality and without void.'[208] 'The Dharma transcends all contemplation practice.'"[209] The Dharma masters all looked at one another, unable to say a word.

SECTION 36. DIALOGUE WITH VINAYA MASTERS (*T.* 51:194B1–194C15)

The Venerable asked the Vinaya Masters, "What are the Vinaya precepts? What is *Vinayaviniścaya* and what is *Vinayottara*?[210] What is the substance of the precepts, and what is the meaning of the Vinaya?" None of the Vinaya Masters dared answer. The Venerable asked the Vinaya Masters, "Do you recognize host and guest or not?"

The Vinaya Masters said, "We request the Venerable to explain the meaning of 'host and guest' for us."

The Venerable replied, "Coming and going is 'guest,' not coming and going is 'host.' If conceptualizations are not produced, then there is neither host nor guest, and this is precisely 'seeing the nature.' The 'thousand thoughts and ten thousand anxieties'[211] do not benefit the principle of the Way, and merely due to agitation one loses the fundamental Mind King. If there are no thoughts and anxieties then there is no birth-and-death.

"The significance of the Vinaya is to regulate and subdue, and the precepts are not blue, yellow, red, or white. Not color/desire and not mind, this is the substance of precepts, this is the fundamental nature of beings, fundamentally complete, fundamentally pure. When deluded thoughts are produced, then one 'turns away from awakening and adheres to dust,'[212] and this is precisely 'violating the Vinaya precepts.' When deluded thoughts are not produced, then one turns away from dust and adheres to awakening, and this is precisely 'fulfilling the Vinaya precepts.' When thoughts are not produced, this is precisely *Vinayottara;* when thoughts are not produced, this is precisely *Vinayaviniścaya.* When thoughts are not produced, this is precisely destroying all mind consciousnesses. 'If one has views of upholding the precepts then one violates the precepts. Whether 'precepts' or 'not precepts,' the two views are a single characteristic. One who is able to know this is a great Master of the Way.'[213] 'One sees that the monks who commit grave offenses do not fall into hell, and sees that those who practice purity do not enter nirvāṇa. If you abide in views like these, this is impartial seeing.'[214]

"These days Vinaya Masters preach about [sense] 'contact' and preach about 'purity,' preach about 'upholding' and preach about 'violating.' They make forms for receiving the precepts, they make forms for decorum, and even for eating food—everything is made into forms. 'If one makes forms, then one is the same as non-Buddhist [practitioners of] the five supramundane powers. If one does not make forms, this is precisely the unconditioned. One ought not have views.'[215] False concepts are defilement, having no false concepts is purity. Grasping 'I' is defilement, not grasping 'I' is purity. Turning things upside down is defilement, not turning things upside down is purity. 'Upholding' and 'violating' are merely restraining the body, and it is not the body that has nothing to restrain. Unless there is nothing whatsoever, how does one capture absolutely everything? 'If what one preaches is all about upholding the precepts, one has neither goodness nor decorum. The nature of the precepts is like emptiness, and those who uphold them are confounded by them.'[216] 'When mind is produced then various dharmas are produced, when the mind is extinguished then various dharmas are extinguished.'[217] 'As one's mind is, so also are the stains of wrongdoing, so also are all dharmas.'[218]

"Nowadays Vinaya Masters are only motivated by fame and benefits. Like cats stalking mice, they take mincing steps and creep along, seeing 'true' and seeing 'false' with their self-styled precepts practice. This is really the extinction of the Buddha-Dharma, it is not the practice of the *śramaṇa.* The *Laṅkāvatāra-sūtra* says, 'In generations to come there will be those whose bodies wear the *kāṣāya,* [but who] delusively preach 'being' and 'nonbeing' and harm my true Dharma.'[219] In generations to come, in my Dharma [there will be those who] having left home delusively preach the Vinaya and ruin the true Dharma. Better that one should destroy *śīla,* and not destroy true seeing. *Śīla* [causes] rebirth in Heaven, adding more [karmic] bonds, while true seeing attains nirvāṇa." Hearing his talk, the Vinaya Masters looked frightened and lost color, got shaky and uneasy.

The Venerable expounded again, "'Transcending characteristics and extinguishing characteristics, forever the characteristic of tranquil extinction, finally returning home to emptiness.'[220] 'Always completely enter the practice of empty tranquility.'[221] 'The Buddha Treasury [of scriptures numerous as] the Ganges sands are completely understood in a single thought.'[222] The Buddha only permitted five years of study of the Vinaya precepts. After five years [the disciple was to] abandon Hīnayāna masters and seek Mahāyāna masters, and study the Dharma of no 'others' or 'self.' If [disciples] did not [practice] like this, the Buddha would severely rebuke them."[223]

When the Vinaya Masters heard this, the web of doubt was suddenly removed, and they told the Venerable, "We petty masters have transmitted deceptions for a long time. [Now] we utterly forsake the precepts and Vinaya and we humbly beg that you compassionately accept us." They made obeisances in unison, weeping a rain of tears.

The Venerable said, "[As for] not-recollecting and not-thinking, [this means] not-recollecting any Dharma at all, not-recollecting either the Buddha-Dharma or worldly dharmas, so much at ease." He asked, "Do you get it?"

The Vinaya Masters said in unison, "We get it."

The Venerable said, "When you truly get it, then you will indeed be genuine Vinaya Masters, and this is precisely 'seeing the nature.' At the time of true seeing, seeing is like transcendence of seeing. When seeing is inadequate, this is precisely 'seeing the Buddha.' At the time of true seeing, even seeing itself is not."

The Venerable expounded for them for them yet again, "Arousing the mind is precisely defilement, movement of thought is precisely the demons' net. So much at ease, not sinking and not floating, not flowing and not revolving, lively like a fish jumping! At all times, everything is meditation." When the Vinaya Masters had heard they leaped with joy, [then] sat silently listening.

SECTION 37. DIALOGUE WITH TREATISE MASTERS (*T.* 51:194C16–195A2)

The Venerable asked the Dharma Masters and Treatise Masters, "What branch of study do you pursue?"

The Treatise Masters replied, "We explicate the *Baifa [lun]* (Treatise on One Hundred Dharmas)."[224]

The Venerable expounded, "Explicating the one hundred Dharmas is one hundred separate calculations,[225] and not explicating at all is no-calculation. No-calculation is thus no-thought. No-thought is thus no-receiving, no-thought is thus no-self, no-thought is thus no-other. It is because beings have thought that one provisionally teaches no-thought, but at the time of true no-thought, no-thought itself is not."

He further questioned the Treatise Masters, "What other scriptures and treatises do you explicate?"

They replied, "We explicate the *Treatise on the Awakening of Faith*."

The Venerable said, "Arousing is precisely not faith, faith is precisely not arousing." He further questioned the Treatise Masters, "What do you take to be 'doctrine'?" The Treatise Masters did not speak.

The Venerable said, "The *Treatise* takes destroying the false and displaying the true as 'doctrine.'[226] The *Treatise* says, 'Transcending the characteristic of verbal explanation, transcending the characteristic of names and characters, transcending the characteristic of mind and causes.'[227] 'Transcending the characteristic of thought is equal to void emptiness; in the entire Dharmadhatu, there is nowhere that is not encompassed.'[228] Nowadays Treatise

Masters merely explicate verbal prescriptions. They do not recognize host and guest, and they explicate scriptures and treatises with the mind of the flux of birth and death, a great error. The treatises saying 'transcend verbal explanation' are in fact [performing] attachment to verbal explanation; [saying] 'transcend names and characters' is in fact [performing] attachment to names and characters. [It is like] only explicating an impure [diet] of dumplings, and not knowing the simple [diet] of jujube.

"The *Laṅkāvatāra-sūtra* says: 'As for the revolving of the mind, this really makes for frivolous treatises. If one does not give rise to distinctions, this person sees his own mind.'[229] 'With no consciousness and discrimination, and no perception and volition, then one fully brings down all heterodoxies.'[230] 'Thoroughly penetrating all Dharma characteristics without hindrance, one bows one's head to the ground like emptiness, without anything on which to depend.'"[231] When the Treatise Masters heard his talk, they joined their palms and made obeisance.

SECTION 38. TRADING QUOTATIONS WITH MASTERS DAOYOU, MINGFA, AND GUANLU (*T.* 51:195A2–12)

There were also Master Daoyou, Master Mingfa, and Master Guanlu. Their Dharma names had long been passed down. They asked the Venerable about a passage: "The *Chanshi jing* says, 'Attachment to the taste of meditation is the bondage of the bodhisattva.'"[232]

The Venerable replied, "That Dharma Masters grasp after characteristics and are attached to characteristics is the bondage of the many beings."

[The masters went on,] "Another scripture says, 'People of dull roots and shallow wisdom, those arrogant ones attached to characteristics—regarding this type, how can one say that they can be saved?'"[233]

The Venerable said, "A scripture says, 'Transcending characteristics and extinguishing characteristics, forever the characteristic of tranquil extinction.'[234] Vinaya Masters and Dharma Masters all disregard the Buddha's teachings. They are attached to characteristics and grasp after characteristics, misrecognize sense objects, and take this as scholarly inquiry. It is like a dog chasing clods of earth—the clods just increase. I, Wuzhu, am not like that. I am like a lion who leaves the clods and goes after the person [throwing them], and the clods then cease on their own.[235] Conceptualizations are noisily active and destroy one's good roots. Awakening to one's nature in peaceful meditation is thus non-outflow wisdom. 'If one seeks after external characteristics, endless eons go by and in the end one is unable to attain [wisdom].'[236] In inner awakened contemplation, in an instant one attains *anuttara-samyak-saṃbodhi.*"

SECTION 39. TAKING ON CHAN DISCIPLES WHILE DRINKING TEA (*T.* 51:195A12–29)

Another time there were Master Guangjing, Master Wuyou, Master Daoyan, and Master Dazhi. All of the above were disciples of Chan Master Jiancheng. They came to the Venerable and sat down. The Venerable was drinking tea at the time. Master Wuyou said to the Venerable, "Drinking three or five cups of tea and sitting with eyes closed. . . . Just like a strong fellow grabbing an emaciated man by the waist, it seems rather affected and pretentious."

The Venerable told Master Wuyou, "Don't indulge in idle talk. You didn't eat mud dumplings in the famine of the Yongchun era (682–683).'"[237] (I.e., "You young whippersnapper.") Wuyou heard this and lost color.

The Venerable said, "You, Master So-and-So, bring a worldly, birth-and-death mind to try to fathom Chan—really stupid. This [illustrates] 'a kick from a *hastināga* is not something an ass can bear.'"[238]

The Venerable told Master Wuyou, "Wuzhu will tell you a story. There was a man standing on a high earthen mound. A number of people were traveling along the road together, and from afar they saw the man standing on the high place. They talked about it among themselves. [One man said,] 'This man surely has lost an animal.' One man said, 'He lost his group.' One man said, 'He's enjoying the coolness of the wind.' The three argued together without deciding. They reached the high place and asked the man on the mound, 'Did you lose an animal?' He replied, "No, I didn't.' Again they asked, 'Did you lose your group?' But neither had he lost his group. Again they asked, 'Were you enjoying the coolness of the wind?' But neither was he enjoying the coolness of the wind. [They asked,] 'Then if it is none of these, why are you standing up high on the mound?' He replied, 'I'm just standing.'"

The Venerable told Master Wuyou, "Wuzhu's Chan is not sinking and not floating, not flowing and not fixed, but it truly has function. It functions without birth or tranquil [extinction], functions without stain or purity, and functions without 'is' or 'is not.' Lively like a fish jumping; at all times, everything is meditation."

SECTION 40. DIALOGUE WITH MASTER XIONGJUN (*T.* 51:195A29–B3)

There was Dharma Master Xiongjun, who asked, "Venerable, does a Chan Master enter meditation?"

The Venerable said, "In meditation there is neither exiting nor entering."

[Master Xiongjun] asked, "Does a Chan Master enter *samādhi*?"

[The Venerable] replied, "'Not entering *samādhi*, not abiding in seated meditation, the mind is without gain or loss.'[239] At all times, everything is meditation."

SECTION 41. DIALOGUE WITH MASTER FAYUAN, ACCOMPANIED BY HIS MOTHER (*T.* 51:195B3–22)

There was also Master Fayuan of Longyou (Shaanxi), whose secular surname was Lü. From afar he heard of the Venerable and, bringing his mother along with him, arrived at the Baiya mountains and made obeisance to the Venerable.[240] The Venerable asked, "On which scriptures and treatises do you lecture?"

He replied, "I lecture on the *Diamond Sūtra*."

The Venerable asked, "Whose commentaries and treatises do you use?'

He replied, "I use the treatises by Vasubandhu and Asaṅga,[241] and the commentaries of Masters Hui, Tan, and Da."

The Venerable asked, "The sūtra says, 'The Dharma of all the buddhas and all the buddhas' *anuttara-samyak-saṃbodhi* (unsurpassed enlightenment) come from this scripture.'[242] What is this scripture? Is it *tāla* tree leaves,[243] is it ink, is it paper?"

Master Fayuan replied, "The *prajñā* characterized by actuality, the *prajñā* of contemplating radiance, and the *prajñā* of texts and characters."[244]

The Venerable told Master Fayuan, "'Texts and characters have nothing actual and nothing on which to depend. Altogether unified in tranquil extinction, fundamentally there is nothing that moves.'[245] 'The Dharma transcends all contemplation practice.'[246] The sūtra says, 'My Dharma is without actuality and without void.'[247] 'If anyone says the Tathāgata preached any Dharma, then they slander the Buddha.'"[248]

The Dharma master replied, "I rely on the explanations of essays and commentaries."

The Venerable said to Master Fayuan, "The [treatises of] Vasubandhu and Asaṅga, and the commentaries of Hui and Tan, et al.—are they as good as the Buddha's explanations?"

Master Fayuan replied, "They are not."

The Venerable said, "Since they are not as good, why don't you rely on the Buddha's teachings? The sūtra says, 'Transcendence of all characteristics is precisely called the Buddha.'[249] 'Someone who sees "I" through form and seeks "I" through sounds is taking a false path, and is unable to see the Tathāgata.'[250] The words of this scripture are none other than this mind. Seeing the nature is the Way of becoming a Buddha. No-thought is thus seeing the nature, no-thought is no-defilements. No-thought is thus no-self, no-thought is thus no-other. No-thought is thus no-Buddha, no-thought is no-beings. At the time of true no-thought, no-thought itself is not."

When Master Fayuan heard this, he joined his palms and said to the Venerable, "I am exceedingly glad that I have been able to meet the Venerable. Fayuan and his aged relative (my mother and I) humbly beg you to compassionately accept us." And so they stayed in the mountains and never left [the Venerable's] side.

SECTION 42. DISCOURSE TO LAY DONORS (*T.* 51:195B23–C13)

[The Venerable said,] "In the Prajñāpāramitā, one does not see the one who repays the kindness, nor does one see the one who does the kindness. I, Wuzhu, practice unconditioned compassion, practice desireless compassion, practice not-grasping compassion, and practice causeless compassion. It is neither that nor this, I do not practice upper, middle, and lower Dharma, do not practice 'conditioned and unconditioned' or 'real and unreal' Dharma. It is not for the sake of increase and not for the sake of decrease, there is no great good fortune and no small good fortune. With nothing that is received, one yet receives all that is received. In the uncompleted Buddha-Dharma, there is also no end to receiving. 'If you want to confess and repent, sit properly and contemplate the characteristic of actuality.'[251] No-thought is thus the characteristic of actuality, thought is thus empty delusion. Confessing and repenting and intoning prayers, all this is empty delusion."

The Venerable expounded, "'Who repays the Buddha's kindness? One who practices according to the Dharma. Who is worthy to receive offerings? One who is not involved in worldly affairs. Who consumes offerings? In the Dharma there is nothing that is taken.'[252] No-thought is thus no-taking, no-thought is thus no-discarding. No-thought is thus no-stain, no-thought is thus no-purity. No-thought is thus no-bonds, no-thought is thus no-ties. No-thought is thus no-self, no-thought is thus no-other. At the time of true no-thought, no-thought itself is not. No-thought is thus Prajñāpāramitā. 'Prajñāpāramitā is the mantra of great spirit, is the mantra of great illumination, the unsurpassed mantra, the unequaled mantra. It is able to do away with all suffering, it is true reality and not void.'[253]

"How about if you *dānapati* (lay donors) root out the source of delusory views and awaken to your unborn substance? Like the roiling of thick clouds and the sun of bright wisdom, the veil of karma will suddenly roll back. Cut delusory conceptualization by emptying the mind, tranquilly not moving. The meaning of *tathātā* is neither principle nor phenomena, it is unborn and undying, it is not moving and not still. If one experiences the twin illumination of the Two Truths, then one truly sees the Buddha. If you *dānapati* would only rely on this Dharma this instant without delay, then even if the border is closed and we are kept far apart, we will always see each other without any alienation. If you dare disregard this meaning, you will be swept along by sense defilements, anxieties and strife will be produced, and the stain of arrogance will be unlimited. Then, though we might often be face to face, it is as difficult to meet as [it is for] the states of Chu and Yue."[254]

SECTION 43. PORTRAIT-EULOGY AND FINAL SCENE (*T.* 51:195C15–196B6)

ACCOUNT OF THE VENERABLE OF THE DALI BAO TANG MONASTERY

Portrait-eulogy, with preface, composed for a disciple of the Chan teachings of sudden awakening in the Mahāyāna.

The mountain man Sun Huan states: "'The Dao is nameless,'[255] those who awaken to the Dao only then know they have attained the origin. The Dharma is without characteristics, those who recognize the Dharma then penetrate its source. Attaining the origin is thus the Dao, and one knows that the substance of the Dao is wondrous being and birthlessness. Recognizing the Dharma is thus the source, and one sees that the nature of the Dharma is perfect luminosity and spontaneity. Existence is without anything that exists, existence is not orientation to 'that' or 'this.' Birth is without anything that is born, birth is not the limit of being or nonbeing.

"Because the twelve divisions of Dharma[256] that Śākyamuni Buddha preached are complete in the mind, his exposition is without anything that is expounded. Our Venerable, as he pointed out the eighty thousand gates of the mound of dust,[257] was directly teaching 'seeing the nature,' and so he pointed without anything at which to point. How well he knew that the Dharma transcends the Dharma of verbal explanation, yet it is not that verbal explanation does not illuminate. The Dharma transcends seeing and hearing, but it is not that the Dharma is not manifest in seeing and hearing. 'Rely on words to make the meaning manifest, and having gotten the meaning, forget the words.'[258] Thus, those who follow verbal explanations manifest words and forget the Dharma, while on the contrary those who see and hear forget the words and manifest the Dharma. Without words there is no 'I,' without 'I' there is nondoing. The substance of nondoing is suchness, the principle of suchness is not one; not one and not self, this is truly bodhi. 'Peerless pure bright mind pervades the Dharmadhātu.'[259]

"Just so did our Venerable ground his teachings and transmit his Dharma. He displayed the meaning of no-thought, not moving and not still. He expounded the teaching of sudden awakening, no-recollection, and no-thought. He often told his disciples, 'The Dharma is just this, it is not something verbal explanation can reach. Our Ancestral Master Dharmatrāta (Bodhidharma) transmitted these essentials of the Dharma, passed from legitimate heir to legitimate heir. It is the secret teaching of the buddhas, it is the Prajñāpāramitā. It is also called the number one meaning, the nondual gate, seeing the nature, suchness, nirvāṇa, and the Chan teachings. Names such as these are the provisional teachings of the tathāgatas of the past, but the meaning of true reality has no name.'

"Sometimes we disciples, obtaining the teaching and practicing according to his explanation, would get a taste of it. Then we would sigh to each other,

'How magnificent! It is like gazing at the empty expanse of the great void, without particle or speck of dust. How oceanic! It is as if looking out over the utter limitlessness of the vast deep, without boundary or shore. Words cannot touch deeply knowing the Dao, subtle mystery, nameless. We are full of gratitude toward our Great Master for having pity on our delusion and dullness, for showing us the true Dharma not through gradual steps but directly arriving at bodhi. If we meet other students we should turn about and show [the true Dharma], but without the characteristics of our master, how are we to manifest it?'

"Accordingly, we secretly summoned a fine artist to paint [the Venerable's] portrait. His appearance is lustrous, his characteristics are fine and successfully rendered. Those who gaze at the portrait are able to destroy evil, those who rely on the Dharma are able to attain the mystery. The deeper places [of his Dharma] I have not yet fathomed. Bowing my head to the ground and raising my gaze with reverence, I exert my strength to speak this eulogy:

"The highest vehicle of the Dharma is neither principle nor phenomena. The many gates of the good teaching all return to nonduality. [Mahā]kāśyapa attained it, and it spread westward to buddha-regions; [Bodhi]dharma received it, and it flowed eastward to the land of the Han. These are matters spanning over one thousand years; the Holy Ones for thirty-four generations have passed it from legitimate heir to legitimate heir, from one generation to the next. The Dharma they obtained tallies with the Dao's source, the robe they transmitted clearly shows true and false. Our teacher secretly received it and graciously displayed it, opening the secret mysterious gates of the buddhas and revealing the complete meaning of the Mahāyāna. Not following conditionality, not relying on *avyākṛta*,[260] transcending qualities and characteristics, not 'dull' and not 'wise,' the true meaning is not being or nonbeing, being and nonbeing are not the true meaning. Contrary to the mind of the ordinary man, going beyond the intent of the virtuous Holy Ones, [our] practice exceeds the three vehicles and suddenly leaps over the ten stages of the bodhisattva path. It is neither cause nor result, it has neither other nor self. 'It functions without birth or tranquil [extinction],' reflection and substance are altogether transcended. Seeing is without bright or dark; no-thought is precisely this.

"Accordingly we summoned the fine artist; secretly he made the painting. [The artist] brandished his brush and produced the characteristics, and gazing at the majestic response body transcending characteristics and emptied of words, we see the expansive vessel of the Dharma. His attainments are like Heaven's gifts, his bones (i.e., intrinsic qualities) are not like those of this world. How silently mysterious and fine! [The portrait] seems to be truly breathing, the face quivers and wants to speak, the eyes dance and are about to see. 'I look up and it is ever loftier, I venerate and it is ever more dear.'[261] Without our master, this Dharma will sink."

On the third day of the sixth month of the ninth year of the Dali era (774), [the Venerable] told his disciples, "Bring me a fresh, clean robe, I wish to bathe." When he had bathed and put on the robe, he asked his disciples, "Is it the time of abstinence (i.e., noon) yet?"

They answered, "Yes."

He bound all his disciples to a promise: "If you are filial, obedient children you will not disobey my teachings. I am at the point of the great practice. After I am gone you are not to knit your brows [in distress], you are not to act like worldly and untrained people. Those who weep, wear mourning garments, and knit their brows shall not be called my disciples. Weeping is precisely the way of the world; the Buddha-Dharma is not thus. 'Transcending all characteristics; this is precisely seeing the Buddha.'"[262]

When he finished speaking, he passed away while remaining in a seated position. The Great Master's springs and autumns amounted to sixty-one.

Lidai fabao ji, in one fascicle.

NOTES

1. INTRODUCTION TO THE *LIDAI FABAO JI* AND MEDIEVAL CHINESE BUDDHISM

1. Zen is the Japanese form of Chan, which is the Chinese transliteration of the Sanskrit word *dhyāna*, meditation.
2. The contrasting term, Hīnayāna (Lesser Vehicle), was coined by the Mahāyānists, who claimed that the early Buddhist followers were only concerned with their own liberation.
3. *Lidai fabao ji, T.* 2075, 51:180c19–23 (Translation Section 4).
4. Yampolsky 1967:130.
5. Yampolsky 1967:132; there is also an alternative version of this verse included in the early *Platform Sūtra.*

2. QUESTIONING WUZHU'S TRANSMISSION

1. *Lidai fabao ji, T.* 2075, 51:194a20–23 (Translation Section 35).
2. *Dīghanikāya* II. 16.2.26. See Walshe, trans., 1995:245.
3. Modification of Yampolsky 1967:146; Dunhuang text 10.
4. Modification of Yampolsky 1967:152; Dunhuang text 14.
5. Modification of Yampolsky 1967:145; Dunhuang text 10.
6. *Dunwu wushang banruo song,* S. 468. In Hu Shi 1970:195.
7. *Da Tang xiyu ji, T.* 2087, 51:919b24–c24.
8. Weiner 1992.

9. Penkower 2000:245–296.
10. Jorgensen 1987:89–133.
11. *Lidai fabao ji, T.* 2075, 51:186a24 (Translation Section 18).
12. *Lidai fabao ji, T.* 2075, 51:185c20–21 (Translation Section 16).
13. *Lidai fabao ji,* . 2075, 51:186b8–17 (Translation Section 18).
14. *Lidai fabao ji, T.* 2075, 51:186c2–9 (Translation Section 18).
15. *Lidai fabao ji, T.* 2075, 51:186c9–13 (Translation Section 18).
16. *Lidai fabao ji, T.* 2075, 51:186c13–28 (Translation Section 18).
17. *Lidai fabao ji, T.* 2075, 51:187b18–20 (Translation Section 18).
18. *Lidai fabao ji, T.* 2075, 51:187c2–3 (Translation Section 18).
19. *Lidai fabao ji, T.* 2075, 51:188a15–23 (Translation Section 19).

3. RADICAL ASPECTS OF WUZHU'S TEACHINGS

1. *Avataṃsaka-sūtra, T.* 278, 9 & 279, 10. The five basic precepts of Buddhism are not killing, not stealing, not indulging in sexual misconduct, not lying, not taking intoxicants. The *Avataṃsaka* included the first four, to which are added: not slandering, not speaking harshly, not speaking frivolously, not being covetous, not being moved to anger, not entertaining false views. See Cleary, trans., 1993:714–721.
2. *Bodhisattvabhūmi, T.* 1581, 30:913b.
3. *Brahmajāla-sūtra, T.* 1484, 24. The *Brahmajāla-sūtra* was alleged to have been translated by Kumārajīva (344–413). However, internal evidence suggests that it could not have been compiled before 431, and a Dunhuang manuscript establishes that it was completed no later than 480.
4. *Brahmajāla-sūtra, T.* 1484, 24:1004a23–24. Filial obedience is also repeated as the first of the vows in the 35th precept (1007b27).
5. Groner 1990:235.
6. McRae 1986:171–172.
7. Yampolsky 1967:141–146.
8. Yampolsky 1967:141.
9. Yampolsky 1967:147.
10. See *Wumen guan,* Case 2.
11. *Lidai fabao ji, T.* 2075, 51:185c26–186a5 (Translation Section 17).
12. *Vimalakīrtinirdeśa-sūtra, T.* 475, 14; Watson, trans., 1997:54, see 54–56 for a translation of the entire passage on the *bodhimaṇḍa.*

13. *Lidai fabao ji, T.* 2075, 51:193a18 (Translation Section 32).
14. *Lidai fabao ji, T.* 2075, 51:189a17–18 (Translation Section 20).
15. *Yuanjue jing dashu chao, ZZ.* I, 14:278c; Broughton, trans., 2004:19 (with minor modifications).
16. *Yuanjue jing dashu chao, ZZ.* I, 14:278d.
17. *Nanyang heshang dunjiao jietuo chanmen zhiliao xing tanyu,* Hu Shi, ed., [1958] 1970:228–229.
18. *Lidai fabao ji, T.* 2075, 51:194b8–16 (Translation Section 36).
19. Interestingly, Daoyi is homophonous with the Dharma name of Mazu Daoyi (709–788), the Hongzhou founder who is said to have been one of Wuxiang's disciples. The characters are different: Daoyi in Mazu's name means "unifying the Way," while one way to read the name of Wuzhu's fellow disciple is "escaping the Way"! The oddness of this Dharma name tempts one to surmise that the *Lidai fabao ji* authors may have been slyly mocking Mazu Daoyi.
20. *Śūraṃgama-sūtra, T.* 945, 19:121b25–26.
21. *Lidai fabao ji, T.* 2075, 51:186c28–187a8 (Translation Section 18).
22. *Lidai fabao ji, T.* 2075, 51:190b24–190c4 (Translation Section 22).
23. *Lidai fabao ji, T.* 2075, 51:194b13–17 (Translation Section 36).
24. Based on the *Viśeṣacintibrahma-paripṛcchā-sūtra, T.* 586, 15:37b3–8.
25. *Lidai fabao ji, T.* 2075, 51:195b27–195c13 (Translation Section 42).
26. *Lidai fabao ji, T.* 2075, 51:195b28 (Translation Section 42).
27. *Yuanjue jing dashu chao, ZZ.* I, 14:278d. Broughton, trans., 2004:21–23, with minor modifications.
28. Gregory 1991:247.

4. WUZHU'S FEMALE DISCIPLES

1. *Biqiuni zhuan* (Biographies of Nuns), *T.* 2063; for this incident see Tsai, trans., 1994:19.
2. See Li Yuzhen 1989 and Georgieva 2000.
3. *Platform Sūtra,* Yampolsky, trans., 1967:159.
4. *Lidai fabao ji, T.* 2075, 51:193a20–26 (Translation Section 32).
5. *Lidai fabao ji, T.* 2075, 51:195b3–22 (Translation Section 41).
6. *Lidai fabao ji, T.* 2075, 51:184c17–21 (Translation Section 15).
7. *Lidai fabao ji, T.* 2075, 51:192b7–18 (Translation Section 30).

5. WUZHU'S LEGACY

1. *Beishan lu, T.* 2113, 52:612c7–8.
2. *Beishan lu, T.* 2113, 52:612c11–16.
3. *Beishan lu, T.* 2113, 52:612c22–27.
4. *Lidai fabao ji, T.* 2075, 51:179a4, repeated in Section 36, 51:194b13.
5. *Lidai fabao ji, T.* 2075, 51:189c15 (Section 21), 193b15 (Section 33), 194b24 (Section 36). The quotation is from the *Dasheng qixin lun, T.* 1666, 32:577b22–23.
6. Backus 1981:69–100.
7. Beckwith 1987:108–172.
8. P. Tib. 116, P. Tib. 121, P. Tib. 813, and P. Tib. 699; see Ueyama 1981.
9. Ba Sangshi was Chinese; he was the son of a Chinese envoy to the Tibetan court who remained in Tibet in the entourage of the future Tibetan emperor Trhi Songdetsen. See Broughton 1983:5.
10. The history and dating of this chronicle of the bSam yas monastery is complex, but there is reason to believe that its account of Wuxiang may stem from eighth-century documents; see Kapstein 2000:72 & 212–214.
11. Eg-chu appears to be a transcription of Yizhou, the Chengdu area; see Kapstein 2000:72.
12. Yamaguchi Zuihō traces the process through which Wuxiang and his tiger become one of the eighteen arhats in Tibet; see Yamaguchi 1984.
13. This is an interesting claim, implying that Wuxiang was being trained by a still more powerful master. There is a distorted reflection of this theme in the *Song gaoseng zhuan* (Song Dynasty Biographies of Eminent Monks) biography of Wuxiang, where it is said that Wuxiang's master Chuji was never wrong in his predictions. Moreover, the biography also has a version of the animal-taming motif: Wuxiang, meditating in the night, remains impervious even when an aggressive bull puts its hoof up his sleeve. *Song gaoseng zhuan, T.* 2061, 50:832b15–21.
14. Kapstein, trans., 2000:71.
15. Kapstein 2000:71–72.
16. Broughton 1983:7.
17. See Tanaka and Robertson 1992:58–59.
18. Kapstein 2000:72–73.
19. Tibetan title: *Cig-char yang-dag-pa'i phyi-mo'i tshor-ba.* See Tanaka and Robertson 1992:58–59.

20. Neatly capturing the dilemma of the not-yet-enlightened yet nondual mind, the Chinese ms. P. 2799 asserts that these two are actually the same person; Tanaka and Robertson 1992:60.
21. P. Tib. 116, fol. 231.2; Tanaka and Robertson, trans., 1992:71.
22. *Yuanjue jing dashu chao, ZZ.* I, 14:279a–b.
23. Minn 1991.
24. *Yuanjue jing dashu chao, ZZ.* I, 14:279a–b. Broughton, trans., 2004:27.
25. *Song gaoseng zhuan, T.* 2061, 50:770c.
26. *Lidai fabao ji, T.* 2075, 51:196a27–196b5 (Translation Section 43).
27. Sutton 1996:242.
28. Sutton 1996:243.

PART II. TRANSLATION OF THE *LIDAI FABAO JI* (RECORD OF THE DHARMA-JEWEL THROUGH THE GENERATIONS)

1. This is probably the result of a miscopied citation from a list of titles in the *Shi Falin zhuan* (Biography of Shi Falin), *T.* 2051, 50:207a17.
2. See bibliography for identification of these works.
3. The following account is based on the *Hanfa neizhuan,* found in the *Xu ji gujin fodao lun heng* (Continued Anthology of Past and Present Buddhist-Daoist Debates), *T.* 2105, 52:397b25–401c25.
4. Fu Yi was an archivist under Emperor Zhang of the Han; see *Hou Han shu* 80:2610–2613.
5. These dates are quoted from a passage in the *Hanfa nei zhuan, T.* 2105, 52:397c14–398a9, quoting from the nonextant *Zhou shu yiji* (Supplement to the Zhou History).
6. The *Sishi'er zhang jing* (*T.* 784, 17) is traditionally held to be China's earliest translated sūtra, but it was probably compiled as an introduction to Buddhism sometime during the Eastern Jin (317–420), with the names of the two translators spuriously added.
7. See *Gaoseng zhuan* (Biographies of Eminent Monks), *T.* 2059, 50:322c15–323a23.
8. On these pickets or gates in a Daoist ritual structure, see Schipper and Wang 1986:189, 195. Burning texts was part of the ritual, not a sign of failure.
9. The "Brāhmanical Voice" is one of the thirty-two characteristics of a Buddha.
10. Kaṇṭhaka is the name of the horse that carried the Buddha when he left home, and Chandaka is the name of the Buddha's charioteer.

11. For a discussion of the identification of bodhisattvas with Confucius and Yanhui, see Zürcher 1959:313–317.
12. A copy of this long-lost scripture was found at Nanatsudera temple, but I have not been able to verify whether or not it includes this passage.
13. The following passage is based on the version in the *Hongming ji, T.* 2102, 52:1a28–7a22.
14. The Yuezhi were nomadic people of West Transoxiana who were instrumental in introducing Buddhism to the Chinese in the Later Han.
15. This passage does not appear in the *Jin shu,* but it reflects passages in the *Gaoseng zhuan* biography of Huiyuan, *T.* 2059, 50:360b18–28, and the *Hongming ji, T.* 2102, 52:29c–32b and 80b–85c. Huan Xuan was the virtual ruler of the Eastern Jin territories from 397 to 404.
16. Quoted in the *Shi Falin zhuan, T.* 2051, 50:211b26–27.
17. This appears to be a paraphrase of a passage describing the various transformations through which the Dharma is disseminated; *T.* 279, 10:435b9–435c27.
18. This is a summary of a much longer passage in which the Buddha tells Śāriputra that after his nirvāṇa the Dharma will spread to each direction in turn; see *T.* 220, 7:593c20–594c17.
19. The following passage is loosely based on the *Fufazang yinyuan zhuan* (Account of the Causes and Conditions of the Transmission of the Dharma Treasury), *T.* 2058, 50.
20. Mihirakula was the second ruler of the Hūṇa people (related to the Hepthalites) who ruled northwest India and Kashmir in the fifth and sixth centuries.
21. This is a rendering of the name of the putative First Patriarch, Bodhidharma, that is unique to the *Lidai fabao ji.*
22. Trepiṭaka is the title of a master of the Tripiṭaka, the Buddhist scriptures.
23. *Lotus Sūtra, T.* 262, 9:37b23–24.
24. *T.* 670, 16.
25. *T.* 671, 16.
26. *T.* 672, 16.
27. This is a pun incorporating the Second Patriarch Huike's name.
28. This exchange is first found in the *Lidai fabao ji* and was probably modeled after the initial exchange between Hongren and the Sixth Patriarch Huineng in Shenhui's "Miscellaneous Dialogues," which was the basis of the well-known *Platform Sūtra* version.
29. This is a pun on Sengcan's name, which means Saṅgha gem.

30. "Elephant-Dragons" is an epithet for peerless monks.
31. A Chinese foot, *chi,* is approximately 14 cm. To say someone is 8 *chi* tall is a trope to describe a distinguished man.
32. *Laṅkāvatāra-sūtra* translation by Śikṣānanda, the version most often quoted by the *Lidai fabao ji* authors:*T.* 672, 16:619b23–24.
33. As with many of the passages below, the *Lidai fabao ji* authors appear to have taken this from a favorite source, the Dunhuang compendium known as the *Zhujing yaochao* (Digest of Scriptures); see *T.* 2819, 85:1196b28–29. The line is actually a pastiche of two different lines from fascicle seven of the *Laṅkāvatāra-sūtra, T.* 672, 16:634c13 & 634c21.
34. *Laṅkāvatāra-sūtra, T.* 672, 16:610a27–28; also found in the *Zhujing yaochao, T.* 2819, 85:1195b1–2.
35. This passage is assembled from different couplets in a verse in fascicle seven of the *Laṅkāvatāra-sūtra, T.* 672, 16:639b21 & 639c12–13.
36. *Vajracchedikā-sūtra, T.* 235, 8:750b9. Also in the *Zhujing yaochao, T.* 2819, 85:1194b2.
37. *Vajracchedikā-sūtra, T.* 235, 8:752a17–18; also in the *Zhujing yaochao, T.* 2819, 85:1194a14–15.
38. Loosely based on the *Viśeṣacintibrahma-paripṛcchā-sūtra, T.* 586, 15:47c11–13. Also in the *Zhujing yaochao, T.* 2819, 85:1196a15–17.
39. Loosely based on the *Viśeṣacintibrahma-paripṛcchā-sūtra, T.* 586, 15:37b3–8.
40. One of the "contemplations of impurity," the "Nine Visualizations" refers to the contemplation of the nine stages of corpse decay in order to overcome attachment to the physical; contemplation of white bones is the eighth stage.
41. The Five Cessations is one of the larger categories of contemplation practices, and includes the contemplations of impurity and breath counting; these practices are designed to counteract greed, anger, ignorance, delusion of self, and a disordered mind.
42. These last five contemplations are included in the sixteen contemplations in the popular *Guan wuliangshou jing* (*Amitāyurbuddhānusmṛti-sūtra*), *T.* 365, 12.
43. This is not a direct quotation, but these improvised examples reflect the general tenor of the *Chan miyaofa jing;* see *T.* 631, 15:246a15–b17 & 251a 13–14.
44. From the *Chanmen jing,* S. 5532.
45. *Laṅkāvatāra-sūtra, T.* 672, 16:602a28.
46. *Faju jing, T.* 2901, 85:1435a21–22.
47. *Vajrasamādhi-sūtra, T.* 273, 9:368a12–13 & 370b3.

48. *Viśeṣacintibrahma-paripṛcchā-sūtra, T.* 586, 15:37c17–18.
49. This is a summary of a passage in the *Vimalakīrtinirdeśa-sūtra, T.* 475, 14:521c3 ff.
50. *Strīvivarta-vyākaraṇa-sūtra,* in the *Foshuo zhuan nushen jing* translation, *T.* 564, 14:916b22–24.
51. A near match is found in the *Vinayaviniścaya-Upālipariprcchā-sūtra, T.* 325, 12:40b7–8.
52. The extant translations do not include this phrase.
53. In the Tang apocryphal *Śūraṃgama-sūtra* this phrase appears frequently; see for example *T.* 945, 19:147a28.
54. The passage in the *Lidai fabao ji* is a pastiche of the three sections from the original; see *Buddhapiṭakaduḥśīlanirgraha-sūtra, T.* 653, 15:790a26–b2.
55. *Buddhapiṭakaduḥśīlanirgraha-sūtra, T.* 653, 15:790b5–8.
56. *Buddhapiṭakaduḥśīlanirgraha-sūtra, T.* 653, 15:803b21–26; also in the *Zhujing yaochao, T.* 2819, 85:1195c2–7.
57. Arhats-in-training who have not yet reached *arhatva,* the fourth and final level before final nirvāṇa.
58. Independently enlightened ones.
59. *Assutavā-bhikkhu* means a monk who practices *samādhi* but does not study, who therefore mistakes the fourth level of *dhyāna* meditation for nirvāṇa. Sunakṣatra is a classic example from the *Nirvāṇa-sūtra;* he falls into Avīci Hell because he mistakes the fourth level of *dhyāna* for nirvāṇa, then says there is no nirvāṇa and that arhats will also be reborn.
60. *Śūraṃgama-sūtra, T.* 945, 19:147a21–b1.
61. I.e., disciples privileged to engage in public dialogue with the master and seek private instruction.
62. There is a similar but not identical list of Hongren's disciples in Section 8 at the scene of Hongren's passing. Here Zhishen is promoted to the head of the list, as he is the protagonist of the next two sections.
63. Gaozong's widow Wu Zetian (623–705) established her own Zhou dynasty in 690, supplanting the Tang heirs.
64. *Ruyao* originally referred to a poison used for suicide, but later referred to an herb (or fungus) with magically efficacious properties that was given as an auspicious gift.
65. This connection is unlikely, but the name Xuanzang represents scholasticism and often serves as a trope in Chan treatises.

66. This may be careless copying from the *Lengqie shizi ji* (Record of the Masters and Disciples of the *Laṅkā Sūtra*) biography of Hongren, in which Hongren says that, among his disciples, both Zhishen and Liu Zhubu have a literary nature.
67. The *Song gaoseng zhuan* (Song Biographies of Eminent Monks) says that the patronage of the Military Commissioner Zhangqiu Jianqiong was the reason Wuxiang was invited to Emperor Xuanzong's court in exile in Sichuan; *T.* 2061, 50:832b28–29.
68. These are tropes from the account of the Buddha's death in the *Nirvāṇa-sūtra.*
69. *Dasheng qixin lun* (Treatise on Awakening of Faith in the Mahāyāna); see Hakeda, trans., 1967:31.
70. In the *Nirvāṇa-sūtra,* the fearless domestic dog represents the passion of anger, difficult to chase away, while the shy forest deer represents compassion, easy to lose; *T.* 374, 12:453c26–28.
71. This is based on a story in the *Dīrghāgama, T.* 1, 1:45b3–c1.
72. "Purity Chan" is a reference to *kanjing,* "viewing purity," a practice associated with the Northern School. McRae points out that for Shenxiu this meant the ultimate pure mind or reality (thus no different from *jian foxing,* seeing buddha nature), and was not used dualistically as Shenhui and his heirs claimed; McRae 1986:229–230.
73. The assembly referred to is the *wuzhe dahui* (unrestricted great assembly) of 732 at Dayun monastery in Huatai, where Shenhui issued a challenge to Shenxiu's heirs.
74. *Nirvāṇa-sūtra, T.* 374, 12:372b26–27.
75. The *Nirvāṇa-sūtra* passage says that if a person can explain the *Nirvāṇa-sūtra,* it means that he has seen buddha nature; *T.* 374, 12:526a29–b1. The *Lidai fabao ji* authors have conflated different parts of their source text, the *Putidamo nanzong ding shifei lun* (Treatise Determining Truth and Falsehood Concerning the Southern Sect of Bodhidharma) in order to make the exchange more confrontational; see Hu Shi, ed., (1958) 1970:277 & 311.
76. This passage is adapted from the *Putidamo nanzong ding shifei lun,* Hu Shi, ed., (1958) 1970:277. Shenhui uses the technical terminology of Buddhist logic and analysis of cognition, where the means of knowledge are divided into categories like direct perception, knowledge based on the scriptures, inference, and deduction of error.

77. Wuzhu's reinterpretation of the bodhisattva precepts ritual is based on the well-known "*bodhimaṇḍa*" passage in the *Vimalakīrti-sutra, T.* 475, 14:542c13–543a8.
78. *Vajrasamādhi-sūtra, T.* 273, 9:371a3.
79. *Vajrasamādhi-sūtra, T.* 273, 9:368a12–13 & 370b3.
80. This is an indication that someone started to write the *Lidai fabao ji* while Wuzhu (714–774) was still alive, based on Wuzhu's own account. It can't mean that he was fifty years old when he took the tonsure, because the text claims he took the tonsure before 749 (and he would have been thirty-four in 749). Nor can we conclude that he spent fifty years as a monk, because then he would have been ten when he was ordained.
81. Perhaps the most famous Buddhist pilgrimage site in China, Mount Wutai was considered the home of the bodhisattva Manjuśri.
82. The Helan mountains had a long-standing reputation as a sacred area.
83. "Below" here refers to the axis of the temple buildings, so the cloister was outside the main temple complex.
84. There are numerous tales concerning this nun, who in some accounts was a beautiful but virtuous nun pursued by men and in other accounts was a former courtesan.
85. A version of this episode is found in the *Ekottarāgama, T.* 125, 2:707c5–708a20, as well as in several later sources more likely to have been known by the *Lidai fabao ji* authors. The *Dazhi du lun* version is very close to the *Lidai fabao ji* version; *T.* 1509, 25:137a.
86. *Śūraṃgama-sūtra, T.* 945, 19:121b25–26.
87. Due to complicated calendrical arrangements, this designates the fourth month of the first year of the Baoying era, 762.
88. Due to support that the eunuch general Du Hongjian (709–769) gave to Emperor Suzong (r. 756–762) during the An Lushan rebellion, he was promoted to the rank of Vice-Marshal. He later served as Chancellor to both Suzong and Dezong (r. 762–779). He was sent to Shu in 766 to put down an uprising by the cavalry officer Cui Gan. In order to quell the uprising, Du criticized Cui's cowardice in his capacity as Military Commissioner. See *Tang shu* (108), 3282–3284 and *Xin Tang shu* (126), 4422–4424.
89. Xiaojin could also mean "Little Kim," so this might refer to another Korean monk who felt himself entitled to succeed Wuxiang.

90. This refers to greater Sichuan province; the name derives from the traditional division of the province into Shujun, Guang Han, and Jianwei.
91. The term "green sprouts" refers to an extra tax that was collected just as the plants were sprouting, not after the harvest; a "green sprouts official" was therefore a tax collector, no doubt an especially unpopular one.
92. *Faju jing*, *T.* 2901, 85:1435a19–21. This passage is meant to point out that the concept of meritorious practice traps the practitioner in attachment to purity. Thus, Wuzhu's use of this phrase in connection with "*mowang*" tallies with his interpretation of "delusion" not as defilements but as objectification of merit.
93. This is an adaptation of a *Vimalakīrti-sūtra* passage stating that seeking the Dharma means practice without attachment to any object; see *T.* 475, 14:546a23–24.
94. *Vajrasamādhi-sūtra*, *T.* 273, 9:369a23–24.
95. *Vimalakīrti-sūtra*, *T.* 475, 14:542b25 and 554b24, with minor variations.
96. *Laṅkāvatāra-sūtra*, *T.* 672, 16:628c19.
97. *Śūraṃgama-sūtra*, *T.* 945, 19:121b2 and 113a18.
98. This appears to be a gloss of a *Viśeṣacintibrahmaparipṛcchā-sūtra* passage, *T.* 586, 15:36b24–28.
99. This appears to be a gloss of *Laṅkāvatāra-sūtra* passages, *T.* 672, 16:588c8–9 and *T.* 671, 16:516b25–28.
100. Cui Gan, a.k.a. Cui Ning, was originally from Henan, and he used his military position to become a virtual ruler in the Sichuan region. Du Hongjian was sent in to control him, but his military power in the area remained uncontested. His biography is in the *Tang shu* (117), 3397–3404.
101. Cui Gan's wife Ren is mentioned in his biography as having bravely fought rebels during an attack on Chengdu while Cui Gan was away at court; see *Tang shu* (117), 3402.
102. Rosaries are made of these seeds, which form in triplets and illustrate the simultaneity of illusion, action, and suffering. They also fall in clusters and thus illustrate numerousness, as here.
103. *Śūramgama-sūtra*, *T.* 945, 19:108b28–c8.
104. *Dasheng qixin lun*, *T.* 1667, 32:586a10–11.
105. *Vimalakīrti-sūtra*, *T.* 475, 14:541b20.
106. *Vajracchedikā-sūtra*, *T.* 235, 8:751b2.

107. This echoes a passage in the apocryphal *Shanhaihui pusa jing, T.* 2891, 85:1407a6–7.
108. This is a paraphrase of several lines in the *Fo yijiao jing, T.* 389, 12:1111c4–6.
109. This is a trope, as for example found in a verse in the *Lotus Sūtra:* "When the bodhisattva hears this Dharma, the net of doubt is completely removed." *T.* 264, 9:143a11.
110. "Host and guest" is used to represent the teaching that the fundamental nature or "host" is covered by adventitious defilements or "guest." However, in Chan texts it is used in a polemical sense to criticize gradualist dualism that reifies original purity as "host."
111. *Laṅkāvatāra-sūtra, T.* 672, 16:610a27–28.
112. Pastiche from the *Laṅkāvatāra-sūtra, T.* 672, 16:630b7 & 633a24–25.
113. This discussion is based on Yogācāra moral epistemology; for an introduction to the Yogācāra system, see Nagao 1991.
114. *Laṅkāvatāra-sūtra, T.* 672, 16:625a27–29.
115. Slightly different from the phrase in T. 672, this matches a *Laṅkāvatāra-sūtra* quotation in the *Zhujing yaochao, T.* 2819, 85:1196c20–21.
116. *Laṅkāvatāra-sūtra, T.* 672, 16:610a2.
117. *Laṅkāvatāra-sūtra, T.* 672, 16:610b28, with slight variations.
118. There is a similar phrase in *T.* 672, 16:601c18.
119. *Laṅkāvatāra-sūtra, T.* 672, 16:616a22–23.
120. *Vimalakīrti-sūtra, T.* 475, 14:556c10.
121. *Vajracchedikā-sūtra, T.* 235, 8:751a5–6, with minor discrepancies.
122. *Zhujing yaochao, T.* 2819, 85:1196a9–12.
123. *Zhujing yaochao, T.* 2819, 85:1196a10.
124. *Zhujing yaochao, T.* 2819, 85:1195a26.
125. This appears to be a gloss of a couplet in the *Dazhidu lun, T.* 1509, 25:118a6–7.
126. This passage was used in Section 20.
127. The *Lidai fabao ji* appears to be the earliest Chan text to use the term *huopopo,* "lively like a fish jumping."
128. The *Treatise on One Hundred Dharmas* refers to Xuanzang's translation of the *Dasheng baifa mingmen lun* (*Mahāyānaśatadharmaprakāśamukha-śāstra*), *T.* 1614, 13. Many people were lecturing on the *Baifa lun* at that time; it is frequently mentioned in monks' biographies.
129. *Laṅkāvatāra-sūtra, T.* 672, 16:631c23; also in the *Zhujing yaochao, T.* 2819, 85:1197a6–7.

130. *Laṅkāvatāra-sūtra, T.* 672, 16:631a7.

131. Four-fascicle *Laṅkāvatāra-sūtra, T.* 670, 16:505b8–9.

132. The *Pusa jie* meant here may be Zhiyi's commentary, the *Pusa jie jing shu, T.* 1811, 40.

133. *Vajrasamādhi-sūtra, T.* 273, 9:371a10, with minor variations.

134. *Laṅkāvatāra-sūtra, T.* 672, 16:633a24–25. Also in the *Zhujing yaochao, T.* 2819, 85:1196a12–13.

135. *Vimalakīrti-sūtra, T.* 475, 14:553a14.

136. *Zhujing yaochao, T.* 2819, 85:1196b11–12.

137. *Laṅkāvatāra-sūtra, T.* 672, 16:633c26–27. Also in the *Zhujing yaochao, T.* 2819, 85:1195a24–25.

138. *Laṅkāvatāra-sūtra, T.* 672, 16:616a22–23.

139. *Laṅkāvatāra-sūtra, T.* 672, 16:610a27–28.

140. *Laṅkāvatāra-sūtra, T.* 672, 16:632a29.

141. *Vajracchedikā-sūtra, T.* 235, 8:750b9; also in the *Zhujing yaochao, T.* 2819, 85:1194b2.

142. *Kanjing,* "viewing purity," is part of Shenhui's negative characterization of Northern School practice:"freeze the mind to enter concentration, fix the mind to view purity, activate the mind for external illumination, and concentrate the mind for internal realization."

143. A well-known quotation from Confucius's *Lunyu* (Analects), 4.8. See Watson, trans., 2007:33.

144. *Vajrasamādhi-sūtra, T.* 273, 9:369a23–24.

145. *Zhujing yaochao, T.* 2819, 85:1196a10.

146. This dialogue is not found in the standard *Nirvāṇa-sūtra* translations, but the key phrase "exhausting all movement of thought . . . is called the *mahāparinirvāṇa*" is found in the *Dabanniepan jing houfen* (Latter Part of the *Mahāparinirvāṇa-sūtra*), translated in the Tang by Jñānabhadra, *T.* 377, 12:904c11–12.

147. *Laṅkāvatāra-sūtra, T.* 672, 16:632a29.

148. Four-fascicle *Laṅkāvatāra-sūtra, T.* 670, 16:480b6–7.

149. Recitation of Mayāyāna scriptures in general and the *Lotus Sūtra* in particular was believed to be meritorious, and there were many tales of miracles resulting from recitation of the *Lotus.*

150. *Lotus Sūtra, T.* 262, 9:37c13–15.

151. *Lotus Sūtra, T.* 262, 9:10a4.

152. *Lotus Sūtra, T.* 262, 9:5c25.

153. *Lotus Sūtra, T.* 262, 9:19c4–5, with minor variations.

154. *Vimalakīrti-sūtra, T.* 475, 14:538a13.

155. *Renwang jing* (Scripture of Humane Kings), *T.* 245, 8:827c21.

156. In the *Platform Sūtra* dialogue between Huineng and the *Lotus* practitioner Fada, there is a similar discussion of "revolving the Lotus/Lotus revolutions"; see Yampolsky 1967:167–168.

157. *Sanzhang wunan* refers to the three obstructions of greed, anger, and ignorance and the five traditional difficulties endured by women, namely the necessity of leaving her own family to be married, menstruation, pregnancy, childbirth, and the obligation to wait on a man; see *Sigālaka-sutta, Dīghanikāya* III. 30. See Walshe, trans., 1995:467.

158. Glossed from the *Vimalakīrti-sūtra, T.* 475, 14:540a16–17.

159. Loosely based on the *Viśeṣacintibrahma-paripṛcchā-sūtra, T.* 586, 15:37b3–8.

160. This verse is in the early eighth-century *Dunwu yaomen;* see *Zen no goroku* no. 6, 103.

161. *Vajracchedikā-sūtra, T.* 235, 8:749b8–11.

162. Adaptation from two different translations of verses from the *Avataṃsaka-sūtra, T.* 278, 9:429a3–14 and *T.* 279, 10:68a25–b5.

163. Adaptation of a simile in the *Faju jing, T.* 2901, 85:1432b28–c1.

164. Adaptation of verses in the *Śūraṃgama-sūtra, T.* 945, 19:131a11 & 131a8.

165. Source unclear.

166. *Vimalakīrti-sūtra, T.* 475, 14:539c23–26.

167. *Vimalakīrti-sūtra, T.* 475, 14:541a17.

168. Adapted from the *Vimalakīrti-sūtra, T.* 475, 14:540a16–18.

169. *Vimalakīrti-sūtra, T.* 475, 14:551c24.

170. *Zhujing yaochao, T.* 2819, 85:1196c4–5.

171. *Vajracchedikā-sūtra, T.* 235, 8:751c23.

172. *Faju jing, T.* 2901, 85:1433c9.

173. *Vajrasamādhi-sūtra, T.*273, 9:368c20. *Ludi zuo* (sitting on dewy ground) refers to escaping from defilements; it was used in the *Lotus Sūtra* to describe the place where the children sat down after escaping the Burning House; *T.* 262, 9:12c15.

174. *Laṅkāvatāra-sūtra, T.* 672, 16:635a25.

175. Pastiche from the *Vajrasamādhi-sūtra, T.* 273, 9:368a12–13 & 370b3.

176. *Faju Jing, T.* 2901, 85:1435a24, with minor variations.

177. *Śūraṃgama-sūtra, T.* 945, 19:131a20–21.

178. *Fo yijiao jing, T.* 389, 12:1111a20.

179. *Faju jing, T.* 2901, 85:1435a23.

180. *Vajrasamādhi-sūtra, T.* 273, 9:370c23.

181. *Vajrasamādhi-sūtra, T.* 273, 9:371a4.

182. Possibly based on the *Fo yijiao jing, T.* 389, 12:1111c11–13.

183. This poem does not appear in the *Wang Fanzhi shiji,* the collected poems of Brahmacarya Wang (d. ca. 670).

184. Tea drinking is one of the distinctive motifs of the *Lidai fabao ji;* in Section 18 Wuzhu's gift of tea to Wuxiang is part of the plot, and in Section 39 Wuzhu snaps at a rude guest who mocks his tea-drinking habits. These are some of the earliest recorded examples showing monks engaged in tea drinking; including such scenes in a Buddhist work marks a literary trend toward showing interactions between teacher and students in everyday settings.

185. From the *Chanmen jing* as quoted in the *Zhujing yaochao, T.* 2819, 85:1196c1–2, with minor variations.

186. *Dasheng qixin lun, T.* 1667, 32:586a10–11.

187. *Vajracchedikā-sūtra, T.* 235, 8:752b28–29.

188. The famous first line of the *Daode jing* (Classic of the Way and Its Power). See Roberts, trans., 2001:27.

189. *Daode jing* Chapter 48, with modifications. See Roberts, trans., 2001:128.

190. Derived from the "*Dazong shi*" section of the *Zhuangzi;* see Watson, trans., 1996:79.

191. These are the key Confucian virtues as developed in *Mengzi* (Mencius) 2A:6 and 6A:16; see Bloom, trans., 2009:35, 121 ff.

192. The original passage refers to the nonaction of the *Yijing* (Classic of Changes) itself; see Lynn, trans., 1994:63.

193. Echoes a passage in the apocryphal *Shanhaihui pusa jing, T.* 2891, 85:1407a6–7.

194. *Daode jing* Chapter 38, with modifications. See Roberts, trans., 2001:106.

195. From the *Heart Sūtra, T.* 251, 8:848c14–15, as quoted in the *Zhujing yaochao, T.* 2819, 85:1196c4–5.

196. *Vajracchedikā-sūtra, T.* 235, 8:751c23.

197. This line is repeated often in the *Śūraṃgama-sūtra;* see for example *T.* 945, 19:117c11.

198. *Vajrasamādhi-sūtra, T.* 273, 9:367c6.

199. *Vajracchedikā-sūtra, T.* 235, 8:749b18.

200. *Laṅkāvatāra-sūtra, T.* 672, 16:597c1–2.

201. *Sarvabuddhaviṣayāvatārajñānālokālaṃkāra-sūtra, T.* 357, 12:248a3–4, as quoted in the *Zhujing yaochao, T.* 2819, 85:1194b5–6.

202. Based on the *Viśeṣacintabrahmaparipṛcchā-sūtra, T.* 586, 15:37c13–14.

203. *Vimalakīrti-sūtra, T.* 475, 14:540a18–19.

204. *Vajracchedikā-sūtra, T.* 235, 8:751c15.

205. *Nirvāṇa-sūtra, T.* 374, 12:520b8–9, with modifications.

206. Based on the *Dasheng yi zhang, T.* 1851, 44:699a20–21.

207. *Faju jing, T.* 2901, 85:1435a13–14.

208. *Vajracchedikā-sūtra, T.* 235, 8:750b29.

209. *Vimalakīrti-sūtra, T.* 475, 14:540a17.

210. As discussed in the *Vinayaviniścaya-Upāliparipṛcchā-sūtra, T.* 325, 12, *Vinayaviniścaya* is Vinaya to remove the gravest transgressions, and *Vinayottara* means the highest Vinaya, referring to the view that the fundamental nature of all dharmas is pure.

211. *Vajrasamādhi-sūtra, T.* 273, 9:366c20.

212. *Śūraṃgama-sūtra, T.* 945, 19:121a2.

213. Based on the *Sarvadharmāpravṛttinirdeśa-sūtra, T.* 651, 15:763a7–8.

214. Based on the *Saptaśatikāprajñāpāramitā-sūtra, T.* 232, 8:728b23–25.

215. *Vimalakīrti-sūtra, T.* 475, 14:541b2–3.

216. *Faju jing, T.* 2901, 85:1435a16–17.

217. *Dasheng qixin lun, T.* 1667, 32:586a10–11.

218. *Vimalakīrti-sūtra, T.* 475, 14:541b20.

219. *Laṅkāvatāra-sūtra, T.* 672, 16:633c26–27.

220. *Lotus Sūtra, T.* 262, 9:19c4–5.

221. *Vimalakīrti-sūtra, T.* 475, 14:538a13.

222. *Renwang jing, T.* 245, 8:827c21.

223. The passage on "five years of study" may be based on a note in the *Zhujing yaochao, T.* 2819, 85:1194c17.

224. *Treatise on One Hundred Dharmas* refers to the *Mahāyānaśatadharmaprakāśamukha-śāstra, T.* 1614, 31.

225. This is a critique of the numerical approach used throughout the *Dasheng baifa mingmen lun.*

226. This appears to be based on the introduction of three kinds of interpretation in the Liang translation of the *Dasheng qixin lun, T.* 1666, 32:576a3–5.

227. *Dasheng qixin lun, T.* 1666, 32:576a12.

228. Based on the *Dasheng qixin lun*, *T.* 1666, 32:576b13.

229. *Laṅkāvatāra-sūtra*, *T.* 672, 16:613c18–19, with minor modifications.

230. *Vimalakīrti-sūtra*, *T.* 475, 14:537c18.

231. *Vimalakīrti-sūtra*, *T.* 475, 14:538a14.

232. The title *Chanshi jing* is unclear, but the quotation is from the *Vimalakīrti-sūtra*, *T.* 475, 14:545b6.

233. Loosely based on a verse in the *Lotus Sūtra*, *T.* 262, 9:9c7–8.

234. Abbreviated from the *Lotus Sūtra*, *T.* 262, 9:19c4–5.

235. Based on an example in the *Mahāprajñāpāramitā-sūtra*, *T.* 220, 7:939a28–b2.

236. Based on the *Chanmen jing*.

237. The famine of the Yongchun era was apparently a leading date for some time; see *Zizhi tongjian* (203), 6406–6407.

238. *Vimalakīrti-sūtra*, *T.* 475, 14:547a26.

239. *Vajrasamādhi-sūtra*, *T.* 273, 9:368a12–13 & 370b3.

240. This is the only mention of a disciple who joined Wuzhu while he was still in the Baiya mountains, from 759 to 766. Thus, Fayuan could be one of Wuzhu's earliest disciples, which might account for the relatively realistic tone of the dialogue.

241. Vasubandhu and Asaṅga's *Vajracchedikā* (Diamond Sūtra) treatises were widely used, in five Chinese translations: *T.* 1510–1514, 25. It was cited as the scripture that enlightened the Sixth Patriarch Huineng at first hearing, and it remained foundational for the Chan school.

242. *Vajracchedikā-sūtra*, *T.* 235, 8:749b24; also in the *Zhujing yaochao*, *T.* 2819, 85:1197a16.

243. *Phallodendron amurence:* the leaves of this tree were used to copy early scriptures.

244. Based on the *Dasheng yi zhang*, *T.* 1851, 44:699a20–21 ff.

245. *Faju jing*, *T.* 2901, 85:1435a13–14.

246. *Vimalakīrti-sūtra*, *T.* 475, 14:540a17.

247. *Vajracchedikā-sūtra*, *T.* 235, 8:750b29.

248. *Vajracchedikā-sūtra*, *T.* 235, 8:751c13.

249. *Vajracchedikā-sūtra*, *T.* 235, 8:750b9; also in the *Zhujing yaochao*, *T.* 2819, 85:1194b2.

250. *Vajracchedikā-sūtra*, *T.* 235, 8:752a17–18; also in the *Zhujing yaochao*, *T.* 2819, 85:1194a14–15.

251. *Guan Puxianpusa xingfa jing* (Scripture of the Methods of Contemplation of the Bodhisattva Samantabhadra), *T.* 277, 9:393b11.

252. Based on the *Viśeṣacintibrahma-paripṛcchā-sūtra, T.* 586, 15:37b3–8.

253. *Heart Sūtra, T.* 251, 8:848c18–20.

254. Two of the most powerful contenders during the Warring States period, Chu and Yue were allies who became enemies; Chu vanquished Yue in 333 B.C.E.

255. Though this wording does not appear in the *Daode jing,* the Dao is frequently referred to as "nameless."

256. This refers to the twelve categories of scriptural literature.

257. This refers to the expedient means that eradicate the eighty-four thousand *kleśa,* defilements.

258. Based on a phrase in the *Zhuangzi;* see Watson, trans., 1996:140.

259. Based on a line in the *Śūraṃgama-sūtra, T.* 945, 19:121b26.

260. As discussed in a dialogue in Section 21, *avyākṛta* is a technical term from Abhidharma exegesis on the moral qualities of dharmas; it means morally neutral, not subject to karmic retribution.

261. Adaptation of Yan Hui's praise of virtue in the *Lunyu* (Analects), 9.10. See Watson, trans., 2007:61.

262. Variation on a line from the *Vajracchedikā-sūtra, T.* 235, 8:750b9.

BIBLIOGRAPHY

CONVENTIONS

Daozang = The Daoist canon, cited according to Schipper's numbering system
P. = Dunhuang manuscripts in the Pelliot collection, Bibliothèque Nationale
P. Tib. = Tibetan Dunhuang manuscripts in the Pelliot collection, Bibliothèque Nationale
S. = Dunhuang manuscripts in the Stein collection, British Library
T. = Takakusu Junjiro 高楠順次郎, ed. (1922–1933). *Taishō shinshū daizōkyō* 太正新修大藏經. 85 vols. Tokyo: Daizō shuppan kai.
ZZ. = Nakano Tatsue 中野達慧, ed. (1905–12). *Dai Nippon zokuzōkyō* 大日本続藏経. 150 vols. Kyoto: Zōkyō shoin.

Abhiniṣkramana-sūtra (Scripture of the Initial Steps on the Path). *Benxing jing* 本行經. *T.* 190, 3.

Adamek, Wendi L. 2007. *The Mystique of Transmission: On an Early Chan History and Its Contexts.* New York: Columbia University Press.

Avataṃsaka-sūtra (Flower Garland Scripture). *Da fangguang fo huayan jing* 大方廣佛華嚴經. *T.* 278, 9 & 279, 293, 10.

Backus, Charles. 1981. *The Nan-chao Kingdom and T'ang China's Southwestern Frontier.* Cambridge: Cambridge University Press.

Baolin zhuan 寶林傳 (Transmission of the Baolin [Temple]). Compiled 801, by Zhiju 智炬. In Tanaka Ryōshō 田中良昭, *Hōrinden yakuchū* 宝林伝訳注 (An Annotated Translation of the *Baolin zhuan*). Tokyo: Uchiyama shoten, 2003.

Beckwith, Christopher I. 1987. *The Tibetan Empire in Central Asia.* Princeton: Princeton University Press.

Beishan lu 北山錄 (Record of North Mountain). Compiled 806, by Shenqing 神清. *T.* 2113, 52.

Bhaiṣajyaguruvaiḍūryaprabhāsapūrvapraṇidhānaviśeṣavistara-sūtra (Elaboration on the Merit of the Previous Vows of the Medicine Master Who Shines Like an Emerald). *Yaoshi jing* 藥師經. *T.* 449–451, 14.

Biqiuni zhuan 比丘尼傳 (Biographies of Nuns). Compiled ca. 516, by Baochang 寶唱. *T.* 2063, 50.

Bloom, Irene, trans. 2009. *Mencius.* New York: Columbia University Press.

Bodhisattvabhūmi (Bodhisattva Stages). By Asaṅga (ca. 4th c.). *Pusadichi jing* 菩薩地持經. *T.* 1581, 30.

Brahmajāla-sūtra (Scripture of Brahma's Net). *Fanwang jing* 梵網經. *T.* 1484, 24.

Broughton, Jeffrey L. 1983. "Early Ch'an Schools in Tibet." In Robert M. Gimello and Peter N. Gregory, eds., *Studies in Ch'an and Hua-yen,* 1–68. Honolulu: University of Hawai'i Press.

——. 2004. "Tsung-mi's *Zen Prolegomenon:* Introduction to an Exemplary Zen Canon." In Steven Heine and Dale S. Wright, eds., *The Zen Canon: Understanding the Classic Texts.* Oxford: Oxford University Press.

Buddhapiṭakaduḥśīlanirgraha-sūtra (Scripture in Which the Admonitions of the Buddha Treasury Are Understood). *Fozang jing* 佛藏經. *T.* 653, 15.

Chanmen jing 禪門經 (Scripture of the Chan Teachings). P. 4646, S. 5532.

Chan miyaofa jing 禪秘要法經 (Scripture of the Secret Essential Methods of Dhyāna). *T.* 613, 15.

Chujia gongde jing 出家功德經 (Scripture on the Merit of Renunciation). *T.* 707, 16.

Cleary, Thomas, trans. 1993. *The Flower Ornament Scripture.* Boston: Shambhala.

Dabanniepan jing houfen 大般涅槃經後分 (Latter Part of the *Mahāparinirvāṇa-sūtra*). *T.* 377, 12.

Daojiao xisheng jing 道教西昇經 (Scripture of the Ascension to the West of the Daoist Teachings). *T.* 2139, 44.

Dasheng qixin lun 大乘起信論 (Treatise on the Awakening of Faith in the Mahāyāna). Apocryphon attrib. to Aśvaghoṣa. *T.* 1666–1667, 32.

Dasheng yi zhang 大乘義章 (Chapters on the Meaning of the Mahāyāna). By Huiyuan 慧遠 (523–592). *T.* 1851, 44.

Da Tang xiyu ji 大唐西域記 (The Tang Dynasty Account of the Western Regions). By Xuanzang 玄奘 (602–664). *T.* 2087, 51.

Dazhidu lun 大智度論 (Treatise on the Great Perfection of Wisdom). *Mahāprajñāpāramitā-śastra,* attributed to Nāgārjuna, as compiled by Kumārajīva 鳩摩羅什. *T.* 1509, 25.

Dīghanikāya. See Walshe, trans., 1995.

Dīrghāgama (The Long Discourses). *Chang ahan jing* 長阿含經. *T.* 1, 1.

Donner, Neal and Daniel B. Stevenson. 1993. *The Great Calming and Contemplation: A Study and Annotated Translation of the First Chapter of Chih-i's* Mo-ho Chih-kuan. Honolulu: University of Hawai'i Press.

Dunwu wushang banruo song 頓悟無生般若頌 (Hymn to the Birthless Wisdom of Sudden Awakening). Compiled ca. 750, by Shenhui 神會. S. 468.

Dunwu yaomen 頓悟要門 (The Essentials of Sudden Awakening). Early 8th c., by Dazhu Huihai 大珠慧海. In *Zen no goroku* 禅の語録, no. 6. Tokyo: Chikuma shobō, 1969.

Ekottarāgama (Numerical Discourses). *Zengyi ahan jing* 增一阿含經. *T.* 125, 2.

Faju jing 法句經 (Verses on Dharma). Apocryphal *Dhammapada-sutta, ca.* 7th c. *T.* 2901, 85.

Faure, Bernard. 1991. *The Rhetoric of Immediacy: A Cultural Critique of Chan/Zen Buddhism.* Princeton: Princeton University Press.

——. 1997. *The Will to Orthodoxy: A Critical Genealogy of Northern Chan Buddhism.* Stanford: Stanford University Press.

Fo yijiao jing 佛遺教經 (Teachings Left by the Buddha). *T.* 389, 12.

Fu fazang yinyuan zhuan 付法藏[因緣]傳 (Account of the Causes and Conditions of the Transmission of the Dharma Treasury). *T.* 2058, 50.

Fuzi 苻子 (The Book of Master Fu). Nonextant.

Gaoseng zhuan 高僧傳 (Biographies of Eminent Monks). Compiled ca. 530, by Huijiao 慧皎. *T.* 2059, 50.

Georgieva, Valentina. 2000. "Buddhist Nuns in China: From the Six Dynasties to the Tang." Ph.D. diss., University of Leiden.

Gregory, Peter. 1991. *Tsung-mi and the Sinification of Buddhism.* Princeton: Princeton University Press.

Groner, Paul. 1990. "The Ordination Ritual in the *Platform Sūtra* Within the Context of the East Asian Buddhist Vinaya Tradition." *Fo Kuang Shan Report of International Conference on Ch'an Buddhism,* 220–250. Kao-hsiung, Taiwan: Fo Kuang Publisher.

Guan wuliangshou jing 觀無量壽經 (*Amitāyurbuddhānusmṛti-sūtra*). *T.* 365, 12.

Guan Puxianpusa xingfa jing 觀普賢菩薩行法經 (Scripture of the Methods of Contemplation of the Bodhisattva Samantabhadra). *T.* 277, 9.

Hakeda, Yoshito S., trans. 1967. *The Awakening of Faith, Attributed to Asvaghosha.* New York: Columbia University Press.

Hanfa neizhuan 漢法內傳 (Inner Commentary on the Dharma in the Han). In the *Xu ji gujin fodao lun heng* 續集古今佛道論衡 (Continued Anthology of Past and Present Buddhist–Daoist Debates). *T.* 2105, 52: 397b25–401c25.

Harvey, Peter. 1990. *An Introduction to Buddhism: Teachings, History and Practices.* Cambridge: Cambridge University Press.

Heart Sūtra. See *Prajñāpāramitā-hṛdaya-sūtra.*

Hongming ji 弘明集 (Anthology for Spreading Enlightenment). By Sengyou 僧祐. *T.* 2102, 52.

Hou Han shu 後漢書 (History of the Later Han). By Fan Ye 范曄 (398–445). Beijing: Zhonghua shuju, 1963.

Hu Shi 胡適. (1958) 1970. *Shenhui heshang yizhi* 神會和尚遺集 (The Surviving Works of the Venerable Shenhui). Taibei: Hu Shi jinian guan.

Jin shu 晉書 (Jin History). Compiled ca. 646–648. Beijing: Zhonghua shuju, 1975.

Jorgensen, John. 1987. "The 'Imperial' Lineage of Ch'an Buddhism: The Role of Confucian Ritual and Ancestor Worship in Ch'an's Search for Legitimation in the Mid-T'ang Dynasty." *Papers on Far Eastern History* 35:89–133.

——. 2005. *Inventing Hui-neng, the Sixth Patriarch: Hagiography and Biography in Early Ch'an.* Leiden: Brill.

Kaiyuan shijiao mu 開元釋教目 (Catalogue of Buddhism in the Kaiyuan Era) (a.k.a. *Kaiyuan shijiao lu* 開元釋教録). *T.* 2154, 55.

Kapstein, Matthew T. 2000. *The Tibetan Assimilation of Buddhism: Conversion, Contestation, and Memory.* Oxford: Oxford University Press.

Kumārakuśalaphalanidāna-sūtra (Scripture of Auspicious Signs). *Shuiying jing* 瑞應經. *T.* 185, 3.

Lalitavistara-sūtra (Scripture of the Unfolding of the Divine Play [of the Buddha]). *Puyao jing* 普曜經. *T.* 186, 3.

Laṅkāvatāra-sūtra (Scripture of the Appearance of the Dharma in Laṅkā). *Lengqie jing* 楞伽經. *T.* 670–672, 16.

Lengqie shizi ji 楞伽師資記 (Record of the Masters and Disciples of the *Laṅkāvatāra-sūtra*). Compiled ca. 720, by Jingjue 淨覺. *T.* 2837, 85.

Lidai fabao ji 曆代法寶記 (Record of the Dharma-Jewel Through the Generations). Compiled ca. 780. *T.* no. 2075.

Liezi 列子 (The Book of Master Lie). *Daozang* 348.668.

Liuzu tanjing 六祖壇經 (Platform Sūtra of the Sixth Patriarch). Compiled ca. late 8th c. Numerous texts; see Yampolsky 1967, Jorgensen 2005.

Li Yuzhen 李玉珍. 1989. *Tangdai de biqiuni* 唐代的比丘尼 (Nuns of the Tang Dynasty). Taibei: Taiwan xuesheng shuju.

Lotus Sūtra. See *Saddharmapuṇḍarīka-sūtra.*

Lynn, Richard John. 1994. *The Classic of Changes: A New Translation of the* I Ching, *as Interpreted by Wang Bi.* New York: Columbia University Press.

Mahāprajñāpāramitā-sūtra (Scripture of the Great Perfection of Wisdom). *Dabanruopoluomiduo jing* 大般若波羅蜜多經. *T.* 220, 5–7.

Mahāyānaśatadharmaprakāśamukha-śāstra (Treatise Elucidating One Hundred Dharmas of the Mahāyāna). *Dasheng baifa mingmen lun* 大乘百法明門論. *T.* 1614, 31.

Manjuśrī parinirvāṇa-sūtra (Scripture of the Final Nirvāṇa of Manjuśrī). *Wenshushili niepan jing* 文殊師利涅槃經. *T.* 463, 14.

McRae, John. 1986. *The Northern School and the Formation of Early Ch'an Buddhism.* Honolulu: University of Hawai'i Press.

——. 2002. "Shenhui as Evangelist: Re-envisioning the Identity of a Chinese Buddhist Monk." *Journal of Chinese Religions* 30:123–148.

——. 2003. *Seeing Through Zen: Encounter, Transformation, and Genealogy in Chinese Chan Buddhism.* Berkeley: University of California Press.

Minn Young-gyu 閔泳珪. 1991. "Shisen kōdan shūi 四川講壇趣拾遺." *Chūgai Nippō* 中外日報 July 26, 29, & 30 (24509:1, 24510:1, & 24511:1–2).

Mouzi 牟子 (The Book of Master Mou) = *Mouzi lihuo lun* 牟子理惑論 (Mouzi's Treatise Settling Doubts). In the *Hongming ji* 弘明集. *T.* 2102, 52:1a28–7a22.

Nagao, Gadjin M. 1991. *Mādhyamika and Yogācāra.* Albany: State University of New York Press.

Nanyang heshang dunjiao jietuo chanmen zhiliao xing tanyu 南陽和上頓教解脫禪門直了性壇語 (The Platform Address of the Venerable of Nanyang on Directly Comprehending the Nature According to the Chan Approach of Emancipation in the Sudden Teaching). Compiled ca. 720. P. 2045 (part 2) in Hu Shi, ed., (1958) 1970:225–252.

Nirvāṇa-sūtra (Scripture of the [Buddha's Final] Nirvāṇa). *Niepan jing* 涅槃經. *T.* 374–375, 12.

Ochiai Toshinori. 1991. *The Manuscripts of Nanatsu-dera.* Trans. and ed. Silvio Vita. Kyoto: Italian School of East Asian Studies.

Penkower, Linda. 2000. "In the Beginning . . . Guanding 灌頂 (561–632) and the Creation of Early Tiantai." *Journal of the International Association of Buddhist Studies* 23, no. 2: 245–296.

Platform Sūtra. See *Liuzu tanjing.*

Prajñāpāramitā-hṛdaya-sūtra (Heart Sūtra). *Banruopoluomiduo xin jing* 般若波羅蜜多心經. *T.* 251, 8.

Pusa jie jing shu 菩薩戒經疏 (Commentary on the Bodhisattva Precepts Scripture). By Zhiyi 智顗 (538–597). *T.* 1811, 40.

Putidamou nanzong ding shifei lun 菩提達摩南宗定是非論 (Treatise Determining the True and False About the Southern School of Bodhidharma). Record of Shenhui's 神會 732 debate, by Dugu Pei 獨孤沛. P. 3047 (part 2), P. 2045 (part 1), and P. 3488 (part 1); in Hu Shi, ed., (1958) 1970:260–314.

Qingjing faxing jing 清浄法行經 (Scripture of the Practice of the Pure Dharma). Six Dynasties apocryphon recently rediscovered at Nanatsudera; see Ochiai 1991:26.

Renwang jing 仁王經 (Scripture of Humane Kings). *T.* 245–246, 8.

Roberts, Moss, trans. 2001. *Dao de Jing: The Book of the Way.* Berkeley: University of California Press.

Saddharmapuṇḍarīka-sūtra (Lotus Sūtra). *Miaofa lianhua jing* 妙法蓮華經. *T.* 262–264, 9.

Saṃyuktāgama-sūtra (Miscellaneous Discourses). *Za ahan jing* 雜阿含經. *T.* 99, 2.

Saptaśatikāprajñāpāramitā-sūtra (The Perfection of Wisdom Scripture in Seven Hundred Verses [Spoken by Manjuśrī]). *Wenshu shuo banruo jing* 文殊說般若經. *T.* 232–233, 8.

Sarvabuddhaviṣayāvatārajñānālokālaṃkāra-sūtra (Scripture on Tathāgata-Adorning Wisdom Light That Enters All Buddha Realms). *Rulai zhuangyan zhihui guangming ru yiqie fojingjue jing* 如來莊嚴智惠光明入一切佛境界經. *T.* 357, 12.

Sarvadharmāpravṛttinirdeśa-sūtra (Scripture of the Fundamental Nonbeing of Dharmas). *Zhufa benwu jing* 諸法本無經. *T.* 651, 15.

Schipper, Kristofer M. and Wang Hsiu-huei. 1986. "Progressive and Regressive Time Cycles in Taoist Ritual." In J. T. Fraser et al., eds., *Time, Science, and Society in China and the West,* 185–205. Amherst: University of Massachusetts Press.

Shanhaihui pusa jing 山海慧菩薩經 (Scripture of the Bodhisattva "Wisdom of Mountains and Seas"). *T.* 2891, 85.

Shi Falin zhuan 釋法琳傳 (Biography of Shi Falin) (a.k.a. *Falin biezhuan* 法琳別傳). Compiled ca. late 7th c., by Yanzong 彥琮. *T.* 2051, 50.

Shi Xushi ji 釋虛實記 (Record of the Monk Shi Xushi). Nonextant.

Sishi'er zhang jing 四十二章經 (Scripture in Forty-two Sections). *T.* 784, 17.

Song gaoseng zhuan 宋高僧傳 (Song Dynasty Biographies of Eminent Monks). Compiled 988, by Zanning 贊寧. *T.* 2061, 50.

Strīvivarta-vyākaraṇa-sūtra (Scripture of the Unstained Radiant Transformation of the Female Body). *Foshuo zhuan nushen jing* 佛說轉女身經. *T.* 562–566, 14.

Śūraṃgama-sūtra (Scripture of the Crown of the Buddha's Head). Tang apocryphon, *Dafoding jing* 大佛頂經. *T.* 945, 19.

Sutton, Donald S. 1996. "Transmission in Popular Religion: The Jiajiang Festival Troupe of Southern Taiwan." In Meir Shahar and Robert P. Weller, eds., *Unruly Gods: Divinity and Society in China,* 212–249. Honolulu: University of Hawai'i Press.

Tanaka, Kenneth K. and Raymond E. Robertson. 1992. "A Ch'an Text from Tunhuang: Implications for Ch'an Influence on Tibetan Buddhism." In Stephen D. Goodman and Ronald M. Davidson, eds., *Tibetan Buddhism: Reason and Revelation.* Albany: State University of New York Press.

Tang shu 唐書 (Tang History). 945, by Liu Xu 劉昫. Beijing: Zhonghua shuju, 1975.

Tsai, Kathryn Ann, trans. 1994. *Lives of the Nuns: Biographies of Chinese Buddhist Nuns from the Fourth to the Sixth Centuries.* Honolulu: University of Hawai'i Press.

Ueyama Daishun 上山大峻. 1981. "Études des manuscrits tibétains de Dunhuang relatifs au bouddhisme de dhyāna. Bilan et perspectives." *Journal Asiatique* 269:287–293.

Vajracchedika-sutra (Diamond Sūtra). *Jingangbanruopoluomi jing* 金剛般若波羅蜜經. *T.* 235–239, 8.

Vajrasamādhi-sūtra (Scripture of Adamantine Concentration). *Jingang sanmei jing* 金剛三昧經. *T.* 273, 9.

Vimalakīrtinirdeśa-sūtra (Scripture on the Expositions of Vimalakīrti). *Weimojie suoshuo jing* 維摩詰所說經. *T.* 474–476, 14.

Vinayaviniścaya-Upālipariprcchā-sūtra (Scripture of the Inquiry of Upāli Regarding Determination of the Vinaya). *Juedingpini jing* 決定毘尼經. *T.* 325, 12.

Viśeṣacintibrahmaparipṛcchā-sūtra (Scripture of the Inquiry of the Deity of Thinking). *Siyifantian suowen jing* 思益梵天所問經. *T.* 585–587, 15.

Walshe, Maurice, trans. 1995. *The Long Discourses of the Buddha: A Translation of the* Dīgha Nikāya. Boston: Wisdom Publications.

Wang Fanzhi shiji 王梵志詩集 (Collected Poems of Brahmacarya Wang). *T.* 85 (2863).

Watson, Burton, trans. 1996. *Chuang Tzu: The Basic Writings.* New York: Columbia University Press.

——. 1997. *The Vimalakirti Sutra.* New York: Columbia University Press.
——. 2007. *The Analects of Confucius.* New York: Columbia University Press.
Weiner, Annette B. 1992. *Inalienable Possessions: The Paradox of Keeping-While-Giving.* Berkeley: University of California Press.
Wumen guan 無門關 (The Gateless Barrier). By Wumen Huikai 無門慧開 (1183–1260). In *Zen no goroku* 禅の語録, no. 18. Tokyo: Chikuma shobō, 1969.
Wu shu 呉書 (The Wu History). Official history, nonextant; spurious Buddhist-Daoist polemical version quoted in the *Chuanfa ji* 傳法記, *T.* 2105, 52:402a9–b17.
Xin Tang shu 新唐書 (New Tang History). 1060, by Ouyang Xiu 歐陽修 and Song Qi 宋祁. Beijing: Zhonghua shuju, 1975.
Yamaguchi Zuihō 山口瑞鳳. 1984. "Tora o tomonau daijūhachi rakanzu no raireki 虎を伴う第十八羅漢図の来歴 (Tracing the Origins of the Image of the Eighteenth Arhat Accompanied by a Tiger)." *Indō koten kenkyū* 6:392–422.
Yampolsky, Philip B. 1967. *The Platform Sūtra of the Sixth Patriarch.* New York: Columbia University Press.
Yanagida Seizan 柳田聖山, ed. 1976. *Shoki no Zenshi II: Rekidai hōbōki* 初期の禅史 *II*—歴代法宝記 (Early Chan History II: *Lidai fabao ji*). *Zen no goroku* 禅の語録, no. 3. Tokyo: Chikuma shobō.
Yang Lengqie Yedu gushi 楊楞伽鄴都故事 (Laṅkā Yang's Stories of Ye). Nonextant.
Yifa. 2002. *The Origins of Buddhist Monastic Codes in China: An Annotated Translation and Study of the* Chanyuan Qinggui. Honolulu: University of Hawai'i Press.
Yingluo jing 瓔珞經 (Gem-Necklace Scripture). *T.* 1485, 24 & 656, 15.
Yin Xi neizhuan 尹喜内傳 (Yin Xi's Inner Commentary). *Daozang* 347.667.
Yuanjue jing dashu chao 圓覺經大疏鈔 (Subcommentary to the Scripture of Perfect Enlightenment). Compiled 823–824, by Zongmi 宗密 (780–841). *ZZ.* I, 14, 3.
Zhou shu yiji 周書異記 (Supplement to the Zhou History). Nonextant.
Zhujing yaochao 諸經要抄 (Digest of Scriptures). *T.* 2819, 85.
Zizhi tongjian 資治通鑑 (Comprehensive Mirror for Aid in Government). By Sima Guang 司馬光 (1019–86). Beijing: Zhonghua shuju, 1976.
Zürcher, Erik. 1959. *The Buddhist Conquest of China: The Spread and Adaptation of Buddhism in Early Medieval China.* 2 vols. Leiden: Brill.

INDEX

Page numbers followed by "q" indicate quotations. Page numbers followed by "+q" indicate discussions plus quotations.

Abatoubao Lengqie jing, 76

abuse of others: in practice centers, 41–42; *upāya* vs., 7–8. *See also* hitting/beating monks

affinity between master and disciple, 21, 25–27

afflictions. *See* defilements

almsgiving, 36

"Amid the Dharma but not practicing," 138

Amitābha: power, 10; visualizing and calling on, 31

Ānanda, 138; the Buddha and, 91, 121–122

antinomianism (in Chan), 35, 37, 58, 60, 61, 64; of the Bao Tang group, 44, 52, 53, 54–55, 56; of the Hongzhou school, 60

anuttara-samyak-sambodhi, 139, 144, 151, 152

appearances: working with, 6–7

army. *See* Tang military

army officers and Wuzhu, 28–29, 113–114, 125–126

arousing the mind, 130, 142, 149

Asian forms for contemporary Zen practitioners, 64

aspiration (spiritual aspiration), 6, 36

attachment: to characteristics, 105, 134, 138, 142, 150; to meditation, 150; to verbal explanation, 129–130, 138

authority: naturalized vs. natural, 7; social contracts and, 5–6; transmission and, 15–16

Avalokiteśvara: visualizing and calling on, 31

Avataṃsaka-sūtra, 31q, 74–75q, 138q, 160n1

avyākṛta, 123–124, 176n260

awakening. *See* enlightenment
Awakening of Faith, 100q, 149

Ba Sangshi, 162n9; Wuxiang and, 57–58
Baifa lun, 128, 149, 170n128
Baiya Mountains. *See* Mount Baiya
Baizhang, 60–61
Baizhang qinggui, 60–61
Bao Tang group/school, 3, 4, 52, 53, 54; antinomianism, 44, 52, 53, 54–55, 56; criticism of, 4, 24, 41, 43–44, 54–56; developmental limits/unsustainability, 4, 5, 43; iconoclasm, 54–55; patronage issue, 39–41, 42–43; practice, 44–45 (*see also* no-thought); teacher (*see* Wuzhu); teacher's record (*see Lidai fabao ji*); Zongmi on, 24, 43–44, 55, 56
Bao Tang monastery, 104
Baolin zhuan, 4, 54, 56
beating/hitting monks, 41, 126, 129
becoming a buddha, 62, 142, 153
beheading: of Daoxin (feigned), 83–84; of Siṃha Bhikṣu, 21–22, 75–76
Beishan lu (Shenqing), 3, 4, 54–55+q
berating monks/students, 41–42, 126
besieged town(s): Daoxin and, 83; Hongren and, 85
Bhaiṣajyaguruvaiḍūryaprabharāja-sūtra, 91q
biographies of Chinese nuns, 47
Biqiuni zhuan, 47
birth-and-death, 40, 100, 105, 109, 122, 142; cutting off the source of, 50
bleeding of white milk, 22, 76, 80, 81
bodhi, 17, 122, 139; *anuttara-samyak-sambodhi,* 139, 144, 151, 152. *See also* enlightenment (awakening); nirvāṇa
bodhicitta, 6
Bodhidharma (Dharmatrāta/Patriarchal Master Dharma), 77, 77–79, 164n21; China journey, 78; death, 78–79; disciples, 49, 79, 80; and Emperor Wu, 11, 30, 78, 79; and Huike, 27, 76, 78–79, 79–80; robe (*see* robe of Bodhidharma); three phrases (*see* three phrases of Wuxiang)
bodhimaṇḍa (place of practice): of Wuxiang, 99; Wuzhu on, 36, 62, 104, 167n77
Bodhiruci, Trepiṭaka: and Bodhidharma, 78; and Huike, 80–81; *Ru Lengqie jing,* 76–77
bodhisattva path, 31
bodhisattva precepts, 30–37; Chan reinterpretation of, 33–35; conventional and ultimate, 34–35; emptiness, 39; formalization of, 31, 160n1; formlessness, 34–35, 62, 63; interiorization of, 33–35; maintaining (*see* maintaining the bodhisattva precepts); practice of (*see* precepts practice); taking (*see* taking the bodhisattva precepts); texts on, 31–33; Wuzhu on, 36–37, 53, 140, 167n77
Bodhisattvabhūmi, 31–32
bodhisattvas, 17, 139, 144; calling on, 30–31; Chinese sages identified

with, 73; perceptions, 9; power (of skillful means), 10, 63–64; vs. śrāvakas, 90–91; sympathetic resonance, 9–10; visualizing, 31. *See also* images
bondage by ignorance, 48
Brahmajāla-sūtra, 32–33, 160nn3,4
Brahmaloka, 123, 144
Brāhmanical Voice, 72, 163n9
brilliance, mental, 133
Buddha (Buddha-Jewel), 17, 146
the Buddha (Śākyamuni): and Ānanda, 91, 121–122; Brāhmanical Voice, 72, 163n9; on Buddhism in China, 75; characteristics, 90; continued direct transmission from, 21; demon warnings, 91–92; and the Dharma, 153; following the Buddha's teachings/words, 89; incarnation, 72–73; vs. Laozi and Zhuangzi, 145; and the nun's order, 46–47; seeing (*see* seeing the Buddha); on śrāvakas, 91; on study of the Vinaya precepts and the Dharma, 148; and Subhuti, 108, 109; transmission of his robe to Maitreya, 19, 92; and Utpalavarṇā, 27, 108–109
Buddha and Yaśas (two Brahmins), 77–78
Buddha image in Emperor Ming's dream, 70, 73
buddha nature (true nature): damask and, 100–101q; mind nature as, 12; as the nature of the precepts, 34; purity, 106; seeing (perceiving), 102–103, 167n75; and social contracts, 39
Buddhapiṭakaduḥśīlanirgraha-sūtra, 91q
buddhas, 17; becoming a buddha, 62, 142, 153; calling on, 30–31, 99–100; Chan masters as living buddhas, 62–63; incarnation of, 74–75; perceptions, 9; power (of skillful means), 10, 63–64; sympathetic resonance, 9–10; visualizing, 31. *See also* images
Buddhism: vs. Daoism, 145–146; Hīnayāna, 159n2; Jesuit criticism of, 53; nun's order, 46–47; soteriology in, 5. *See also* Buddhism in China; Mahāyāna
Buddhism in China, 73–74; Bodhidharma's arrival, 78; the Buddha on, 75; growth, 8–9, 11–12, 16, 75; persecution of, 9, 12, 32, 59, 82; ruler's role, 32–33, 74; transmission accounts (*see* master-disciple narratives). *See also* Chan; Huayan Buddhism; Tiantai school
Buddhism in India: master-disciple narratives, 20–21, 21–22
Buddhist rituals, 16; ordination rituals, 19, 33; performance (*see* sacred performance); and power distribution in practice centers, 64; professionalization of, 33; resistance to, 37; for taking the bodhisattva precepts, 30, 31–32, 33, 88–89; Tiantai school and, 33–34
Buddhist texts. *See* texts

Buddhists: Daoists vs. Buddhists in ritual combat, 70–72, 163n8; Western Buddhists, 63–64

Cai Yin, 70
calling on buddhas/bodhisattvas, 30–31, 99–100
Cao Gui and Wuzhu, 25–26, 38–39, 106–107
Caoqi: Huineng at, 87, 88
Chan (Chan Buddhism): antinomianism (*see* antinomianism [in Chan]); berating monks, 41, 126; the challenge for, 14; contestation of rivals, 15, 22–23, 29, 61; development of, 6, 12–14, 22–24, 61; and devotional practices, 8 (*see also* . . . and merit practices, *below*); foundational narrative, 12–14; hitting/beating monks, 41, 126, 129; iconoclasm (*see* iconoclasm [in Chan]); Jesuit criticism of, 53; kinship model, 61; lineage (*see* lineage [of Chan]); masters (*see* Chan masters); and merit practices, 8, 11, 12, 30; the Middle Way in, 61; monastic code, 60–61; nuns (*see* Chan nuns); patriarchy in, 20, 23–24; patriarchy mythos, 12–13, 18–19, 23; polemics, 22–23; Purity Chan (*see* viewing purity); reinterpretation of the precepts, 33–35; in Sichuan (*see* Sichuan Chan); Tathāgata Chan, 102; in Tibet, 57–59; transmission accounts (*see* master-disciple narratives); transmission ideology, 12, 15, 18, 22–24, 65; Wuzhu's Chan, 151–152; Wuzhu's reputation in, 4, 53, 56. *See also* Zen
Chan literature: the *Lidai fabao ji* and Song Chan literature, 62; Tibetan appropriations of, 57–58
Chan masters (Venerables): desires, 96; as living buddhas, 62–63; as neither Southern nor Northern, 128; portrayal of, 54; wild animals and, 82, 99. *See also specific masters*
Chan men jing, 90q
Chan miyao jing, 90q
Chan nuns: Wuzhu's disciples, 50–52, 135–136; Zongchi, 49, 79
Chan texts. *See Lidai fabao ji; Platform Sūtra; and other specific texts*
Chandaka, 72, 163n10
Changjingjin: Wuzhu and, 50, 135–136
Chanmen jing, 78
Chanshi jing, 150q
Chanyan qinggui, 60–61
Chaoran. *See* Zhiyi
Chaozang. *See* Jingzang
characteristics: attachment to, 105, 134, 138, 142, 150; of the Buddha, 90. *See also* transcending characteristics
Chen Chuzang and Wuzhu, 24, 105–106
China (imperial China): dynastic succession in, 23; hierarchy in, 7. *See also* Buddhism in China
Chinese nuns: biographies, 47. *See also* Chan nuns
Chinese texts: on the bodhisattva precepts, 32–33. *See also specific texts*

Chongyuan (Yuan): Shenhui and, 102–103
Chu shanxin, 71
Chuji (Tang), 57, 97–98, 162n13; Shenhui on, 103–104; and Wuxiang, 98, 98–99, 110; Zhishen and, 97, 97–98
clergy: patronage issue, 39–41, 42–43; professionalization of, 23
collective practices, 33
commentaries, reading, 130
community: hierarchy in, 7. *See also* Bao Tang group/school
compassion: Wuzhu on, 153–154
compounding poisons, 129
comprehending sūtras, 127
compulsions. *See* defilements
conceptualization. *See* thought(s)
conditionality: and awakening, 142
confession. *See* repentance practice
Confucius: the Buddha vs., 145–146; Kumara as, 73; on nonconceiving and nondoing, 143–144
consciousness: of the Dharma, 140; extinguishing (Zongmi), 44, 55
consciousnesses, sixth through ninth, 124
"consulting one's own feelings," 55, 56
contemplative practices, 89–90, 165nn40,41; concentrating on sense objects, 90, 123, 143, 150. *See also* meditation; *samādhi*
contestation of rivals, 15, 22–23, 29, 61
corpse decay contemplation, 165n40
critique of religion, 5–6, 15
Cui Gan (Vice-Director): Du Hongjian and, 168n88, 169n100; invitation of Wuzhu, 116, 117; and the monks of Jingzhong and Ningguo monasteries, 115, 116; and Wuzhu, 117–118, 121–126
cultivating one's own practice, 137
Cunda, 102–103
cutting off the source of birth and death, 50

Da Tang xiyu ji (Xuanzang), 19
damask and buddha nature, 100–101q
Dao, 155, 176n255
Daoan, 88–89
Daode jing (Laozi): teachings, 143, 144, 145
Daoism: Buddhism vs., 145–146
Daoists: vs. Buddhists in ritual combat, 70–72, 163n8; Wuzhu and, 142–146
Daoxin, 82–84; death, 84; and Hongren, 84, 84–85; Sengcan and, 82, 82–83; and Wenwu (Emperor), 83–84
Daoyan: Wuzhu and, 151
Daoyi, 40, 109–110
Daoyou: Wuzhu and, 150–151
Daoyu, 79
Dasheng wusheng fangbian men, 34
dazhangfu, 51, 52
Dazhi: Wuzhu and, 151
death: of Bodhidharma, 78–79; of Daoxin, 84; of Hongren, 85–86; of Huike, 80–81; of Huineng, 88; of Sengcan, 82; of Siṃha Bhikṣu, 21–22, 75–76; of Wuxiang, 99, 112; of Wuzhu, 63, 157; of Zhishen, 97. *See also* birth-and-death

decreasing day by day, 144
deer, 100, 176n70
defilements (*kleśa*), 7, 142, 144, 147, 149, 172n157; awakening and defilement, 77; escape metaphor, 172n173; exhaustion of, 144; Huineng on, 18; removing, 30, 165n41 (*see also upāya*); thoughts as, 104–105; wedge metaphor, 125; Wuzhu on, 104–105, 125, 142, 144, 147, 149, 154. *See also* ignorance
delusion(s), 122; Huineng on, 18; the three trainings on, 38
demon warnings from the Buddha, 91–92
desires of masters, 96
destinies, 121–122
devotion: and sympathetic resonance, 9–10
devotional practices: Chan and, 8; and patronage, 39–41, 109; and power distribution in practice centers, 64; Western Buddhists and, 64; Wuzhu on, 39–40. *See also* merit practices; precepts practice; purification practices
Dhammapada, 90q, 120q, 138q
dhāraṇi, 16
Dharma (Dharma-Jewel), 17–18, 146; "Amid the Dharma but not practicing," 138; the Buddha and, 153; the Buddha on study of, 148; consciousness of, 140; expounding/explaining/explicating, 127, 146, 149; grasping at, 125, 138; "How could one teach it?," 139; knowing, 17, 146; manifesting, 155; as nothing to attain, 139, 144; *śramaṇa* Dharma, 91, 129–130, 148. *See also* teaching(s) . . .
"Dharma" illness, 139–140
Dharma master groups: Wuzhu and, 128–130, 146, 150–152
Dharma transmission. *See* transmission (of the Dharma)
Dharmaratna, 70, 72
dharmas: emptiness, 134–135; mind and, 122, 142, 148; as true/wrong, 120–121, 127
Dharmatrāta. *See* Bodhidharma
dhyāna. *See* contemplative practices; meditation; *samādhi*
Diamond Sūtra (Vajracchedikā), 89q, 138q, 152–153, 175n241
difficulties endured by women: obstructions and, 50, 135, 172n157
direct mind: taking refuge in, 37
discipline. *See śila*
discrimination: nondiscrimination vs., 44
distinctions, making, 120–121, 127, 128, 150
"do not be deluded" phrase (Wuxiang), 37, 38, 100, 119
"do not forget" phrase (Wuxiang), 37–38, 107, 119
doctrines, studying, 130
dog metaphors, 100, 150, 176n70
Dōgen and *shikantaza*, 6
donation practices, 9, 10–11. *See also* patronage; receiving offerings/donations

Dong Xuan and the transmission of the robe to Wuzhu, 27–28, 99, 110–112
Donglin monastery, 77
Dragon Princess in the *Lotus Sūtra,* 46, 48
Du Ang, 115–116
Du Hongjian (Lord Minister): and Cui Gan, 168n88, 169n100; invitation of Wuzhu, 115, 116, 117; robe story told to, 28–29, 114; search for Wuxiang's successor/Wuzhu, 112–114; and Wuzhu, 117, 118–121
dualism in Wuzhu's teaching, 60
Dunhuang, 57; *Lidai fabao ji* manuscripts, 3, 67; social documents, 49; Tibetan manuscripts, 57–59
dynastic succession in China, 23
Dzogchen: Sichuan Chan and, 59

effort, good, 120, 169n92
emptiness: of the bodhisattva precepts, 39; of dharmas, 134–135; of good and evil, 63; returning home to, 148; sitting in (*see* sitting in idleness/emptiness). *See also* nonduality
enlightenment (awakening): conceptualization and, 138; conditionality and, 142; and defilement, 77; gradual awakening, 12; and maintaining the bodhisattva precepts, 35; in meditation, 151; and practice, 14, 62; realization, 124; self-awakening, 142; sudden (*see* sudden awakening/enlightenment). *See also bodhi*; liberation; nirvāṇa
eschatological theories, 22
eulogy for Wuzhu, 154–157
everyday mind, 60
"everything is meditation," 132, 149, 152
expedient means. *See upāya*
expounding/explaining/explicating the Dharma, 127, 146, 149
"extinguishing consciousness" (Zongmi), 44, 55
"extinguishing of the mind" (Shenqing), 54–56

Falun: Wuzhu and, 133–134
family ties: of monks, 48–49, 152–153; old men wishing to give up, 48, 140–141
Fangguang jing, 138q
Faru, 85, 87, 92
Faure, Bernard: on Chan polemics, 22
Fayuan: Wuzhu and, 48–49, 152–153, 175n240
feelings: "consulting one's own . . . ," 55, 56
Fei Shucai, 71
filial piety as *śila,* 33
finger: pointing with, 129–130
Five Cessations, 89, 165n41
five difficulties, three obstructions and, 50, 135, 172n157
flag blowing in the wind: Huineng on, 93
following the Buddha's teachings, 89
"form is emptiness, emptiness is form," 6

formless practice, 4, 56; sitting in idleness/emptiness, 6, 40, 45, 53, 109–110. *See also* no-thought
formlessness: of the bodhisattva precepts, 34–35, 62, 63; immanence vs., 60
foundational narrative of Chan, 12–14
fourth *dhyāna* unlearned monk, 92, 166n59
Fu fazang zhuan succession stories, 21–22, 75–76
Fu Yi, 70, 73q, 163n4
Fujian of the Qin and Daoan, 88
fulfilling the Vinaya precepts, 39, 147–148
"fundamental" illness, 139–140
fundamental nature of beings, 145

Gaoseng zhuan, 164n15
Gaozong, Emperor: and Hongren, 85
generosity: power of, 10
getting ravings by rote, 40, 109
Goddess in the *Vimalakīrtinirdeśa-sūtra,* 46, 48
good and evil: nonduality/emptiness, 35, 63
good effort, 120, 169n92
gradual awakening: Shenhui on, 12
gradual development/cultivation: and sudden awakening/enlightenment, 26–27, 44–45
grasping at meanings, 89, 123
grasping at the Dharma, 125, 138
Gregory, Peter: on laissez-faire spontaneity, 44
Groner, Paul: on ordination rituals, 33
Guanding: on Tiantai lineage and transmission ideology, 21
Guangtong: and Bodhidharma, 78; and Huike, 80–81
Guanlu: Wuzhu and, 150–151
Guifeng Zongmi. *See* Zongmi
Guṇabhadra, Trepiṭaka, 76

Hanfa neizhuan, 70, 163n3
Heart Sūtra phrase, 6
Helen mountains, 106, 168n82
hemp, silver, and gold story, 101
hierarchy in community vs. imperial China, 7
Hīnayāna (Hīnayāna Buddhism), 159n2
hitting/beating monks, 41, 126, 129
Hongren, 84–86; Daoxin and, 84, 84–85; death, 85–86; disciples, 85, 86, 92; and Huineng, 13, 85, 86–87, 92–93; and Zhishen, 97
Hongzheng, 126
Hongzhou school: Wuxiang and, 59–61; Zongmi's criticism of, 24, 44, 60
host and guest, 123, 147, 170n110
"How could one teach it?," 139
Huairang, 60
Huan Xuan, Emperor, 74, 164n15
Huayan Buddhism: Fifth Patriarch (*see* Zongmi); jewel net analogy, 9
Hui sanjiao (Wu), 74q
Huike, 79–81; Bodhidharma and, 27, 76, 78–79, 79–80; death, 80–81; and Sengcan, 80, 81, 81–82, 164n28; transmission of the robe to, 78–79, 80

Huiming (Fochuan Huiming?): Wuzhu and the disciples of, 128–130
Huiming (former general): Huineng and, 87
Huiming and Yixing: Wuzhu and, 134–135
Huineng, 86–88, 92–94; on the bodhisattva precepts, 34–35; death, 88; disciples, 87–88, 93–94, 95–96, 106; on the flag blowing in the wind, 93; hiding and emergence, 93–94; Hongren and, 13, 85, 86–87, 92–93; and Huiming, 87; and laymen, 48; ordination, 93–94; on purity, 18; vs. Shenxiu (verses), 13–14; successor, 87–88; and the transmission of the robe of Bodhidharma, 27–28, 87–88, 104; transmission of the robe to, 85, 86; Wu Zetian and, 27–28, 94–95; and Yinzong, 93–94. *See also Platform Sūtra*
Huisi and Zhiyi, 21
Huiwen and Nāgārjuna, 21
Huiyi: Wuzhu and, 128
Huiyuan (Yuan), 74; and the two Brahmins, 77

iconoclasm (in Chan), 37, 53, 59, 60, 61, 64; of the Bao Tang group, 54–55
ideology of transmission: in Chan, 12, 15, 18, 22–24, 65; Tiantai ideology, 21
ignorance, 100, 139; bondage by, 48; and *prajñā*, 100q
images: Buddha image in Emperor Ming's dream, 70, 73; of female realization in Mahāyāna texts, 46, 48; reproduction of, 8–9; soteriological function, 9–10
immanence: vs. formlessness, 60; and the Middle Way, 61
imperial minister. *See* Du Hongjian
incantations, 16
incarnation of buddhas, 74–75
increasing day by day, 144
India. *See* Buddhism in India
indulging others vs. oneself, 137
intention: nonintention, 130; quality of, 137
interdependent reflective functioning, 9
interiorization of the bodhisattva precepts, 33–35
"the intimate place of the wise," 134

Jesuit criticism of Buddhism, 53
Jesus. *See* Mishihe
jewel net analogy, 9
Jiajiang performances, 64–65
Jiancheng: Wuzhu and the disciples of, 151–152
Jiannan. *See* Sichuan
Jin Shu, 74, 164n15
Jingde chuandeng lu, 23, 56, 61
Jingjue: *Lengqie shizi xuemo ji*, 76
Jingzang (Chaozang): Wuzhu and, 130–131
Jingzhong monastery: Daoyi with Wuxiang at, 40, 109–110; Du Hongjian at, 112–113; Vinaya masters at, 29, 115; Wuzhu and the monks of, 27, 108–109; Wuzhu with Wuxiang at, 26, 107–108

Jingzhong school: on the three phrases of Wuxiang, 37–38, 106–107
Jorgenson, John: on Chan patriarchy, 23
just sitting, 6. *See also* sitting in idleness/emptiness
"just this": Wuzhu on, 155

Kamalaśila vs. Moheyan, 58
Kaṇṭaka, 72, 163n10
karmic cause, 140
karmic reward, 123, 144; destinies, 121–122
kāṣāya robe of verification. *See* robe of Bodhidharma
Kaśyapa, Bhadra: Shenhui and, 103
Kāśyapamātraṅga, 70, 71–72
Ke. *See* Huike
Kim of Yizhou. *See* Wuxiang
kinship model of Chan, 61
kleśa. *See* defilements
"knowing" illness, 139
knowing the Dharma, 17, 146
Konghui monastery: Wuzhu's descent to, 117–118
kongxian zuo. *See* sitting in idleness/emptiness
Kumara as Confucius, 73

laissez-faire spontaneity, 44
Laṅkāvatāra-sūtra: on the consciousnesses, 124; on grasping at meanings, 89, 123; on making distinctions, 128, 150; on the mind, 127; on no-thought, 120; on preachers (delusive), 129–130, 148; on the real vs. verbal explanation, 127, 133; on seeing the Buddha, 121; translations of, 76–77, 164n32; wedge metaphor, 125; on wrong views, 89, 90
Laoan, 85, 92, 95, 96
Laozi: the Buddha vs., 145–146; Mahākāśyapa as, 73; on nondoing, 143, 144–145; on virtue, 144; on the Way, 145
the Law: the Dharma as, 17
lax practice criticism of Wuzhu, 39–40, 42
lay practice, 48
lay supporters: Wuzhu and, 42–43, 153–154
laypeople (laymen): collective practices, 33; Huineng and, 48; merit practices, 8–9; support from (*see* patronage); Wuzhu and, 36–37, 42–43, 48, 118–126, 140–141, 153–154
laywomen: practice spheres, 47
legitimacy of transmission, 16
Lengqie jing versions, 76–77
Lengqie shizi xuemo ji (Jingjue), 76
Lengqie Yedu gushi, 81
Liaojianxing: Wuzhu and, 50–51, 52, 136
liberation, 36; merit and, 10. *See also* enlightenment (awakening)
Lidai fabao ji, 3; on the Chan lineage as linked to Bodhidharma through Wuzhu, 22; criticism of, 3, 54–56; determinative characteristics, 4; Dunhuang manuscripts, 3, 67; fate, 56, 57–59; as the robe of Wuzhu,

65–66; Shenqing on, 3, 54–56; and Song Chan literature, 62; sources, 69–70, 164n32, 165n33; sūtra quotations section, 89–92; Tibetan traces, 57–59; tone, 52; women in (*see* women in the *Lidai fabao ji*); writers of, 51 (*see also* Bao Tang group/school); writing of, 168n80; writing style, 4
lineage (of Chan), 75–76; contestation of rivals, 15, 22–23, 29, 61; the end of the line, 21–22; as linked to Bodhidharma through Wuzhu, 22; transtemporal relationships, 21. *See also* master-disciple narratives
Lion's Roar section (*Nirvāṇa-sūtra*), 102q
Liu Zhubo, 85, 92, 166n66
Liuzu tanjing. *See Platform Sūtra*
living buddhas: Chan masters as, 62–63
Lotus Sūtra, 21; Dragon Princess in, 46, 48; recitation of, 134–135, 171n149; on Trepiṭakas, 76–77

Ma Liang, 113
Ma Xiong, 104
magic: incantations, 16
Mahākāśyapa: as Laozi, 73; and the transmission of the Dharma, 19
Mahāmaudgalyāyana, 108
mahāparinirvāṇa, 133, 171n146
Mahāprajāpatī Gotamī, 46
Mahāprajñāpāramitā-sūtra, 75q
Mahāyāna (Mahāyāna Buddhism), 6–7, 124, 129
Mahāyāna texts: on the bodhisattva precepts, 31–32; female realization images in, 46, 48. *See also* sūtras
maintaining the bodhisattva precepts, 34, 36, 101; enlightenment and, 35. *See also* precepts practice; taking the bodhisattva precepts
Maitreya: transmission of the robe of the Buddha to, 19, 92; visualizing and calling on, 31
making distinctions, 120–121, 127, 128, 150
man standing story, 151
manifestation of practice, 54
manifesting the Dharma, 155
Manjuśri: as not far, 141; and Vimalakīrti, 139
mantra, transmission. *See* three phrases of Wuxiang
mantric arts, 16
marketplace: Wuzhu in, 66
master-disciple narratives (Buddhist transmission accounts), 20–22; unreliability, 23; Wuxiang and Wuzhu, 25–27
masters. *See* Chan masters
Mazu Daoyi, 61; Wuxiang and, 59–60
means, skillful/expedient. *See upāya*
meditation: attachment to, 150; awakening in, 151; everything as, 132, 149, 152; studying doctrines and, 130; Wuzhu on, 128, 130, 132, 152. *See also* contemplative practices; *samādhi*; sitting in idleness/emptiness
Meng: and Wuzhu, 110

mental brilliance, 133
merit, 8; and liberation, 10; transfer of, 9–10
merit practices, 8–9, 10–11, 63; Chan and, 8, 11, 12, 30; good effort, 120, 169n92; as self-purification methods, 30–31; Western Buddhists and, 64
Messiah (Mishihe, Jesus), 75, 76
Middle Way in Chan, 61
mieshi, 44, 55
Mihirakula (king of Kashmir), 21–22, 75–76, 164n20
military. *See* Tang military
mind, 36, 40, 100, 105, 109; arousing, 130, 142, 149; brilliance, 133; and dharmas, 122, 142, 148; everyday mind, 60; "extinguishing of the mind," 54–56; no-mind, 129; of quiet sitting, 139; stingy mind, 137; and suffering, 120; taking refuge in direct mind, 37; the Three Jewels as of one's own, 17–18. *See also* thought(s) (conceptualization)
mind nature: as buddha nature, 12. *See also* buddha nature (true nature)
Ming (former general). *See* Huiming
Ming (of Mount Daoci), 106
Ming, Emperor (Xiaoming), 73–74; legend of, 70–73, 73
Mingfa: Wuzhu and, 150–151
Mishihe (Messiah, Jesus), 75, 76
Mogao caves, 3
Mohe zhiguan (Tiantai Zhiyi), 21
Moheyan vs. Kamalaśila, 58
Momanni (Mani), 75, 76
monastic rules, 88; *Brahmajāla-sūtra,* 32–33; Chan code, 60–61; for nuns, 47, 88. *See also* Vinaya
monks: berating, 41, 126; family ties, 48–49, 152–153; fourth *dhyāna* unlearned monk, 92, 166n59; hitting/beating, 41, 126, 129; robes, 19; senior monks, 62; Wuxiang's fellow monks, 110; Wuzhu and the Jingzhong monks, 27; Wuzhu's fellow monks, 40, 43, 109–110 (*see also* Shenqing; Zongmi)
morally good or bad categories, 124
morally neutral categories, 123–124, 176n260
mother, monk with. *See* Fayuan
Mount Baiya (Baiya Mountains), 99, 113; Wuzhu's invitation and descent from, 115, 116, 117–118
Mount Lu, 74, 77, 78
Mount Pingmao, 85
Mount Shuangfeng (Potou), 83
Mount Wutai, 168n81; pilgrimage to, 141; Qingliang monastery, 25, 106
mountain practice, 40, 99, 109–110; vs. plains practice, 40, 109. *See also* sitting in idleness/emptiness
Mouzi, 73–74+q, 163n13
mowang (in the third phrase of Wuxiang), 37–38, 39; *wang* character, 38, 119–120, 121
mystique of transmission, 15, 20, 24, 26–27, 39; in the Chan community, 61

Nāgārjuna as a spiritual ancestor, 21
naturalized authority vs. natural authority, 7
nature: fundamental nature of beings, 145; no-nature, 133; seeing the nature, 105, 107, 142, 147, 149, 153. *See also* buddha nature
Neng. *See* Huineng
nihilism: Wuzhu as accused of, 55–56
Nine Vizualizations, 165n40
Ningguo monastery: Du Hongjian at, 112–113
nirvāṇa, 105, 122; mahāparinirvāṇa, 133, 171n146
"nirvāṇa" illness, 139–140
Nirvāṇa-sūtra, 100q, 102–103+q, 133
Niu Wangxian on Wuzhu, 113–114
no-mind: *śramaṇa* Dharma as, 129
no-nature, 133
no-practice, 105, 120; "Amid the Dharma but not practicing," 138. *See also* no-thought
no-recollection: ritual and, 65; Wuzhu on, 48, 141, 148, 155
"no-recollection" phrase (Wuxiang), 37, 38, 100, 106, 119
no-religion. *See* formless practice
no-thought (*wunian*): as "extinguishing consciousness" (Zongmi), 44, 55; as "extinguishing of the mind" (Shenqing), 54–56; the *Platform Sūtra* and, 14; and precepts practice, 56; ritual and, 65; Wuxiang on, 100, 101 (*see also* "no-thought" phrase); Wuzhu on, 8, 36, 40, 45, 48, 50, 51, 53, 105, 109, 119, 120, 122, 131, 131–132, 132, 133–134, 135, 135–136, 141, 148, 149, 153, 154; Wuzhu's robe as a costume of, 65–66
"no-thought" phrase (Wuxiang), 37, 38, 100, 106–107, 119
no-wisdom, 139
nonaction. *See* nondoing
nonconceptualization (nonconceiving), 59; Confucius on, 143–144. *See also* no-thought
nondiscrimination vs. discrimination, 44
nondoing (nonaction/nonactivity), 17, 36, 146; Confucius on, 143–144; Laozi on, 143, 144–145; not abiding in, 144–145; Shenqing on, 55; Zhumo's despising of Wuzhu's "not doing," 129
nonduality, 36; of good and evil, 35; of just sitting, 6. *See also* emptiness
nonintention, 130
Northern Chan masters as not Northern, 128
Northern School (of Chan): Southern School vs., 12–14; text on the precepts, 34
not abiding in nondoing, 144–145
"not born," 145
"not doing" (Wuzhu): Zhumo's despising of, 129
not having views, 147
nothing to attain, 139, 144
nun's order, 46–47

nuns: Chinese nuns' biographies, 47; Mahāprajāpatī Gotamī, 46; monastic rules for, 47; Utpalavarṇā, 27, 108–109. *See also* Chan nuns

objectifications of practice, 37
objects: soteriological function, 9–10. *See also* images; sūtras
obstructions and difficulties endured by women, 50, 135, 172n157
offerings (donations): receiving, 41, 42–43, 89, 126–127, 136–137, 153–154
old men wishing to give up family ties: Wuzhu and, 48, 140–141
omens of Wuzhu's descent, 117
"one" illness, 140
one shoe story of Bodhidharma, 79
ordinary beings: perceptions, 9
ordination: of Huineng, 93–94; for nuns, 47; rituals, 19, 33; of Wuzhu, 25, 106

Patriarchal Master Dharma. *See* Bodhidharma
patriarchy (in Chan), 20, 23–24; mythos, 12–13, 18–19, 23
patronage (lay support): devotional practices and, 39–41, 109; precepts practice and, 41–43. *See also* receiving offerings/donations
Pelliot Tibetan 116, 58–59
Penkower, Linda: on Tiantai lineage and transmission ideology, 21
perceiving buddha nature. *See* seeing buddha nature
perceptions of buddhas and bodhisattvas vs. ordinary beings, 9
performance. *See* sacred performance
"perils of the patriarchs" hagiography style, 54
persecution of Buddhism in China, 9, 12, 32, 59, 82
pilgrimage to Mount Wutai, 141
place of practice. *See bodhimaṇḍa*
plains practice: mountain practice vs., 40, 109
Platform Sūtra, 13, 20, 56; on the bodhisattva precepts, 34–35; on the Chan lineage as linked to Bodhidharma, 22; Huineng vs. Shenxiu (in verses), 13–14; and no-thought, 14; setting, 33; on taking refuge in the Three Jewels, 17–18
poetry. *See* verses
pointing with a finger, 129–130
poisons: compounding, 129; three poisons, 7
polemics of Chan, 22–23
politics: soteriology and, 5–8; of transmission, 15
portrait of Wuzhu, 156–157
power: of buddhas and bodhisattvas, 10, 63–64; distribution in practice centers, 64; salvation and, 5–8; of skillful means, 10; social contracts and, 5–6
practice: Bao Tang practice, 44–45; cultivating one's own, 137; and

enlightenment, 14, 62; formless (*see* formless practice); lax practice criticism of Wuzhu, 39–40, 42; lay practice, 48; laywomen's spheres, 47; manifestation of, 54; no-practice (*see* no-practice); objectifications of, 37; the place of (*see bodhimaṇḍa*); of the precepts (*see* precepts practice); sudden practice, 34, 37; true practice, 34
practice centers: abuse of others in, 41–42; power distribution in, 64
practices: collective practices, 33; contemplative practices, 89–90, 165nn40,41; contestation of rivals over, 15, 22–23; mountain practice, 40, 99, 109–110; self-directed practices, 33. *See also* devotional practices; merit practices; no-practice; no-thought; precepts practice; purification practices; sitting in idleness/emptiness
prajñā, 37, 100, 101, 102, 119, 134; Dharma Master on, 146; Fayuan on, 152; ignorance and, 100q
Prajñāpāramitā, 75
Prajñāpāramitā mantra, 154
Prajñāpāramitara, 79, 80
pratyekabuddhas, 145, 166n58
preachers, delusive, 129–130, 148
precepts: basic precepts, 160n1; practice of (*see* precepts practice); pure precepts, 32. *See also* bodhisattva precepts; monastic rules; Vinaya precepts
precepts ceremonies, 31–32, 34; mass assemblies, 35
precepts platform, 33
precepts practice: evolution of, 31–37; no-thought and, 56; and patronage, 41–43. *See also* maintaining the bodhisattva precepts; taking the bodhisattva precepts
precepts retreats, 33
production/nonproduction of thoughts, 147
professionalization of the clergy/rituals, 23, 33
pure precepts, 32
purification practices (self-purification methods): merit practices as, 30–31; Shenhui on, 34
purity, 147; of buddha nature, 106; Huineng on, 18. *See also* viewing purity
Purity Chan. *See* viewing purity
"purity" illness, 139–140
Pusa jie, 129

Qin Hua, 117, 118
Qin Jing, 70
Qin Ti on Wuzhu, 114
Qingjing faxing jing, 73q, 163n12
Qingliang monastery, 25, 106
Qingyuan: Wuzhu and, 121, 123

ravings: getting by rote, 40, 109
reading commentaries, 130
the real vs. verbal explanation, 127, 133

realization, 124. *See also* enlightenment (awakening)
"realization" illness, 139–140
receiving offerings/donations, 41, 42–43, 89, 126–127, 136–137, 153–154
receiving the bodhisattva precepts. *See* taking the bodhisattva precepts
recitation: calling on buddhas, 30–31, 99–100; of the *Lotus Sūtra,* 134–135, 171n149
refuge. *See* taking refuge . . .
relationships: subitism and, 65. *See also* master-disciple narratives
religion: critique of, 5–6, 15; no-religion (*see* formless practice); without religion, 64
removing defilements, 30, 165n41. *See also upāya*
Ren (wife of Cui Gan), 121, 169n101
repentance practice, 30, 33; Wuzhu on, 43, 154
resource allocation: social contracts and, 5–6
"the [response] that follows pervades all," 143, 144
restraining oneself vs. others, 137
returning home to emptiness, 148
"rhetoric of immediacy," 22
rituals: Daoists vs. Buddhists ritual combat, 70–72, 163n8. *See also* Buddhist rituals
robe of Bodhidharma (*kāṣāya* robe of verification), 18, 18–20; Huiming and, 87; Shenhui on, 19, 65, 103; Shenqing on, 54; symbolic importance, 19–20, 65–66, 78, 80. *See also* transmission of the robe of Bodhidharma
robe of the Buddha: transmission to Maitreya, 19, 92
robes of monks, 19
roots, two kinds, 122
Ru Lengqie jing, 76–77
rudrākṣa seeds, 121, 169n102
ruler's role in Buddhism in China, 32–33; Huan Xuan, 74
rules. *See* monastic rules

sacred performance: contemporary ritual performances, 64–65; of masters as living buddhas, 62–63; Wuzhu's passing away, 63, 157
Saddharmapuṇḍarīka-sūtra. See Lotus Sūtra
śaikṣas, 166n57
salvation: and power, 5–8
samādhi, 37, 100, 101, 102, 119; contemplative practices, 89–90, 165nn40,41; Subhuti in, 108, 109; and thought, 138; true *samādhi,* 142
Saṅgha (Saṅgha-Jewel), 18
Śāriputra: the Buddha and, 91
Sba-bzhed, 57–58q, 162n10
Scripture in Forty-two Sections, 70, 73, 163n6
seated meditation: Wuzhu on, 128, 130. *See also* sitting in idleness/emptiness
seeing (true seeing), 149; vs. *śila,* 148
seeing buddha nature, 102–103, 167n75
seeing each other, 154

seeing the Buddha, 40, 63, 90, 100, 108–109, 109, 121, 140, 141, 149, 154
seeing the nature, 105, 107, 142, 147, 149, 153
self-administered vows, 33
self-awakening, 142
self-directed practices, 33
self-tonsuring of Liaojianxing, 52
Sengcan, 81–82; and Daoxin, 82, 82–83; death, 82; Huike and, 80, 81, 81–82, 164n28
senior monks, 62
sense objects: concentrating on, 90, 123, 143, 150
Shen. *See* Zhishen
Shenhui, 101–104; Bodhidharma story, 11; and Chongyuan, 102–103; foundational narrative of Chan, 12–14; and Kaśyapa (Bhadra), 103; patriarchal mythos, 11, 18–19; on purification practices, 34; on the robe of Bodhidharma, 19, 65, 103; on Shen, Tang, and Tang's disciples, 103–104; vs. Shenxiu, 12, 102, 167nn72,73; on the three trainings, 37–38; on Wuxiang (Kim of Yizhou), 25, 104; and Wuzhu, 25, 38, 106; and Zongmi, 24, 38
Shenqing: *Beishan lu,* 3, 4, 54–55+q; on the *Lidai fabao ji,* 3, 54–56
Shenxiu, 13, 76, 85, 92, 95, 96; Huineng vs. (in verses), 13–14; Shenhui vs., 12, 102, 167nn72,73
shikantaza, 6. *See also* sitting in idleness/emptiness
Sian: *Zhaiwen,* 89
Sichuan, 168n90; imperial minister in (*see* Du Hongjian); military campaigns from, 57
Sichuan Chan: and Dzogchen, 59; and Song Chan, 61. *See also* Bao Tang group/school; Chuji; Hongzhou school; Jingzhong monastery; Shenqing; Wuxiang; Wuzhu
Śikṣānanda: *Lengqie jing,* 77
śila, 37, 100, 101, 102, 119; filial piety as, 33; seeing vs., 148
Siṃha Bhikṣu: beheading of, 21–22, 75–76
Sishi'er zhang jing. See Scripture in Forty-two Sections
sister of Wuxiang, 49, 98
sitting in idleness/emptiness (*kongxian zuo*), 6, 40, 45, 53, 109–110
sixth through ninth consciousnesses, 124
skillful means. *See upāya*
social contracts: and power, 5–6; true nature and, 39
Song Chan: Sichuan Chan and, 61
Song Chan literature: the *Lidai fabao ji* and, 62
Song Yun and Bodhidharma, 79
Songdetsen, Trhi, 58
soteriological function of objects, 9–10
soteriology: in Buddhism, 5; and politics, 5–8
Southern School (of Chan): vs. Northern School, 12–14
spiritual aspiration (aspiration), 6
splitting wood metaphor, 125
spontaneity, laissez-faire, 44

śramaṇa Dharma, 91, 129–130, 148
śrāvakas, 145; vs. bodhisattvas, 90–91; the Buddha on, 91
stains: viewing purity as, 131
stingy mind, 137
Strīvivarta-vyākaraṇa-sūtra, 90q
studying doctrines, 130
studying the Vinaya precepts and the Dharma: the Buddha on, 148
Subhuti: and the Buddha, 108, 109
subitism: and relationships, 65
suchness (*tathātā*), 129, 154, 155
Sudden Awakening to the Fundamental Reality, 59
sudden awakening/enlightenment: and gradual development/cultivation, 26–27, 44–45; Shenhui on, 12
sudden practice, 34, 37
suffering: the mind and, 120
Sumedha as Yanhui, 73
Sun Huan: eulogy for Wuzhu, 154–157
Śūraṃgama-sūtra: on conceptualization and awakening, 138; on destinies, 121–122; on the mind, 40, 109, 120; on wrong views, 91–92
sūtras: *Brahmajāla-sūtra,* 32–33, 160nn3,4; comprehending, 127; *Heart Sūtra* phrase, 6; *Mahāprajñā-pāramitā-sūtra,* 75q; *Nirvāṇa-sūtra,* 100q, 102–103+q, 133; quotations section in the *Lidai fabao ji,* 89–92; soteriological function, 9–10; *Vajra-samādhi-sūtra,* 90q, 120q; *Viśeṣacin-tibrahma-paripṛcchā-sūtra,* 89q, 90q, 120–121q, 127q. *See also Avataṃsaka-sūtra; Laṅkāvatāra-sūtra; Lotus Sūtra; Platform Sūtra; Śūraṃgama-sūtra;* texts; *Vajracchedikā-sūtra; Vimalakīrtinirdeśa-sūtra; and other specific sūtras*
Sutton, Donald: on contemporary ritual performances, 64–65
Suzuki, D. T.: writings on Chan, 53
sympathetic resonance (of buddhas and bodhisattvas), 9–10

Taiwu, Emperor (of the Northern Wei), 9
taking refuge in direct mind, 37
taking refuge in the three bodies of the Buddha, 34–35
taking refuge in the Three Jewels, 17–18
taking the bodhisattva precepts, 31; ceremonies, 31–32, 34, 35; retreats, 33; rituals for, 30, 31–32, 33, 88–89. *See also* maintaining the bodhisattva precepts; precepts practice
talismans: as signs of legitimacy, 19. *See also* robe of Bodhidharma; robe of the Buddha
Tang. *See* Chuji
Tang imperial minister. *See* Du Hongjian
Tang military: campaigns from Sichuan, 57; officers on Wuzhu, 28–29, 113–114, 125–126; Wuzhu's connections to, 7–8, 24, 57
Tangwen: Wuzhu and, 128
Tathāgata Chan, 102
tathātā (suchness), 129, 154, 155

tea drinking challenge to Wuzhu, 151–152
tea verse, 141–142
teaching(s). *See below, specific teachings, and under specific masters*
teaching(s) of the Buddha: following, 89. *See also under* the Buddha; sūtras
teaching(s) of Wuxiang, 25–29, 37–39, 99–101; Tibetan traces, 58–59
teaching(s) of Wuzhu: on *bodhimaṇḍa,* 36, 62, 104, 167n77; on the bodhisattva precepts, 36–37, 53, 140, 167n77; on bondage, 48; on compassion, 153–154; on defilements, 104–105, 125, 142, 144, 147, 149, 154; on devotional practices, 39–40; dualism in, 60; on family ties, 48; for laypeople, 36–37, 42–43, 48, 118–126; loss and reappearance of, 66; on meditation, 128, 130, 132, 152; on no-recollection, 48, 141, 148, 155; on no-thought, 8, 36, 40, 45, 48, 50, 51, 53, 105, 109, 119, 120, 122, 131, 131–132, 132, 133–134, 135, 135–136, 141, 148, 149, 153, 154; on receiving donations, 41, 42–43, 126–127; on repentance practice, 43, 154; responses to criticism, 39–45, 54–56, 109–110, 126–127, 128–130, 151–152; as sacred performance, 62–63; tea verse, 141–142; on texts, 146, 152–153; on the Three Jewels, 17; on the three phrases of Wuxiang, 37, 38, 39; Tibetan traces, 58–59; on transcending characteristics, 17, 36, 51, 63, 104, 131, 134–135, 136, 146, 148, 149–150, 153; on the Vinaya precepts, 39, 147–148
temple donations. *See* patronage
Tendai sect: monastic rules, 32–33. *See also* Tiantai school
texts (Buddhist texts): on the bodhisattva precepts, 31–33; Chan (*see Lidai fabao ji; Platform Sūtra; and other specific texts*); reproduction of, 8–9; Tibetan manuscripts, 57–59; transmission of, 16; Wuzhu on, 146, 152–153. *See also* sūtras; *and other specific texts*
thought(s) (conceptualization), 40, 109; and awakening, 138; as defilements, 104–105; making distinctions, 120–121, 127, 128, 150; nonconceptualization, 59; production/nonproduction of, 147; reading commentaries and, 130; and *samādhi,* 138. *See also* mind; no-thought
three bodies of the Buddha: taking refuge in, 34–35
The Three Groups of Pure Precepts, 32
Three Jewels, 17–18, 146
three obstructions and five difficulties, 50, 135, 172n157
three phrases of Wuxiang, 37–39, 100, 101, 106–107, 119
three poisons, 7
three trainings, 37–38
Tiantai school: and Buddhist rituals, 33–34; lineage and transmission ideology, 21. *See also* Tendai sect
Tiantai Zhiyi: Huisi and, 21

Tibet: Chan and *Lidai fabao ji* traces in, 57–59
Tibetan empire, 57
Tibetan manuscripts, 57–59
Tiwu: Wuzhu and, 41–42, 126–127
transcending characteristics: Shenqing on, 55; *Vajracchedikā-sūtra* on, 89; Wuzhu on, 17, 36, 51, 63, 104, 131, 134–135, 136, 146, 148, 149–150, 153
transcending verbal explanation, 128, 149–150
transfer of merit, 9–10
transmission (of the Dharma), 15–18; accounts of (*see* master-disciple narratives); and authority, 15–16; Chan ideology, 12, 15, 18, 22–24, 65; contestation of rivals, 15, 22–23, 29, 61; continued direct transmission from the Buddha, 21; forms/levels, 15, 16; as imperiled, 22; legitimacy, 16; Mahākāśyapa and, 19; mystique (*see* mystique of transmission); the robe as verification of (*see* robe of Bodhidharma; robe of the Buddha); special transmission in Chan (*see . . .* Chan ideology, *above*); the Three Jewels in, 17–18; Tiantai ideology, 21; to Wuzhu from Wuxiang, 26–27, 27–29, 38–39, 99, 110–112. *See also* transmission of the robe of Bodhidharma
transmission mantra. *See* three phrases of Wuxiang
Transmission of the Lamp. *See Jingde chuandeng lu*
transmission of the robe of Bodhidharma, 18–20; to Chuji, 97; to Daoxin, 82; to Hongren, 84; to Huike, 78–79, 80; to Huineng, 85, 86; Huineng and, 27–28, 87–88, 104; to Sengcan, 81; Shenhui on, 103; Shenqing on, 54; the Vinaya masters and, 29; Wu Zetian and, 27–28, 49, 87, 94–95, 96; to Wuxiang, 98, 99; to Wuzhu, 27–29, 99, 111–112, 114; to Zhishen, 28, 49, 96
transmission of the robe of the Buddha to Maitreya, 19, 92
transtemporal relationships, 21
Treatise Masters: Wuzhu and, 149–150
Treatise on One Hundred Dharmas, 128, 170n128
Treatise on the Awakening of Faith, 100q, 149
Trepiṭaka Brāhmana: Zhishen and, 95–96
Trepiṭakas, 76–77, 164n22. *See also* Bodhiruci; Trepiṭaka Brāhmana
true nature. *See* buddha nature
true practice, 34
true *samādhi,* 142
two Brahmins, 77–78
Two Truths, 9, 10
two vehicles people, 145

"unborn," meaning of, 145
Unimpeded Wisdom and Yem, 59, 162n20
universe: jewel net analogy of, 9

upāya (skillful/expedient means), 6–7, 36, 104; vs. abuse of others, 7–8; power of, 10, 63–64
upholding the Vinaya precepts, 39, 147–148
Utpalavarṇā, 168n84; the Buddha and, 27, 108–109

Vajracchedikā-sūtra (Diamond Sūtra), 89q, 138q, 152–153, 175n241
Vajrasamādhi-sūtra, 90q, 120q
Venerables. *See* Chan masters
verbal explanation: attachment to, 129–130, 138; the real vs., 127, 133; transcending, 128, 149–150
verses: Huineng vs. Shenxiu, 13–14; Wang's poem, 140; Wuzhu's tea verse, 141–142
viewing purity (Purity Chan), 87, 102, 131–132, 167n72, 171n142
views: not having, 147; wrong views, 89, 90, 91–92
Vimalakīrti: Manjuśri and, 139
Vimalakīrtinirdeśa-sūtra, 36q, 90q, 120q, 139q; Goddess in, 46, 48
Vinaya, 16; Wuzhu on, 39, 147
Vinaya masters: at Jingzhong monastery, 29, 115; on Wuxiang, 113; on Wuzhu, 29, 115–116; Wuzhu and, 39, 42, 146–149; Wuzhu on, 147–148, 150–151. *See also* Guangtong
Vinaya precepts: the Buddha on study of, 148; violating/fulfilling/upholding, 39, 147–148
Vinayaviniścaya, 147, 174n210
Vinayaviniścaya-Upālipariprcchā-sūtra, 90–91q
Vinayottara, 147, 174n210
violating the Vinaya precepts, 39, 147–148
virtue: high and low, 144
Viśeṣacintibrahma-pariprcchā-sūtra, 89q, 90q, 120–121q, 127q
visualizing buddhas and bodhisattvas, 30–31
vows: self-administered vows, 33. *See also* bodhisattva precepts; repentance practice
vyākṛta, 124

Wang, Brahmacarya: poem, 140
wang character, 38, 119–120, 121
Wang Huang, 98, 99
Wang Jian, 115–116
Wang Xuiyan, 118
Wang Zun, 73
waves and water metaphor, 101q
the Way: Laozi on, 145
wedge metaphor, 125
Wei Zhejiao, 118
Wenwu, Emperor: and Daoxin, 83–84
Western Buddhists: contemporary Zen practitioners, 63–64; and devotional/merit-oriented practices, 64
White Horse Monastery, 70, 71
white milk: bleeding of, 22, 76, 80, 81
wild animals and Chan masters, 82, 99
"wisdom" illness, 139
women: laywomen's practice spheres, 47; obstructions and difficulties

women (*continued*)
endured by, 50, 135, 172n157; realization images in Mahāyāna texts, 46, 48. *See also* nuns; women in the *Lidai fabao ji*
women in the *Lidai fabao ji*, 47–52; Changjingjin, 50, 135–136; Liaojianxing, 50–51, 52, 136; Ren (wife of Cui Gan), 121, 169n101; sister of Wuxiang, 49; Wuzhu's disciples, 50–52, 135–136; Zongchi, 49, 79. *See also* Wu Zetian, Empress
working with appearances, 6–7
wrong views, 89, 90, 91–92
Wu, Emperor (of the Xiao Liang): Bodhidharma and, 11, 30, 78, 79; *Hui sanjiao*, 74q
Wu, Emperor (of the Zhou): persecution of Buddhism, 82
Wu Zetian, Empress, 94–96, 166n63; and Huineng, 27–28, 94–95; and the transmission of the robe of Bodhidharma, 27–28, 49, 94–95, 96; and Zhishen, 95, 96
wunian. *See* no-thought
Wutaishan. *See* Mount Wutai
Wuxiang (Kim of Yizhou), 25, 49, 57–58; and Ba Sangshi, 57–58; Chuji (Tang) and, 98, 98–99, 110; and Daoyi, 40, 109–110; death, 99, 112; fellow monks, 110; and the Hongzhou school, 59–61; and Mazu, 59–60; mountain practice, 99, 110; on no-thought, 100, 101 (*see also* "no-thought" phrase); search for his successor/Wuzhu, 112–114; Shenhui on, 25, 104; sister, 49, 98; sitting in idleness/emptiness, 110; teaching(s), 25–29, 37–39, 58–59, 99–101; three phrases, 37–39, 100, 101, 106–107, 119; Tibetan traces, 57–59; transmission of the robe to, 98, 99; transmission to Wuzhu, 26–27, 27–29, 38–39, 99, 110–112; Vinaya masters on, 113; vocation to become a monk, 49, 98; and Wuzhu, 25–29, 38–39, 40, 59, 99, 106–112, 119; Zhangqiu and, 99, 167n67
Wuying: Wuzhu and, 121, 123–125
Wuyou: Wuzhu and, 151–152
Wuzhu, 3, 24–29, 105–112; as ahead of his times, 5; army officers and, 28–29, 113–114, 125–126; on *bodhimaṇḍa*, 36, 62, 104, 167n77; on the bodhisattva precepts, 36–37, 53, 140, 167n77; on bondage, 48; Cao Gui and, 25–26, 38–39, 106–107; Chan (his own), 151–152; Chan reputation, 4, 53, 56; and Changjingjin, 50, 135–136; Chen Chuzang and, 24, 105–106; on compassion, 153–154; criticism of and responses from, 39–45, 54–56, 109–110, 126–127, 128–130, 151–152; and Cui Gan, 117–118, 121–126; and Daoists, 142–146; death (passing away), 63, 157; on defilements, 104–105, 125, 142, 144, 147, 149, 154; descent from Mount Baiya, 117–118; on devotional practices, 39–40; and Dharma master groups, 128–130, 146, 150–152; on Dharma masters, 150–151;

disciples, 48–49, 50–52, 130–136, 141–146, 152–153, 156–157 (*see also* Bao Tang group/school); and Du Hongjian, 117, 118–121; early wanderings, 24–26, 105–107; eulogy for, 154–157; and Falun, 133–134; on family ties, 48; and Fayuan, 48–49, 152–153, 175n240; fellow monks, 40, 43, 109–110 (*see also* Shenqing; Zongmi); female disciples, 50–52, 135–136; and Huiming and Yixing, 134–135; and Huiming's disciples, 128–130; and Huiyi, 128; invitations to descend from Mount Baiya, 115, 116, 117; and Jiancheng's disciples, 151–152; and Jingzang, 130–131; and the Jingzhong monks, 27, 108–109; and lay supporters, 42–43, 153–154; and laypeople, 36–37, 42–43, 48, 118–126, 140–141, 153–154; legacy, 53–66; and Liaojianxing, 50–51, 52, 136; in the marketplace, 66; on meditation, 128, 130, 132, 152; and Meng, 110; military connections, 7–8, 24, 57; mountain practice, 40, 99, 109–110; on no-recollection, 48, 141, 148, 155; on no-thought, 8, 36, 40, 45, 48, 50, 51, 53, 105, 109, 119, 120, 122, 131, 131–132, 132, 133–134, 135, 135–136, 141, 148, 149, 153, 154; and the old men, 48, 140–141; ordination, 25, 106; portrait of, 156–157; practice (*see* no-thought); and Qingyuan, 121, 123; on receiving donations, 41, 42–43, 126–127; record (*see Lidai fabao ji*); on repentance practice, 43, 154; robe of verification, 65–66; search for as Wuxiang's successor, 113–114; Shenhui and, 25, 38, 106; sitting in idleness/emptiness, 6, 40, 45, 53, 109–110; tea drinking challenge to, 151–152; tea verse, 141–142; teaching(s) (*see* teaching[s] of Wuzhu); on texts, 146, 152–153; on the Three Jewels, 17, 146; on the three phrases of Wuxiang, 37, 38, 39; and Tiwu, 41–42, 126–127; on transcending characteristics, 17, 36, 51, 63, 104, 131, 134–135, 136, 146, 148, 149–150, 153; transmission from Wuxiang, 26–27, 27–29, 38–39, 99, 110–112; transmission of the robe to, 27–29, 99, 111–112, 114; and Treatise Masters, 149–150; on the Vinaya, 39, 147; and Vinaya masters, 39, 42, 146–149; on Vinaya masters, 147–148, 150–151; Vinaya masters on, 29, 115–116; on the Vinaya precepts, 39, 147–148; Wuxiang and, 25–29, 38–39, 40, 59, 99, 106–112, 119; and Wuying, 121, 123–125; and Xiongjun, 152; and Zhengbianzhi, 50, 135, 136; and Zhiyi (Chaoran), 131–132; and Zhongxin, 132–133; Zizai and, 25, 106

Xiao (Vinaya Master), 115

Xiaojin (of Jingzhong monastery), 115, 168n89

Xiaoming, Emperor. *See* Ming, Emperor

Xin. *See* Daoxin

xinmie, 55–56
Xiongjun: Wuzhu and, 152
Xiu. *See* Shenxiu
Xuan. *See* Dong Xuan
Xuanjie: Huineng and, 87
Xuanyue, 85, 92, 95, 96
Xuanzang, 166n65; on the transmission of the robe of the Buddha, 19; and Zhishen, 97
Xuanze, 85, 92, 95, 96; Hongren and, 85

Yanhui: Sumedha as, 73
Yaśas and Buddha (two Brahmins), 77–78
Yem: Unimpeded Wisdom and, 59, 162n20
Yijing: Wuzhu and, 128–130
Yijing (Book of Changes): Confucius on, 143–144q
Yingyao (Vinaya Master), 115, 116
Yinzong and Huineng, 93–94
Yixing. *See* Huiming and Yixing
Yizhou, 162n11
Yuan. *See* Chongyuan; Huiyuan
Yuanjue jing dashu chao (Zongmi), 43–44q
Yuanyi: Daoxin and, 84
Yuezhi, 73, 164n14

Zen (Zen Buddhism), 159n1; contemporary practitioners, 63–64; and spiritual aspiration, 6. *See also* Chan
Zetian. *See* Wu Zetian, Empress
Zhaiwen (Sian), 89
Zhang (of Ningguo monastery), 115
Zhang Chanqi, 94, 95
Zhang Huang on Wuzhu, 114
Zhang Qian, 73
Zhangqiu and Wuxiang, 99, 167n67
Zhengbianzhi: Wuzhu and, 50, 135, 136
Zhishen (Shen), 85, 92, 96–97; and Chuji, 97, 97–98; death, 97; Hongren and, 97; Shenhui on, 103; transmission of the robe to, 28, 49, 96; and the Trepiṭaka Brāhmana, 95–96; writings, 97; and Wu Zetian, 95, 96, 97
Zhiyi (Chaoran): Wuzhu and, 131–132
Zhiyi (Tiantai Zhiyi): Huisi and, 21
Zhongxin: Wuzhu and, 132–133
Zhuangzi: the Buddha vs., 145–146; teachings, 143, 145
Zhumo: Wuzhu and, 128–130
Zizai and Wuzhu, 25, 106
Zongchi: Bodhidharma and, 49, 79
Zongmi (Guifeng Zongmi), 24, 38, 61; on the Bao Tang school, 24, 43–44, 55, 56; on the Hongzhou school, 24, 44, 59, 60; Shenhui and, 24, 38; on the three phrases of Wuxiang, 37–38

TRANSLATIONS FROM THE ASIAN CLASSICS

Major Plays of Chikamatsu, tr. Donald Keene 1961

Four Major Plays of Chikamatsu, tr. Donald Keene. Paperback ed. only. 1961; rev. ed. 1997

Records of the Grand Historian of China, translated from the Shih chi of Ssu-ma Ch'ien, tr. Burton Watson, 2 vols. 1961

Instructions for Practical Living and Other Neo-Confucian Writings by Wang Yang-ming, tr. Wing-tsit Chan 1963

Hsün Tzu: Basic Writings, tr. Burton Watson, paperback ed. only. 1963; rev. ed. 1996

Chuang Tzu: Basic Writings, tr. Burton Watson, paperback ed. only. 1964; rev. ed. 1996

The Mahābhārata, tr. Chakravarthi V. Narasimhan. Also in paperback ed. 1965; rev. ed. 1997

The Manyōshū, Nippon Gakujutsu Shinkōkai edition 1965

Su Tung-p'o: Selections from a Sung Dynasty Poet, tr. Burton Watson. Also in paperback ed. 1965

Bhartrihari: Poems, tr. Barbara Stoler Miller. Also in paperback ed. 1967

Basic Writings of Mo Tzu, Hsün Tzu, and Han Fei Tzu, tr. Burton Watson. Also in separate paperback eds. 1967

The Awakening of Faith, Attributed to Aśvaghosha, tr. Yoshito S. Hakeda. Also in paperback ed. 1967

Reflections on Things at Hand: The Neo-Confucian Anthology, comp. Chu Hsi and Lü Tsu-ch'ien, tr. Wing-tsit Chan 1967

The Platform Sutra of the Sixth Patriarch, tr. Philip B. Yampolsky. Also in paperback ed. 1967

Essays in Idleness: The Tsurezuregusa of Kenkō, tr. Donald Keene. Also in paperback ed. 1967

The Pillow Book of Sei Shōnagon, tr. Ivan Morris, 2 vols. 1967

Two Plays of Ancient India: The Little Clay Cart and the Minister's Seal, tr. J. A. B. van Buitenen 1968

The Complete Works of Chuang Tzu, tr. Burton Watson 1968

The Romance of the Western Chamber (Hsi Hsiang chi), tr. S. I. Hsiung. Also in paperback ed. 1968

The Manyōshū, Nippon Gakujutsu Shinkōkai edition. Paperback ed. only. 1969

Records of the Historian: Chapters from the Shih chi of Ssu-ma Ch'ien, tr. Burton Watson. Paperback ed. only. 1969

Cold Mountain: 100 Poems by the T'ang Poet Han-shan, tr. Burton Watson. Also in paperback ed. 1970

Twenty Plays of the Nō Theatre, ed. Donald Keene. Also in paperback ed. 1970

Chūshingura: The Treasury of Loyal Retainers, tr. Donald Keene. Also in paperback ed. 1971; rev. ed. 1997

The Zen Master Hakuin: Selected Writings, tr. Philip B. Yampolsky 1971

Chinese Rhyme-Prose: Poems in the Fu Form from the Han and Six Dynasties Periods, tr. Burton Watson. Also in paperback ed. 1971

Kūkai: Major Works, tr. Yoshito S. Hakeda. Also in paperback ed. 1972

The Old Man Who Does as He Pleases: Selections from the Poetry and Prose of Lu Yu, tr. Burton Watson 1973

The Lion's Roar of Queen Śrīmālā, tr. Alex and Hideko Wayman 1974

Courtier and Commoner in Ancient China: Selections from the History of the Former Han by Pan Ku, tr. Burton Watson. Also in paperback ed. 1974

Japanese Literature in Chinese, vol. 1: *Poetry and Prose in Chinese by Japanese Writers of the Early Period*, tr. Burton Watson 1975

Japanese Literature in Chinese, vol. 2: *Poetry and Prose in Chinese by Japanese Writers of the Later Period*, tr. Burton Watson 1976

Love Song of the Dark Lord: Jayadeva's Gītagovinda, tr. Barbara Stoler Miller. Also in paperback ed. Cloth ed. includes critical text of the Sanskrit. 1977; rev. ed. 1997

Ryōkan: Zen Monk-Poet of Japan, tr. Burton Watson 1977

Calming the Mind and Discerning the Real: From the Lam rim chen mo of Tsoṇ-kha-pa, tr. Alex Wayman 1978

The Hermit and the Love-Thief: Sanskrit Poems of Bhartrihari and Bilhaṇa, tr. Barbara Stoler Miller 1978

The Lute: Kao Ming's P'i-p'a chi, tr. Jean Mulligan. Also in paperback ed. 1980

A Chronicle of Gods and Sovereigns: Jinnō Shōtōki of Kitabatake Chikafusa, tr. H. Paul Varley 1980

Among the Flowers: The Hua-chien chi, tr. Lois Fusek 1982

Grass Hill: Poems and Prose by the Japanese Monk Gensei, tr. Burton Watson 1983

Doctors, Diviners, and Magicians of Ancient China: Biographies of Fang-shih, tr. Kenneth J. DeWoskin. Also in paperback ed. 1983

Theater of Memory: The Plays of Kālidāsa, ed. Barbara Stoler Miller. Also in paperback ed. 1984

The Columbia Book of Chinese Poetry: From Early Times to the Thirteenth Century, ed. and tr. Burton Watson. Also in paperback ed. 1984

Poems of Love and War: From the Eight Anthologies and the Ten Long Poems of Classical Tamil, tr. A. K. Ramanujan. Also in paperback ed. 1985

The Bhagavad Gita: Krishna's Counsel in Time of War, tr. Barbara Stoler Miller 1986

The Columbia Book of Later Chinese Poetry, ed. and tr. Jonathan Chaves. Also in paperback ed. 1986

The Tso Chuan: Selections from China's Oldest Narrative History, tr. Burton Watson 1989

Waiting for the Wind: Thirty-six Poets of Japan's Late Medieval Age, tr. Steven Carter 1989

Selected Writings of Nichiren, ed. Philip B. Yampolsky 1990

Saigyō, Poems of a Mountain Home, tr. Burton Watson 1990

The Book of Lieh Tzu: A Classic of the Tao, tr. A. C. Graham. Morningside ed. 1990

The Tale of an Anklet: An Epic of South India—The Cilappatikāram of Iḷaṅkō Aṭikaḷ, tr. R. Parthasarathy 1993

Waiting for the Dawn: A Plan for the Prince, tr. with introduction by Wm. Theodore de Bary 1993

Yoshitsune and the Thousand Cherry Trees: A Masterpiece of the Eighteenth-Century Japanese Puppet Theater, tr., annotated, and with introduction by Stanleigh H. Jones, Jr. 1993

The Lotus Sutra, tr. Burton Watson. Also in paperback ed. 1993

The Classic of Changes: A New Translation of the I Ching *as Interpreted by Wang Bi*, tr. Richard John Lynn 1994

Beyond Spring: Tz'u Poems of the Sung Dynasty, tr. Julie Landau 1994

The Columbia Anthology of Traditional Chinese Literature, ed. Victor H. Mair 1994

Scenes for Mandarins: The Elite Theater of the Ming, tr. Cyril Birch 1995

Letters of Nichiren, ed. Philip B. Yampolsky; tr. Burton Watson et al. 1996

Unforgotten Dreams: Poems by the Zen Monk Shōtetsu, tr. Steven D. Carter 1997

The Vimalakirti Sutra, tr. Burton Watson 1997

Japanese and Chinese Poems to Sing: The Wakan rōei shū, tr. J. Thomas Rimer and Jonathan Chaves 1997

Breeze Through Bamboo: Kanshi of Ema Saikō, tr. Hiroaki Sato 1998

A Tower for the Summer Heat, by Li Yu, tr. Patrick Hanan 1998

Traditional Japanese Theater: An Anthology of Plays, by Karen Brazell 1998

The Original Analects: Sayings of Confucius and His Successors (0479–0249), by E. Bruce Brooks and A. Taeko Brooks 1998

The Classic of the Way and Virtue: A New Translation of the Tao-te ching *of Laozi as Interpreted by Wang Bi*, tr. Richard John Lynn 1999

The Four Hundred Songs of War and Wisdom: An Anthology of Poems from Classical Tamil, The Puṛanāṇūṛu, ed. and tr. George L. Hart and Hank Heifetz 1999

Original Tao: Inward Training (Nei-yeh) *and the Foundations of Taoist Mysticism*, by Harold D. Roth 1999

Lao Tzu's Tao Te Ching: *A Translation of the Startling New Documents Found at Guodian*, by Robert G. Henricks 2000

Po Chü-i: Selected Poems, tr. Burton Watson 2000

The Shorter Columbia Anthology of Traditional Chinese Literature, ed. Victor H. Mair 2000

Mistress and Maid (Jiaohongji), by Meng Chengshun, tr. Cyril Birch 2001

Chikamatsu: Five Late Plays, tr. and ed. C. Andrew Gerstle 2001

The Essential Lotus: Selections from the Lotus Sutra, tr. Burton Watson 2002

Early Modern Japanese Literature: An Anthology, 1600–1900, ed. Haruo Shirane 2002; abridged 2008

The Columbia Anthology of Traditional Korean Poetry, ed. Peter H. Lee 2002

The Sound of the Kiss, or The Story That Must Never Be Told: Pingali Suranna's Kalapurnodayamu, tr. Vecheru Narayana Rao and David Shulman 2003

The Selected Poems of Du Fu, tr. Burton Watson 2003

Far Beyond the Field: Haiku by Japanese Women, tr. Makoto Ueda 2003

Just Living: Poems and Prose by the Japanese Monk Tonna, ed. and tr. Steven D. Carter 2003

Han Feizi: Basic Writings, tr. Burton Watson 2003

Mozi: Basic Writings, tr. Burton Watson 2003

Xunzi: Basic Writings, tr. Burton Watson 2003

Zhuangzi: Basic Writings, tr. Burton Watson 2003

The Awakening of Faith, Attributed to Aśvaghosha, tr. Yoshito S. Hakeda, introduction by Ryuichi Abe 2005

The Tales of the Heike, tr. Burton Watson, ed. Haruo Shirane 2006

Tales of Moonlight and Rain, by Ueda Akinari, tr. with introduction by Anthony H. Chambers 2007

Traditional Japanese Literature: An Anthology, Beginnings to 1600, ed. Haruo Shirane 2007

The Philosophy of Qi, by Kaibara Ekken, tr. Mary Evelyn Tucker 2007

The Analects of Confucius, tr. Burton Watson 2007

The Art of War: Sun Zi's Military Methods, tr. Victor Mair 2007

One Hundred Poets: One Poem Each: A Translation of the Ogura Hyakunin Isshu, tr. Peter McMillan 2008

Zeami: Performance Notes, tr. Tom Hare 2008

Zongmi on Chan, tr. Jeffrey Lyle Broughton 2009

Scripture of the Lotus Blossom of the Fine Dharma, rev. ed., tr. Leon Hurvitz, preface and introduction by Stephen R. Teiser 2009

Mencius, tr. Irene Bloom, ed. with an introduction by Philip J. Ivanhoe 2009

Clouds Thick, Whereabouts Unknown: Poems by Zen Monks of China, Charles Egan 2010

The Mozi: A Complete Translation, tr. Ian Johnston 2010

The Huainanzi: A Guide to the Theory and Practice of Government in Early Han China, by Liu An, tr. John S. Major, Sarah A. Queen, Andrew Seth Meyer, and Harold D. Roth, with Michael Puett and Judson Murray 2010

The Demon at Agi Bridge and Other Japanese Tales, tr. Burton Watson, ed. with introduction by Haruo Shirane 2011

Haiku Before Haiku: From the Renga Masters to Bashō, tr. with introduction by Steven D. Carter 2011

The Columbia Anthology of Chinese Folk and Popular Literature, ed. Victor H. Mair and Mark Bender 2011

Tamil Love Poetry: The Five Hundred Short Poems of the Aiṅkuṟunūṟu, tr. and ed. by Martha Ann Selby 2011

GPSR Authorized Representative: Easy Access System Europe, Mustamäe tee 50, 10621 Tallinn, Estonia, gpsr.requests@easproject.com

www.ingramcontent.com/pod-product-compliance
Lightning Source LLC
Chambersburg PA
CBHW072234290426
44111CB00012B/2084
9780231150231